Children of Ol' Man River

The Life and Times
of a Showboat Trouper

Billy Bryant and His Family
left to right: Betty (daughter), Billy, Josephine (wife),
Florence (sister), Sam (father), Violet (mother)

The Lakeside Classics

CHILDREN
OF OL' MAN RIVER

The Life and Times
of a Showboat Trouper

By
Billy Bryant

EDITED BY
MARTIN RIDGE

The Lakeside Press

R. R. DONNELLEY & SONS COMPANY

CHICAGO

Christmas, 1988

PUBLISHERS' PREFACE

REGULAR readers of the *Lakeside Classic* series and others who have become familiar with the lifestyles of the pioneers and early settlers are probably of the opinion it was all work and no play. As the colonists made their way through the Allegheny Mountains into what is now known as the Middle West, nearly everyone faced the fears of unknown enemies. Those involved in conflicts or violence lived on the thin edge between life and death. And the settlers—farmers, ranchers, or miners—seemed to face a never-ending succession of back-breaking chores mixed with frequent natural disasters just to eke-out a bare existence. Stories or personal accounts took little, if any, notice of what our forebears did during their leisure time. And yet, even though it is difficult to imagine, there was time to occasionally relax, socialize, and be entertained.

One major source of enjoyment came from the frontier theater—traveling companies or individual actors, singers, and musicians who closely followed the westward movement. There were also traveling menageries, museums, and various displays of art and artifacts that utilized the in-town theaters or *floating theaters called showboats* that plied the Ohio and Mississippi Rivers and their major tributaries.

This year's *Lakeside Classic* selection, "Children of Ol' Man River," is the life of a showboat family, the Bryants, as related by son Billy. It is a story that could easily have been written by Horatio Alger and titled "It Could Only Happen in America." Truly rags-to-riches, it offers readers a full range of emotions—from pathos to a chuckle or two. Further, it brings an added dimension to our long running series—the importance of the rivers and river people to America's westward expansion.

The Bryant family after a variety of false starts finally find their niche in life after building a showboat and performing from its stage. Although the Bryants were late-comers to the "Showboat Era," which began about 1830 and lasted almost a century, their experiences were quite similar to those who had previously brought pleasure to those who used the rivers or lived nearby. It was Billy Bryant who was slowly attracting attention among river audiences while a brilliant entertainer named George M. Cohan and his family had quickly become the toast of Broadway. Cohan's meteoric rise was a continuing irritation to Billy, whose own recognition took almost a lifetime, but in the end, Bryant, too, left an indelible mark on the entertainment world. And finally, too, his jealousy of Cohan changed to appreciation and warm friendship.

If you have reached the age of fifty or more and grew up on or near a middle western river, this story will probably bring back memories—*good* if you were fortunate enough to be part of a showboat audience and experience the emotions brought forth from true melodrama; or *bad* if you were caught in one of the many disasterous floods or ice jams that plagued the inland waterways before controls were established. Yes, before the automobile and paved roads became an American staple, the rivers were our ancestors' interstate highways and Billy Bryant's story will give you a good idea what early river life and river people were all about.

After finding this story, which seemed to us to be somewhat out of the ordinary, we felt we needed an editor who could dig deeply into a subject where there was limited expertise available. Our first call went to Dr. Martin Ridge, Senior Research Fellow at the Huntington Library and Professor of History at The California Institute of Technology. We have known Dr. Ridge for some time, but didn't know that he had become acquainted with showboats during his teaching years at Indiana University. This background, plus his research acumen, paid off with a Prologue that provides interesting information about frontier theater, as well as the development of showboating long before the Bryants came on the scene. We're pleased to report that Dr. Ridge became so interested in the subject matter and the Bryant family that he has also provided an Epilogue or "rest of the story." Our editor, who has just completed his term as President of the Western History Association, is a prolific writer of books, essays, and scholarly papers. His writing has been recognized with "Best Book Awards" and he has repeatedly been called to serve as Chairman of the Pulitzer Prize Jury for Biography.

Because the story is of rather recent vintage, we were able to find a sizeable number of illustrations of showboatmen and their showboats. Included are full-color photographs of showboat posters, several of which were used by the Bryants. We are pleased to recognize Alex Gildzen and Kathleen Noland of the Kent State University Library, Kent, Ohio for their help in supplying information and illustrations from the collection of the late Professor G. Harry Wright.

Developing the two maps used in the book was ably handled by Donnelley cartographers. The maps have been placed in the text close to the mention of numerous river locations visited by the Bryants. The various river courses are shown as they appeared in 1905 along with major geographical features referred to in the text. Several hamlets and landings were found to no longer exist. Rare documents and pilot charts to help spot remote locations were provided for our research by Jim Akerman of the Hermon Dunlap Smith Center for the History of Cartography in the Newberry Library, Chicago.

Since its inception in 1903, the underlying objective of the *Lakeside Classics* has never changed: to produce a top-quality book using modern technology and systems. At this time we would like to recognize the Donnelley employees who have provided their personal skills to the various components of bookmaking—electronic composition, platemaking, color separation, web offset printing, case-making, gathering and binding, cartoning, and shipping. There are also those who expertly handle the myriad of details connected with material purchasing, warehousing, and testing. Finally, there are the quality technicians who work with the various operating crews to assure us of a job well done.

Three Donnelley facilities have shared production responsibilities—our Technical Documentation Services Division in Chicago provided composition; web-offset printing, binding, and distribution were handled by the Crawfordsville (Indiana) Manufacturing Division; and the maps were prepared by our Cartographic Group in Lancaster, Pennsylvania. All-in-all, this volume is an example of our ability to handle the *complete* manufacturing and distribution requirements whether it be for books, catalogs, magazines, directories, or financial literature.

The early years of our enterprise were characterized by a combination of publishing and printing. Publishing helped to keep the presses busy when there was a drop in demand for commercial printing. It became evident well before the turn of the century that publishing and printing were two quite different types of business, though closely related. Often, it is necessary to explain that the Company is not a publisher, save for this annual volume. Why this exception? It does provide for an appropriate

opportunity to extend our appreciation and greet-
ings to our many friends within and without the
Company. We are proud to be able to produce a
book of quality with the best of materials, employ-
ing the same skills, techniques, and equipment as
used for our many book publishing customers. It is
also an opportunity to record the highlights of the
past year for those interested now and in the future.

A year ago, we stated that we had not observed
any severe effects of that year's October 19th stock
market crash. The same holds true for 1988, except
understandably in our Financial Printing Group,
yet even there, progress was notable. Company-wide,
sales increased for the thirtieth consecutive year
bringing us close to the three billion dollar mark
which allows us to remain an international leader
in our industry. Operating profits grew, continuing
a long-term trend interrupted only in 1974, when
the LIFO method of accounting was adopted. This
has supported a seventy-eight year history of divi-
dends, with increases the last sixteen. Payment to
shareholders has always been modest, approximately
a third of the previous year's net earnings. This
continuing practice, coupled with conservative accounting methods, provides for modernization and
for growth in personnel, plant, and working capital.
Also, when especially attractive opportunities are
presented beyond the availability of retained earnings, there has been little hesitation to borrow, though
infrequently and on a reasonable scale.

Our industry is rapidly changing in technology and services provided. We strive to meet, even anticipate, the needs of our customers and prospects. Not to provide the best in quality, service and value would be fatal in our race with keen competition. Many of our competitors of a generation ago are no longer with us, and we have no intention of joining their demise.

One of our new services is facilities management. Many organizations need in-house rapid response printing services, which are becoming increasingly sophisticated. Lawyers are better lawyers than printers; bankers better bankers than printers. Our Company can supply technical expertise, management, and supervision on their premises, thereby freeing valuable time and attention, improving services, and reducing costs.

PULSAR™, a new Donnelley service, is a proprietary customer-based preliminary system using the latest electronic hardware and software technology. PULSAR™ is designed to increase publishers' efficiency with important improvements in schedules and productivity gains. Already installed in the catalog market, we have high hopes this will be a major opportunity for publishers to become more effective in a highly competitive world.

In recognition that there was a growing amount of expertise outside our Company, we entered into a joint venture with Eastman Kodak Company to develop and market selective gathering and imaging equipment designed to personalize printed products. In this day of high paper, production, and mailing costs, this service is expected to have real value for our customers in their continuing drive for efficiency and readership.

This program, as well as facilities management, is now included in the Information Services Group, which was formed at the beginning of this year with Barron W. Schoder, Jr. as President. Its charge is to focus the Company's efforts and resources toward informational businesses that are new, high growth, and have a technical orientation. Documentation Services facilities, which serve the unique needs of computer manufacturers and software publishers, have been expanded in the Portland, Oregon directory plant and Crawfordsville, Indiana book plant.

The former Directory Group is now designated the Telecommunications Group. The Group services the publishers of telephone and other business directories. It had a strong year, thanks in part to the evolving directory market. At Dwight, Illinois two wide-web, four-color offset presses started up successfully. A similar press was installed in the Lancaster, Pennsylvania Division, plus a four-color flexographic press, a new process for our Company.

The Catalog Group serves the catalog and insert markets, by gravure and offset printing. In Spartanburg, South Carolina, an expansion will house a new web gravure press and several high speed binders. Preliminary and cylinder making are also expanding to increase capacity and improve schedules. Major press replacements in Warsaw, Indiana will provide the latest equipment available. In the new Reno, Nevada Division a new gravure press had a most successful startup.

The Book Group enjoyed a strong demand across all its markets. A special module for Bibles commenced production in Harrisonburg, Virginia. In Crawfordsville, Indiana, a new preliminary facility was established. In Barbados, production of one and two color film has been underway for approximately one year.

The Magazine Group had an exceptionally fine year. President Robert G. Myers, who is taking early retirement after many years of fine service, will be succeeded by Jack S. Oberhill. Virtually all of our major magazine contracts have been extended. New press and binding equipment is being added in each of our magazine divisions to provide additional capacity for our customers.

In the Financial Printing Group, there is also a new President, Donald N. Reeves. His predecessor, James R. Donnelley, has assumed new responsibilities as Group President, Corporate Development. As stated previously, 1988 was not the best year for financial printers. However, both the new facilities in New York and London contributed significantly to sales growth in the face of well-established competition. The new Communications Composition System links together all of our worldwide financial centers. It extends from Los Angeles, Chicago, Lancaster and New York to London, Singapore, Hong Kong and Tokyo, with intermediate stations in the United States. The recent acquisition of Dowa Printing Company in Tokyo improves our ability to serve Japanese financial printing requirements.

In England, Ben Johnson continues successfully to be the major supplier of telephone directories and airline guides. It also produces a large range of catalogs, regular and newspaper magazines. New press equipment is being added at Dunstable and York, and we are expanding our Documentation Services capabilities.

This was Metromail's first full year of operation with our Company. Its growth compared to 1987 was good despite very large postal and paper cost increases that impacted the demand for Metromail's mailing list services. During 1988, Metromail acquired Market Compilation & Research Bureau, a leader in life cycle direct mail marketing services, and constructed a new data center in Lincoln, Nebraska. This acquisition and facility will help us to serve the rapidly growing direct mail industry.

It is evident that change in the printing industry is accelerating: technology, markets, and services. Our research and development professionals are constantly alert and striving to keep the Company in the forefront. They benefit from the advice of our Technical Advisory Council, made up of distinguished outside scientists and engineers. The purchasing function throughout the Company insures that the equipment we obtain and the materials we use for our customers' products are the best for their value.

Since ours is a service business, as well as manufacturing, nothing is produced until a sale is made. This emphasizes the importance of our many marketing and sales personnel scattered across all groups, in the United States and abroad. New sales facilities in San Francisco and Dallas bring the total to thirty-eight. While most salespeople specialize in one field, there is a good deal of cross-selling for production in manufacturing facilities of other groups, helping to maintain steady activity.

As we look to the future, we expect to grow in our core activities, mainly preliminary, presswork, binding and distribution. Our sales represent only a small percentage of our industry, and so fortunately there is room to grow. We are looking at possible acquisitions, but only if they will either add to or enhance the core business, and management is available. Generations ago, our predecessors recognized that paper, board, ink and cloth—our major materials—are best made by others.

In the past century and a quarter of our Company's history, many fine people have dedicated their careers and talents to its success—more now than ever, in many different capacities. Their dedication to high quality and fine spirit continue to be key ingredients now and in the future. To work together effectively requires an ever more sophisticated organization, not necessarily a more complex one. The key seems to be decentralization, with authority and responsibility delegated with requisite accountability and communications in return.

Good communications, are in fact, a most important element for ongoing and successful relationships. They are encouraged, at and between every level. Besides a formal grievance procedure, which provides for hearings at various levels, we have a long-standing Open Door Policy. This provides any employee with direct access to the President or Chairman of the Board, or any manager. Neither procedure is abused. We are also proud of our various benefit programs for active and retired employees, which seem much appreciated and certainly are well earned.

Effective January 1, 1989, John R. Walter will become Chief Executive Officer, continuing as President. John B. Schwemm, who has been Chairman and Chief Executive since 1983, will continue as Chairman. Also, Carl K. Doty, President of the Catalog Group, was elected to be Executive Vice President, Operations. A comparable post was held by Donald M. Hackbert, who earlier this year took early retirement after a long career of dedicated service to the Company.

We welcome to our Board of Directors Martha Layne Collins, former Governor of Kentucky, and John M. Richman, Chairman of Kraft, Inc. We say a fond farewell to William W. Darrow and Frederick G. Jaicks, who have served so well, but reached this year the normal retirement age for directors. It is with great sadness we note the untimely passing of Richard B. Ogilvie, a most distinguished citizen and lawyer, soon after his election to our Board. The counsel and interest of our outside board members, who make up the majority, are highly valued and important to our continued success. In addition to bringing their experience and wisdom to the Board's deliberations, they also serve on various committees.

We are constantly reminded of our debt to so many others who have contributed to our success. At this time of the year and by this book, we express our warmest thanks and best wishes of the Season to all our friends.

THE PUBLISHERS

Christmas, 1988

CONTENTS

xxi

ILLUSTRATIONS

PROLOGUE

WHEN Billy Bryant started his recollections by
saying that "My family and I began our lives
on the river as a mussel does—at the bottom," he
told the pure and unvarnished truth; and it makes
the good-natured story of his rise to riverboat captain and successful showboat entertainer all the
more remarkable. His parents were impoverished
English immigrants who drifted into the Middle
West because they could not scratch out a decent
living in Brooklyn. Although somewhat skilled as a
carpenter, his father became a charlatan, an inept
magician, a trickster who tried to peddle an inflam-
mable balm made of gasoline and cayenne pepper
to gullible country folk. His mother, merely sixteen
when she married and migrated to America, had enjoyed a fleeting experience with an English touring
theatrical company, where she learned to sing "Little Buttercup." At times her voice and her guitar
were used to draw a crowd around his father's medicine show wagon so he could make his pitch. They
drifted as far west as Oklahoma for the opening of
the Cherokee Strip in 1889. They were not, however, typical "sooners" looking for free land to farm
but hucksters seeking suckers who would buy father
Bryant's brew.

The Bryants' struggle to find a place in American
society eventually brought them back to the Ohio

Valley. Mother Bryant, because of her talent and theatrical adventures as a youth, knew that she would not be happy unless she brought the family into the theater. But it was not an easy task. As they moved from job to job, they experienced a short tenure on a showboat. It was a marvelous experience and one they all longed to recapture but, seemingly, to no avail. The Bryants often found themselves in desperate financial straits. Each of them took odd jobs, many of them menial, and drifted down the social and economic ladder until father Bryant, at his wife's urging, decided he would turn his carpenter's skill to advantage and build his own showboat. Thus began the Bryant family saga that included the publication of Billy Bryant's own recollections.

In a unique way, within their lifetime, the Bryants reproduced in miniature the history of the showboat and the frontier theater. The gallant Bryants and the story of their rise from "mussels on the river bottom" to stars on the Broadway stage can only be understood in terms of the history of the Ohio-Mississippi River showboat, a uniquely American institution that was an important part of frontier culture and entertainment.

From the time of the colonists the ever-moving western frontier was a raucous place where people of every trade, vocation, and calling—honest and dishonest—tried to capitalize on the business opportunities that came with rapid development. After the Revolution, thousands of settlers crowded across the Appalachian Mountains into the Ohio and Mississippi River Valleys. By 1825, perhaps as many as five million people spread out over millions of acres of land to build towns, dig coal, and plant wheat, corn, tobacco, and cotton. Most of them lived along the rivers which were their main highways because the roads were so primitive as to be almost impassable in rainy seasons. Even as the population increased, outside of a handful of large cities, the majority of people lived quasi-isolated lives on farms and in very small towns and villages.

The expanding frontier left a thin veneer of culture in its wake, a people starved for social contact and entertainment. Every small town with aspirations of becoming a metropolis boasted a theater for local amateur players and visiting companies of actors, many of questionable reputation.

In fact, so bad was the reputation of itinerate actors in Frankfort, Kentucky, in 1815 that Noah Miller Ludlow, a successful actor, learned from his widowed landlady that she would not have rented him a room if she had known his profession.[1]

Farm folk and villagers desperately craved any entertainment that came from beyond their small world. Thousands of rural people were attracted to week-long camp meetings as much for the communal atmosphere and enthusiasm as for the religious

[1] N. M. Ludlow, *Dramatic Life as I Found It* (St. Louis, 1880), p. 57.

experience, which were in themselves sometimes theatrical and bizarre. They were thundered at and preached to for hours on end by teams of zealous evangelists. Little wonder that frontier folk welcomed traveling menageries, exhibitions, museums, freak shows, circuses, and even serious actors who were willing to attempt Shakespeare in the common rooms of inns and taverns.

Entertainers traveled overland in all forms of conveyance from wagons to stagecoaches, but from the earliest days many took advantage of the rivers and made their way to the town theaters by boat. Samuel Drake, who led a company of actors from New York to Kentucky in 1815, drifted with the current downstream from Olean on the Allegheny River to Pittsburgh. Traveling when the river was high because of rains and the melting snow in the mountains, the flatboat passed safely over sandbars and rapids, which were called chutes. Drake's boat, only twenty-five feet long and fifteen feet wide, was essentially an oblong box with a raked bow. The inside was divided into several small rooms to provide privacy for the members of Drake's family and for the young women of the company; the men were expected to rough it by sleeping with the company's luggage.

Later in the season, the same company of actors now under the leadership of Noah Ludlow departed Nashville in a keelboat—which the actors called *Noah's Ark*—on an adventurous voyage down the

Cumberland, Ohio, and Mississippi to Natchez. Unlike Drake's flatboat that counted on a steersman and wide oar-like sweeps to stay in the current, Ludlow's keelboat was a more sophisticated craft that could be directed both by steering and by men pushing poles into the river bottom to control it.

The *Ark* made its way safely to Natchez.[2] After closing the season there, the town fathers extracted a promise from Ludlow that he would return with the company the following year and perform a new play. Here was a pattern that was to be followed for more than a century.[3] Successful performances established lasting contacts for Noah Ludlow in 1816 just as they would for Billy Bryant and other showboat companies nearly 100 years later.

One family in the 1830s—the unusually talented Chapmans—significantly changed western theater. William Chapman, senior, his wife, two sons, two daughters, various assorted family members through marriage, as well as a grandmother and grandchildren were all experienced actors. Chapman, who had performed at London's Covent Garden Theatre, brought the family to America after one of his sons emigrated and began an active theatrical career in New York. Perhaps because they were clannish or because opportunity for them as a group appeared better in the West, the Chapmans moved on to Pittsburgh.

[2] *Ibid.*, pp. 125–26.
[3] *Ibid.*, p. 135.

Having bad luck in securing a theater in Pittsburgh as well as wanting to perform in other river
towns may have led William Chapman to build the
first showboat. Although little is known about the
dimensions of Chapman's *Floating Theatre*, Noah
Ludlow, who saw it in the early 1830s, years later
recalled it as "a large flatboat, with a rude kind of
house built on it. . . . "[4] More than likely the interi-
or of the theater was crude, with benches for seating
and tallow candles for footlights. The Chapmans
intended to drift down the Ohio and Mississippi
and to land wherever an audience could be gathered to see them perform on the boat. In this way
they would avoid the cost of renting theaters and
escape the threat of exclusion by competitors who
might control small-town playhouses. Moreover,
they could reach people who could not otherwise
attend a play because they lived in extremely isolated communities.

From the beginning the Chapmans mastered the
river. They learned, for example, to start early in
the morning to avoid winds that would push them
out of the river channel. They performed in the
South when the northern rivers were frozen, and
they drifted downstream during the rainy season so
as to go easily over sandbars and chutes. They did
this until 1836 when they bought a small steamboat—Chapman's *Theatrical Steamboat*—which allowed them not only to visit small towns that were

[4]*Ibid.*, p. 568.

on the tributaries of the Ohio River because they could travel upstream, but also to give performances up and down the lower Mississippi before they returned home each year from New Orleans.

They developed a technique for attracting audiences that was to be perfected by showboat owners half a century later. When the Chapman boat approached a village or a plantation landing they would unfurl a banner and blow a trumpet to signal their arrival. This no doubt startled villagers during the Chapman's initial season, but after their first visit the friendly trumpet alerted the community to their presence.[5] Later, when they were more successful, they would send someone ahead to set out announcements of their coming. After each performance, the elder Chapman personally bade his audience good night as he stood at the gangplank. Like Ludlow before him, Chapman sealed a lasting relationship with river folk.

With the death of William Chapman the company began to disperse. Talented children and grandchildren found leading roles in theaters from New York to San Francisco. Mrs. Chapman may have operated the boat until 1847 but by then most of the Chapmans had left the river. They were the first successful showboat family on the river and even Billy Bryant would agree that the Chapmans were distinguished show people.

[5] Tyrone Power, *Impressions of America* (Philadelphia, 1836) Vol. 11, p. 133.

In the place of serious theater as offered by the Chapmans came a new world of river entertainment that satisfied a more robust and less sophisticated audience. These were minstrel shows and circuses with museums of wax figures and stuffed exotic animals. Some were traveling companies that moved their equipment by water but performed on land in theaters and tents, but others learned the convenience that came from the avoidance of loading and unloading stage materials and began to perform or show on boats.

The best known early shows and circuses are associated with G. R. Spaulding who ran his American Circus for several years before he merged it with one owned by Charles Rogers. Spaulding and Rogers pioneered in the field of circus entertainment by being among the first to transport a circus by train for a season (1853), by water but performing on land (1848), and ultimately by building a showboat that could accommodate an entire circus company (1852). This was an expensive venture for the partners because providing space for a circus troop to live as well as to perform required an enormous boat.

In fact the Spaulding and Rogers *Floating Palace* reputedly cost $40,000, was 250 feet long and 60 feet wide, and could comfortably seat an audience of more than 2000. It was the equal of virtually any western theater. Its amphitheatre boasted elegant box seats, a large gallery, an organ, and gas lighting.

Announcement in the Baton Rouge Gazette

October 12, 1852

Courtesy Kent State University Library, Kent, Ohio

The *Floating Palace* was towed during its first season by the steamer *North River* and not only successfully navigated the Ohio and Mississippi but also survived a coastal voyage in the Gulf of Mexico to Mobile, Alabama, and up the Tombigbee River. After the *James Raymond* was built in 1853, this more powerful steamer—it was 177 feet in length and 30 feet in width—accompanied the *Floating Palace* both up and down-river. Assisted by the *James Raymond*, the *Floating Palace* could maintain a schedule, and an advance agent was sent out to put up advertising posters in places where the boat would play. In addition the *James Raymond* was resplendent, according to minstrel performer Ralph Keeler, with "a concert-saloon" of "great elegance and convenience, and called the 'Ridotto,'" where various skits, musicals, and minstrel shows were performed.[6]

After an audience experienced the wonders of the museum on the *Floating Palace* they enjoyed a show on the *James Raymond*. The *Floating Palace* was an attraction from Pittsburgh to New Orleans, and its scheduled arrival in any town highlighted that community. Both the *Floating Palace* and *James Raymond*, however, were Civil War casualties.[7] The *Floating Palace* was confiscated by the

[6]Ralph Keeler, *Vagabond Adventures* (Boston, 1870), p. 173.
[7]The Great American Water Circus of 1905 was the last floating circus on the river. See Graham, *Showboats*, p. 36.

Confederacy and converted to a hospital ship in
New Orleans. The *James Raymond*, according to
legend, escaped the clutches of the Confederacy by
steaming north.

On the eve of the Civil War the few large vessels
and established companies faced competition from
a plethora of small-boat owners who found it a simple and cheap way to earn a living. The cost of buying a barge or building a flatboat was so low that
hucksters of all kinds capitalized on it to use the
river as a public highway on which to do business.
The itinerate work force—inhabitants of shanty
boats—that lived along the river verged on being as
impoverished as the derelict homeless of today.
Since many of these people made up the disreputa-
ble part of the petty showboat community, little
wonder that the perception of small-boat operators
as scoundrels and cheats lasted for decades. More
than half a century later, the family of Billy Bryant
deeply resented being associated in any way with
the so-called shanty-boat trash. Although the Bryants may have been down on their luck, they always
thought of themselves as legitimate showboat performers and well above other shanty boaters.

The world of the antebellum showboat operators
was swept away by the Civil War; however, in the
years after the war, as the economy grew, expendi-
tures to improve river transit increased. Canals and
locks were constructed or improved around chutes
and falls, the channels were more carefully charted,

NOVELTY, INSTRUCTION, *Amusement.*

MUSEUM
—AND—
CONCERT.

The former containing upwards of

100,000 Curiosities.

Will exhibit at BATON ROUGE, on

MONDAY, Dec. 31, TUESDAY, Jan. 1st,

on board the

FLOATING PALACE
—AND—
JAMES RAYMOND.

The Museum contains a complete

ZOOLOGICAL EXHIBITION

of every wild & rare animal existing in

Europe, Asia, Africa and America,

INCLUDING a full grown ELEPHANT, and magnificent GIRAFFE; innumerable specimines of Birds from the gigantic OSTRICH to upward of one hundred specimens of the fairy HUMMING BIRD.

A Statue Gallery,

Of figures the size of life, among which are—
CHRIST PREACHING IN THE TEMPLE; THE SHAKS-PEAREAN GALLERY; SIAMESE TWINS; THE FAMILY OF NAPOLEON; WASHINGTON AND LAFAYETTE; WM. WALLACE & HELENA MAR; TAM O'SHANTER; SOUTER JOHNY; THE LANDLORD & LANDLADY. THE CHIEF UTICA—IN THE DRESS HE WORE WHEN LIVING.
HUNDREDS OF ANCIENT & INDIAN WAR WEAPONS.

A Panoramic View of the World,

Mineral and Vegetable Curiosities without number; Ancient Relics from Egypt, Greece, Rome, Pompeii and Herculaneum.

ONE HUNDRED AND FIFTY OIL PAINTINGS.

Admis'n 50cts. Doors open 2 & 7 P. M.

An Entertainment & Concert.

Will be given in a beautiful Concert Room, on the
JAMES RAYMOND,
Immediately after the exhibition on the PALACE, consisting of
Ethiopian Melodies;
Fancy and Comic Dancing;
Characteristic Delineations.
By a talented troupe of Male and Female Artists.

Admission .... 25 Cents.

Announcement in the
Baton Rouge *Weekly Comet*
December 23, 1855

Courtesy Kent State
University Library, Kent, Ohio

xxxvii

and federal money—perhaps as much as $70 million—was invested in new schemes to lengthen the commercial season.

Yet, the great era of the showboat seemed over. Some circus boats and other vessels did try to recapture the earlier spirit but the economy was too weak, especially along the lower Mississippi. The post-war hard times in the South were followed by the nationwide Panic of 1873, which left both the Middle West and the South in a depression. Even that genius of circus performers and entrepreneurs, Dan Rice, who had once competed strenuously against Spaulding and Rogers before the war and who had enjoyed a fleeting period of prosperity after it, failed in the 1870s, plagued by bad luck and financial problems that culminated when his steam-powered showboat *Damsel* hit a snag and burned.

The post-Civil War renaissance of the showboat is usually attributed to a single individual, A. B. French. "Gus" French was born Augustus Byron Dolen in the 1830s at Palmyra, Missouri. His family broke up with his mother's death when he was nine. He lived briefly with his grandmother, with foster parents in Cincinnati, and then as an apprentice, in Augusta, Kentucky. Educated by catch-as-catch-can, French seemed destined to join the flotsam and jetsam labor force of the Ohio Valley. Story has it that he ran away to join a circus, and in 1849, while in his late teens, hired on as a deckhand on a steamboat headed for New Orleans. Incapable of hard work, French was exiled to the galley, where he did menial kitchen tasks.

North of Natchez the packet tied up next to a shanty flatboat named *Quickstep*. The shanty boat was owned by a man named Church, who, along with his daughter Celeste, drifted down-river and performed wherever they could gather an audience. Celeste could sing and dance; Church could do minor magic tricks and Gus French, who could play the banjo, decided to join Church and become an entertainer. He learned to dance, sing, and work rudimentary magic tricks. He remained with the Churchs for two years, then during the next few years French became a minor performer on circus boats. He worked for both Dan Rice as well as for Spaulding and Rogers, but he was never a major success or a star.

After the Civil War he returned to life with the circus, but by 1870 he had changed. He owned a general store in Clarksburg, Ohio. Approaching middle age, French was married, a respectable small-town businessman with a reputation for advocating the virtues of the Victorian era—especially abhorrence of debt—and headed for a sedate future life. A few years later his wife died, and his life took a startlingly different turn. In his mid-forties he took an option on a small circus, which he renamed French's New Sensation, sold his general store, and began a new career. Moreover, he married sixteen-year-old Callie Leach whom he had known since she was a child. They were to be happily married for the remaining quarter century of French's life.

Nothing in his experiences prepared Gus French for the summer of 1878. He had the misfortune of launching his New Sensation Circus during perhaps the wettest year of the decade. There were impassable roads, torrential rains that forced the cancellation of performances, and a totally disappointing season. Faced with losses, disgruntled employees, and hungry animals, French decided before the year was out, so legend has it, that he had suffered enough; if he had to see so much water he would rather live above it than below it—he would build himself a showboat.

He and Callie went to Cincinnati, where, according to one source, they bought an eighty-five foot long, sixteen foot wide, barge.[8] Over this they built a single-story superstructure, including a porch at each end, so the boat's length was extended by almost twenty feet. The width was also extended by runways that added an additional four feet to the boat. Called *French's New Sensation*, the showboat was equipped with two large sweeps or oars on each side of the roof, and a third sweep on the stern to serve as a rudder. The *New Sensation* housed the company, which also doubled as a crew, and had space for a rather plain auditorium that seated about ninety people. The seats closest to the stage

[8]Duane Eldon Reed, "A History of Showboats on Western Waters," p. 59.

were padded and cost more—thirty-five cents, the others were a quarter. The married couples had rooms to themselves, single men slept in the auditorium, and the company shared a common kitchen and dining room at the back of the boat. For all practical purposes French's *New Sensation* differed little from the Chapman's *Floating Theatre* of forty years earlier.

Thus, the showboat, in its simplest form, returned to the river. Gus French had not invented the idea. He had reinvented the thing itself in its primitive form and he was to manage it so well that the modern showboat era is said to have originated with him.

Immediately after launching, French decided that he had to start south as soon as possible, despite the lateness of the season, because he was virtually out of money. The *New Sensation* left Cincinnati in early November, 1878, although ice was already forming on the upper Ohio River.

It must have been a difficult journey. Cold and fog ruled the river in winter, and the crew of entertainers had much to learn of hidden obstacles and sandbars. They performed where an audience of at least twenty-five people could be gathered. Finally, they made it to New Orleans and Callie French, many years later, remembered that she was the only woman who completed the trip.

There is little doubt that French's initial season was successful despite its inauspicious beginnings.

French's First Showboat, New Sensation

Courtesy Kent State University Library, Kent, Ohio

He had taken his small company on a trip that exposed them not only to the trials of the river but also to audiences far cruder than those that had welcomed even the Chapmans. Moreover, French may have produced a popular variety show but he never surrendered his high moral standards; and the *New Sensation*'s performances were intended for the whole family. French was fighting to overcome a double problem: on the one hand, he wanted to attract a large audience by offering wholesome family entertainment often with performers whose personal habits were unacceptable, while on the other hand, he had to overcome the residue of suspicion among river folk about the moral character of showboat performers and their shows that resulted from some of the cheap and tawdry shanty-boat companies that still worked the river. From the beginning French determined to establish a lasting common bond with his audiences because he wanted to return time and time again to perform for them.

Even if French had successfully survived his first season on the river he still had much to learn not only about showboating but about the river as well. During the 1879 season, one of the poorest ever because of both weather and business conditions, the *New Sensation* hit a snag and sank in less than five feet of water almost within arm's reach of the shoreline at Vidalia, Louisiana. There was no way to raise the boat, and Gus French's career as a showboat entertainer seemed finished. But somehow he persuaded two affluent Vidalia businessmen to lend him enough money to buy a new barge. One was bought at Natchez, floated across the river to Vidalia, and the superstructure of the first *New Sensation* was sawed off and shifted to the body of the new barge to create the second *New Sensation*.

Not all seasons were so perilous as the early ones. The Frenchs continued to operate their boat and to make changes in their procedures that influenced the development of showboating. They learned, for example, to begin the season earlier, to find new performers and to retain successful acts, to have the *New Sensation* towed up-stream to the small coal colliers and industrial towns on the Ohio's northern tributaries, where an ardent working-class audience—one much in tune with the family-style of entertainment that French offered—awaited them, to cruise the cotton regions of Tennessee and Mississippi after ginning time, when farmers and hired hands were flush with spending money, and to invade the bayous of the Louisiana "sugar coast" in late December after the grinding of the cane harvest when the labor force had both the time and the cash for entertainment. They also learned which locales had predominantly impoverished populations which might not be able to provide the proper number of ticket sales to warrant a show.

French also pioneered the idea of the free or promotional attraction. The usual manner of bringing in an audience was to send some of the company ashore to post notices or to blow a trumpet to announce the showboat's arrival. French did more. During the 1882 season, when the *New Sensation* prepared to open a show, a cannon was fired, musicians played, a rope was stretched between the boat's two masts, and a trapeze set out on the boom attached to the front mast. Then Callie French, already an accomplished slack wire performer, did a brief act on the rope; she was followed by an acrobat who did a headstand; and a gymnast who performed on the trapeze. Years later the promotional attraction included a street parade and the cast who could "double in brass"—that is play a horn—gave a small concert in the town square. Then tickets were sold and the show started.

Innovations brought added successes, a larger company, and a sound reputation on the river, but it was still a constant struggle to earn profits. As a small businessman, Gus French was always undercapitalized. To consolidate his position he needed constantly to improve the quality both of the *New Sensation* and of his show.

This lack of capital led him into partnerships, two of which were simply unsuccessful and one that had lasting consequences for the history of showboating. The latter occurred shortly after the *New Sensation* tied up next to a shanty boat named *Sylvan Stream*, which had been converted into a photographic studio. The owner of this river novelty was Edwin A. Price, a tight-fisted, small-bodied man who had at one time given illustrated lantern lectures and who existed on the edge of show business. French and Price lashed their two "floaters" together. When they arrived in a town, Price made tintypes by day and French's company performed in the evening. Apparently Price wanted to be a partner at strategic periods, hoping to make a good deal of money when the *New Sensation* was profitable and asking to be bought out when it was not. When he and French parted company as partners for the last time, Price bought a showboat himself and became French's major competitor.

During the 1885–86 season Gus French decided that he would no longer be a "floater," dependent exclusively on the river. He bought a small tug, the *Martin Murphy*. It was not powerful enough to push the *New Sensation* upstream. It could, however, keep it in the river channel and protect it from high winds that might blow it toward dangerous sandbars or the river bank. The next year he traded the little tug for the *Sentinel*, a much more powerful boat that could control the *New Sensation* even in difficult water.

Whether French was aware of his changing economic position or merely making rational business choices, after nine seasons with a "floater" that was small and aging, he decided to build a larger and more modern showboat. He was beginning to face genuine competition. His former partner, Edwin A. Price, was also on the river with a small showboat

Two of the Later French's New Sensations
Courtesy Kent State University Library, Kent, Ohio

bidding to hire his performers and trying to beat him to the best places. Regardless of the quality of Price's show, once he performed at a small town, plantation or colliery that community's money was spent. French had to play leapfrog to keep ahead of him on the river.

Now with the completion of the second *New Sensation* showboating had finally recovered from the shock of the Civil War. Gone were the days when Gus French had to struggle to avoid every sandbar and sunken log. He was an experienced pilot and captain who knew the river, because as one of the actors once wryly observed, they had already hit every sandbar in it.

French would still face competition, but he was the primary force in showboating in 1889. Just a year later, when a potential competitor, Captain C. F. Breidenbach, launched the *New Floating Theatorium*, perhaps the most lavish showboat built since before the Civil War, French was not intimidated because he had not only a reputation and an economically viable boat but also knowledge and cash. Breidenbach took the beautiful 700-seat *New Floating Theatorium* down-river, but one voyage with meager profits or perhaps a serious loss was probably sufficient to erase any romantic notions he may have had about show business. He put the boat up for sale, and French immediately bought it. He thus quickly eliminated a powerful rival and secured at a bargain price the newest and best boat on the river. He sold his small boat and renamed the *Theatorium* the *New Sensation*.

A similar thing happened in 1895. Eugene Robinson, a New Orleans showman representing a business syndicate that had built the elegant showboat *Blow Out* in the late 1880s—it was the equal in size, quality, and fittings to the *Theatorium*—faced financial problems and had to auction it off. French bought it! Once again he had not only eliminated a top competitor but also acquired a splendid boat. Only this time he did not sell the *New Sensation*. But since he refused to have any boat he owned go by any other name than his own, the Robinson boat became *French's New Sensation No. 2*.

By now Callie, who had been with Gus on the river for more than fifteen years and knew parts of its channels as well as he, was also a licensed pilot and captain. She took over as captain and show producer of the *New Sensation No. 1*. She was among a small pioneering group of women who were both pilots and riverboat captains.

Gus French assumed control of the new boat. The performers and crew members were switched back and forth between the boats to keep friendships and families together and to provide first-class entertainment. The Frenchs could now rightfully claim that they played from the Monongahela to the Gulf of Mexico and from St. Paul to New Orleans.

At what was certainly the pinnacle of his influence on the river, the aging Gus French decided to

Opulent Interior of French's New Sensation

Courtesy Missouri State Historical Society, St. Louis

slow down. He sold *New Sensation No. 1* to his former partner and long-time rival Edwin A. Price, but he did not sell its name. He leased *French's New Sensation No. 2* to a family friend and experienced employee, John McNair. Gus and Callie went off to Europe for a holiday; they returned to disaster. The *New Sensation* had burned. There was no loss of life, but for the first time in twenty-two years there was no *New Sensation* on the rivers.

Gus French, affluent and in his late sixties, could have retired but he wanted another and better boat. This latest *New Sensation* was, indeed sensational. Double decked, it had electric lights and fans; and it contained a first-class theater with seating for almost 1000. Gus French never saw a performance in his last showboat. He was on his way to meet the *New Sensation* when he died in Cincinnati in May of 1902. Callie operated what was certainly a luxurious showboat until 1907, then she realized that competition from the newer showboats was cutting deeply into her profits. Finally, she sold her boat to Edwin A. Price.

Edwin A. Price was in several ways like Gus French. He came from a broken home, and was essentially self-educated. He was also quite different. French was outgoing and enjoyed the company of men, Price was a very private person who rarely gave interviews. He was also highly excitable and is often described as pulling at his muttonchop whiskers and scratching his leg at the same time during moments of crisis or anxiety. Although he had some minor theatrical experience before he met French in 1883, Price knew nothing about the showboats. Moreover, his shanty-boat daguerrotype business could not have been very profitable, although it may have been a good promotional attraction for French. But Price learned enough about showboating from French to realize that he could enter the business with little capital and successfully compete with his former partner.

Price's approach to running a showboat was simple: copy the success of others but do them more cheaply. His first boat—a floater with sweeps—was virtually identical to French's showboat. It was painted the same way, and Price even wanted to name it *Price's New Sensation.* Finding that he could not, he called it *Price's Floating Opera.* When he had two boats, like French he named the second "*No. 2.*" He produced the same type of variety show that French did, and he tried to hire the same performers. Price's shows were usually less expensively produced than French's but he gave his customers full measure. He either agreed with French's middle-class values and morality or he copied them because Price's shows were scrupulously pure.

His penchant for economy did make him a leader in an important way on the showboat circuit. Since he always wanted inexpensive performers, Price often hired newcomers who were just beginning to make their way in the profession. He gave promising actors, who might otherwise have had to wait years before they made it to a real showboat, a chance to see what showboat life was like. The New York City *Clipper*, the theatrical trade journal, frequently carried a Price announcement that read: "Novelties and people wanted. Give full particulars and if you double in brass and lowest salary."[9]

The Bryant family's first experience on a showboat came when they worked for Price. Billy Bryant never forgot his mother standing in the middle of the small, sparsely-furnished stateroom on Price's *Water Queen* and wondering at its comfort and cleanliness. Although Price fired all of his company at the end of the season when his boat reached New Orleans, for beginning entertainers Price's frugality paid off. He gave them a chance.

Price also recognized and encouraged genuine talent and energy when he found it. Ralph Waldo Emerson Gaches whom Price met as a river pilot became in time his advance man, ship captain, and friend. When Price owned more than one vessel, Ralph Waldo Emerson, as he preferred to be called because no one could correctly pronounce his surname, managed Price's other showboat.

The successes of Gus French and Ed Price in the 1890s, however different, lured a flock of serious competitors into showboating. They ranged from the family-owned small flatboat, where the family, crew, and entertainers were all the same people, to

[9] *Ibid.*, p. 232.

magnificent floating palaces—owned by entrepreneurs—where electric lights blazed, fans flattered the audience, and crews of rivermen and cooks kept highly paid entertainers happy. Two men who represented the extreme differences between showboat owners after the turn of the century are Ellsworth E. Eisenbarth and W. R. Markle.

Captain E. E. Eisenbarth was among the most respected of the newer showboat captains. He had grown up in river towns, came from a profoundly religious family that wanted him to be a minister, was himself deeply devout, but early in life had been captivated by circuses, wild west shows, and showboats. Eisenbarth produced legitimate plays. He not only put on Goethe's *Faust* but also managed to stage *Uncle Tom's Cabin* successfully even in the deep South. His wife, Julia Henderson, shared and encouraged his interest in the legitimate theater. Their showboat, known as the Eisenbarth-Henderson *Floating Theatre* or the *Modern Temple of Amusement*, became so successful that after 1901, Edwin A. Price, always looking for a sure thing, also began producing legitimate plays to compete for Eisenbarth's more cultured audiences.

Even the dignified, refined, and temperate Eisenbarth, however, was vulnerable to vagaries and dangers of the river. In 1902 his *Floating Theatre* had a freak accident while tied up at Grand Tower, Illinois, preparing for a performance. The gigantic tug *Sprague* on a voyage from Dubuque to St. Louis

The Eisenbarth-Henderson Floating Theatre

Courtesy Kent State University Library, Kent, Ohio

came round a bend in the Mississippi, inexplicably moved straight ahead rather than following the channel, and before a crowd of shocked on-lookers, plowed directly into the *Floating Theatre* sending it to the bottom. Fortunately, no lives were lost. Although he was compensated for the loss of the boat, Eisenbarth had to forfeit part of the season. He eventually secured a new boat and continued his prosperous career. There is no doubt that his puritanical attitude toward his audiences and his actors made him appear overly straightlaced. He, too, may have recognized that although he was financially successful, he was increasingly out of step with the times. Finally, in 1909, when business was good but competition had become increasingly keen, he sold his boat and retired.

W. R. Markle, long known along the river as "Double R" Markle, was the antithesis of Ellsworth Eisenbarth. Flamboyant, excessive, and a gambler, Markle was neither riverman nor showman. He had been reared in Ohio, where he had seen showboats, and as a promoter by nature he felt that the showboat business was wide open to an imaginative and daring investor. The time had come, Markle believed, to build spectacular big boats that would sweep the rivers clean of petty competitors and make fortunes for their owners. "Double R" began saving money from his winnings and contracted with the Pope Dock Company to construct a showboat of unparalleled quality. To pay for the boat he entered a partnership with a card-playing acquaintance, Matt O. Swallow, who had made money in the oil fields of West Virginia. Swallow knew nothing of boats or show business and came into the venture purely as an investor.

Swallow & Markle's *New Grand Floating Palace*, launched in 1901, may have exceeded even "Double R's" expectations. Not only was it planned for electric lights and fans but also for steam heat and commodious quarters; and its auditorium, with opera chair seating for a thousand customers, was richly carpeted and brilliantly decorated in gold and white. Since it drew only eighteen inches of water, it could travel almost anywhere; and seemed unusually graceful despite its 40-foot width and 150-foot length. It set, at once, the standard of excellence.

Markle set other standards as well. He employed the best orchestra leader on the river and best producer. He boasted outrageously about the quality of his show—he had the best musicians, the best performers, and the best entertainment. He also set new standards of profit because river audiences virtually stormed the *New Grand Floating Palace*.

Markle was so successful that he bought out Swallow's interest and began looking for a larger role in showboating. He sold the *New Grand Floating Palace* to Emerson, and ordered a new boat from Pope Dock Company—the *Sunny South*, which, when launched in 1905, was larger, grander, but less ostentatious in its exterior than its predecessor.

Showboat Sunny South

Courtesy Kent State University Library, Kent, Ohio

The interior, however, was almost without rival. Like the previous successful showboatmen, "Double R" allowed no coarse jokes nor double-entendres. Increasing profits and puritanical performances went hand-in-hand. If anything, this new boat was more profitable than the old one. There is no doubt that Markle ruled showboating, although he owned only one boat. In 1909 he sold the *Sunny South* and launched the *Goldenrod*. It was the grandest showboat ever built. No expense was spared. The auditorium was the peer of any first-quality, land-based theater, and overall the vessel proved superior in every detail to any showboat on the river.

The luck of gamblers, whether on land or the river, sooner or later runs out. Markle was slow to recognize that taste was changing, audiences wanted more drama or melodrama than variety acts and the movies claimed an increasing amount of the public's entertainment dollar. Moreover, he lost his tow *Connie Neville* in a storm and a few year's later he rammed a pleasure yacht and had to pay heavy damages. Draining expenses led him to continue gambling on horse races, and in 1913 he was forced into bankruptcy. The *Goldenrod* went at auction for a fraction of its value. It was bought by Ralph Waldo Emerson, the self-proclaimed "Showboat King." Markle's life reads like a tragic film script, but he will always be remembered as the promoter who built three of the finest showboats in American history.

Eisenbarth and Markle represented the extreme types of showboat management that characterized the pre-World War I years. There were men like Ralph Waldo Emerson, who had grown up on the river and learned the trade through experience, and others like John W. Cooley who owned a hotel but was intrigued with the showboat life and became first an investor and later an owner. He knew little of the river and less of the theater, but he had money. There were performers, producers, and advance men like the Menke brothers who failed when they first tried boat ownership but ended up with the *Goldenrod* after Emerson gave it up.

Ralph Waldo Emerson's motto was supposed to be "After the Minnows Comes the Whale." He believed, as did Markle, that the day of the small boats, like those operated by Callie French or Ed Price was over. The floating giants would "devour" them because audiences would flock onto the grandiose boats to enjoy the ambiance as well as the show. He was in part correct, for many people who lived in many small towns and cities still lacked electric lights in their homes and what they saw on the showboat stage was close to fantasy-come-to-life. The deftness of the magician, the artistry of sleight of hand, the skilled professional musicians, the singers and dancers, and the actors who performed melodramas continued to draw audiences from the upper Ohio to the Mississippi delta. But the cost of making each boat more spectacular than its competitor, of attracting the best players, of presenting what was new and vital, all boosted up prices and forced the owners to seek not only larger markets, where a boat could tie-up for a few days or even weeks, but also to attract a wealthier clientele. The heyday of the showboat era was one of many large, lavishly decorated and staffed "whales" in a critical competition with each other. For people who lived along the main traveled routes of the showboats, they would never again have an opportunity to see so much talent, so much glitter, and so much romance for so little cost.

But the whales could not devour the minnows. There were many small-time river families that put on shows along with selling medicine, general merchandise, and junk. There were others who operated showboats as modest as Gus French's first *New Sensation*, humble in comparison with the river queens—in fact, like the first showboat the Bryant family launched, it was homemade of scrap lumber and "borrowed" nails. More often than not, these primitive family showboats could not afford tows, except to get back home at the end of the season, so they drifted downstream like Chapman and French had done many decades earlier. They could not be driven from the river by the biggest or most lavish of competitors. For of the dozen or so great showboat owners, very few could afford to continuously tap the small showboat markets which were found to be either too far upstream or simply too expensive to make a stop worthwhile for a floating palace.

The smaller showboat operators, however, confronted one another, each trying to reach the head of navigation on a profitable river first—the Kanawha, the Green, or the Illinois—so they could start drifting downstream when the river was up, using their sweeps to stay in the channel, shooting the chutes, renewing old friendships while trying to make new ones, and being the first to take the limited entertainment dollars away from other forms of recreation as well as other showboat competitors. If these primitive showboats offered isolated country folk a glimpse of glitter and glamor, the working entertainers who were both performers and crew knew the hard side of show business.

This was the highly competitive world of showboating after 1900. It was the world into which the Bryants in 1907 launched their *Princess*, perhaps the smallest of the large boats. The story of how these English immigrant entertainers and their children became a noteworthy showboat family is a look back into the American past, when rural life was real—not long past the frontier era—and not the subject of nostalgia. Billy Bryant's tale tells us what it was like to grow up in that world. It is on the one hand a success story and on the other hand a narration of the demise of a long tradition. No one can recount the Bryant's family history better than Billy, whose personal adventures describe the transition in America from the avenues of Gus

French, Ed Price, "Double R" Markle, and Ralph Waldo Emerson to the world of New York's Great White Way in the 1930s, World War II, and the era of radio and television.

MARTIN RIDGE

The Huntington Library
The California Institute of Technology
July, 1988

Children of Ol' Man River
*The Life and Times
of a Showboat Trouper*

Author's Introduction

MY FAMILY and I began our lives on the river as the mussel does—at the bottom. Mother and Dad, my sister Florence and I, all went through about as many kinds of thrills and depressions as any one could anywhere. More than once the river got us down. More than once it pushed us up again. It all but tore us apart sometimes, but now we seem securely afloat.

Yet in spite of our many adversities along the inland waterways, I still love the rivers, all of them: the picturesque Allegheny over whose friendly face I skipped stones as a boy and in whose cooling shallows I waded, catching crawdads and shiners from under flat rocks; the smoky Monongahela with its lovable coal miners; the Ohio, childhood nurse of many of America's finest men of letters; the Little Kanawha at whose mouth I experienced the terror which accompanied the final destruction of the first real home I ever knew; the Big Kanawha; the Big Sandy; the Kentucky; the Green; the Tennessee; the Illinois, the greatest showboat river of them all; the mighty Mississippi, along which Sam Clemens cried, "Mark Twain!" until the entire world heard him; the Red River of the North; the Achafalaya,

3

where we found a section of lost America—the largest torrent and the smallest trickle that finds its way into America's great system of inland streams is a part of my life.

To me James Whitcomb Riley's poem, "Noon time, June time, down along the river" describes the finest set of circumstances in which a man, as well as a boy, can find himself.

When I am away from the river I am away from home and homesick. I miss the long gone, but still familiar whistle of the side-wheeler *Kate Adams*,[1] deep in the bend, and the long coils of smoke rising skyward from "the lovin' Kate's stacks." My ears still listen for those soft mellow tones of the *Queen City's*[2] bell and the murmur of her breast waves rolling onto the shores. I wait in vain to hear the mournful bawl of a motherless calf at midnight aboard an up-river packet bound for the Pittsburgh market. I long for the thrill of the Louisville Falls and the sound of the *Tom Greene's*[3] escape at Gun

---

[1] This is probably the third *Kate Adams*, a steel hull packet, built in Jeffersonville, Indiana, by Howard in 1888. The boat burned at the Memphis levee on January 8, 1927.

[2] The *Queen City* was a stern wheel, wooden hull packet built in Cincinnati, Ohio, by the Cincinnati Marine Railway Company in 1897. This was a deluxe packet designed to cater to an elite patronage. The vessel sank on the falls at Louisville on February 17, 1914.

[3] The *Tom Greene* was a stern wheel, steel hull packet built at Point Pleasant, West Virginia, by the Marietta Manufacturing Company in 1923. The vessel ended its career at Paducah, Kentucky, as a landing boat office in the 1950s.

Powder Chute, the sandbars at Diamond Island in midsummer, the sight and smell of fishermen tarring their nets at Enterprise Landing. I miss diving with my clothes on from the ferryman's flat into the muddy Ohio at the challenge of "Last one in—."

In my mind I can see the large pecan trees at Pecan Point above Memphis, hear the whippoorwill's call at twilight, see a full June moon turning the Mississippi into a bright stream of running silver, watch a golden sunset at the mouth of the Red River, daybreak at Natchez Bend, a sunrise at Cairo Point. Frogs in rhythm announce the approach of rain to my listening imagination and the patter of an April shower on a showboat roof follows close on their prophecy.

I miss the mad rush of minnows on the surface of the stream in their hasty retreat from a hungry bass, the shooting of wild geese near Baton Rouge at Christmas time, the silver bridge at Point Pleasant after a heavy frost, Cincinnati's illumined skyline and the picturesque Kanawha Valley hills in early summer strewn with wild flowers, red buds and dogwoods—all call to me with a siren insistence.

And through all my visions of the rivers run the colorful showboats of the past and present, the penetrating notes of their steam calliopes, the charming personnel of their casts and crews, the gay friendliness of their audiences. Showboating has been my life for the past thirty years and the river longer than that. I want to tell people about it.

Comparatively little has ever been truthfully written about the history of the showboat although it is generally known along the rivers that Captain A. B. French[4] and Captain E. A. Price,[5] rival rivermen, were founders of the modern floating theater. The book which will tell this story still waits to be written. Someday I may try to write it.

Primarily the showboat furnishes entertainment for country people. Yet not all the river audiences are farmers and miners and grocery clerks and housewives from little out-of-the-way communities. We ourselves have had many notable visitors. Flo Ziegfeld,[6] a showboat fan and producer of the musical version of *Show Boat*,[7] came to us to check up on some of the details of his settings and direction; Dick Powell,[8] enjoying a happy afternoon with us wanted us to play Little Rock, Arkansas, his favorite port; Fifi D'Orsay[9] nearly caused mutiny among

[4]Augustus Byron French (1832-1902) was the father of American showboating.

[5]Edwin A. Price (1847-1930) was, next to French, the most successful showboat manager.

[6]Florenz "Flo" Ziegfeld (1867-1932) was the most famous American producer of his day. His name remains virtually synonymous with theatrical excellence and extravagance. His production of the stage version of *Show Boat* in 1927 was hailed as a high point in the American theater.

[7]The film was based on Edna Ferber's novel *Show Boat*, which was published in 1926.

[8]Richard "Dick" Powell (1904-63) was a film actor, as well as a Hollywood director and producer.

[9]Fifi D'Orsay (1904-?) was a film actress who was notorious for outlandish behavior off the screen.

Captain Augustus B. French

Captain Edwin A. Price
Courtesy Kent State University Library, Kent, Ohio

7

the crew when she sat on the front porch of our boat in a one-piece bathing suit, and dove from the top of the boat into the Ohio before a battery of news cameras; and Harry Langdon,[10] spending a weekend with us, nearly gave me heart failure by insisting on steering the boat.

And there was that night in Cincinnati when I would willingly have crawled into the mouth of a red-tail sucker, and could have, had I been as small as I felt. I was feeling especially crabby and not overjoyed at the prospects of what looked like a dull evening, when a well-dressed party of people came up to the boat just a little before the show. They didn't go to the box office, but came to me.

"Do you recognize the profession?" one of them asked.

"Oh, I suppose so," I said rudely. "How many?"

Instead of telling me the number he told me their names: Walter Hampden, Fay Bainter, Vincent Lopez, James Barton,[11]—but I didn't hear any more, I was so busy getting them seated.

And the very next night I did it all over again. Just as the show was about to start I noticed a very

[10] Harry Langdon (1885-1944) was a popular stage and screen actor and comedian.

[11] Walter Hampden (1879-1955) was the most famous classical actor in America during his lifetime. He performed many Shakespearean roles and was also well known for his lead role in *Cyrano*. Fay Bainter (1892-1968) was a distinguished actress on both the stage and screen. Vincent Lopez was a popular orchestra leader in the 1930s. James Barton (1890-1962) was a popular film actor.

bulky gentleman standing on the outside guardrail back by the stage with his head and one shoulder squeezed through one of the windows, gossiping with members of the cast. I rushed up with a show of great importance.

"See here," I said, taking him by the arm, "these are the actors' quarters and only professional people are allowed on this end of the boat."

He smiled with cherubic good nature.

"Now take it easy, son. There are some people who think I'm an actor."

It was Walter Connolly.[12]

One more and then I'll stop this and go into less embarrassing memories. We were getting a radio show ready when a tall, middle-aged gentleman, slightly stooped, came up to the platform and began very graciously to offer some suggestions about the way the people out on the air would like to hear the showboat itself described. With considerable asperity I asked him what he knew about it, whereupon he handed me his card and I saw that I was talking to Graham McNamee.[13]

Yes, you'd be quite surprised at the great cross-section of people who find their way to the river and its showboats.

I was telling John Golden, the New York theatri-

[12]Walter Connolly (1887–1940) was well known as both a stage and screen actor.

[13]Graham McNamee (1888–1942) pioneered successful sport and news broadcasting. His lively style gave him the status of a celebrity and entertainer.

cal producer,[14] about some of my river experiences one night several years ago when he suddenly exploded with a suggestion.

"Good Lord!" he cried, "if you'd put some of that in a book they'd surely make you Secretary of the Navy!"

That's the only thing that has kept me from writing a book before. I don't want to be Secretary of the Navy. I might have to go to sea some time and I'd feel as lost on any boat that draws more than three feet of water as I do on land. But awhile ago I learned that you have to have schooling to be a member of the President's cabinet, and that disqualifies me.

So here is my book. It is for you. And it is for my mother, my father, and the river; the three grandest parents any man ever had.

[14]John Golden (1874–1955) was a highly successful lyricist and Broadway producer. He owned his own theater. Although quite sophisticated, he preferred to produce what he called wholesome plays. His autobiography, *Stage-Struck, John Golden*, is a lively introduction to theater in the first third of the twentieth century.

I

From Buckingham Palace to Texas

MOTHER was fond of watercress. Dad liked flowers. And these two loves, quite by accident, brought them together. I don't know where Mother got her fondness for cress, but Dad's love of flowers is easy to explain. His father was a landscape gardener to Queen Victoria, and Dad grew up among the spacious gardens and hedged lanes of Buckingham and Windsor.

When he was about twenty-five, he went to Bristol to see a famous flower show. He didn't know the city and was blundering around trying to find the show when, stepping aside to let a group of girls pass and following them with his eyes, he bumped squarely into another, knocking a basket of watercress out of her hands.

In an instant he was down on his knees, muttering profuse embarrassed apologies, and picking up the cress. When he looked up at the laughing face above him he forgot all about the girls who had passed by. He wanted to keep looking, so instead of putting all of the greenery back in the basket at once he began to nibble at it, stalling for time.

"Pretty good watercress," he said lamely. "Did you grow it?"

It was a silly question to ask anyone with hands as white and smooth as those which were arranging the basket, and the girl only laughed and told him that she was singing in the new Gilbert and Sullivan operetta and really wouldn't have much time to grow cress or know how if she had.

"I could show you," Dad offered hopefully; then, suddenly self-conscious, asked if she could direct him to the flower show. She did, and he went along, but his mind wasn't on flowers much.

That night he was in a shilling stall at Gilbert and Sullivan's famous hit. But even when he heard

> *I'm called Little Buttercup,*
> *Sweet Little Buttercup,*
> *Though I could never tell why . . . ,*[1]

he still couldn't think of flowers, but only of the girl who sang the words.

After that he began to save his money for a velocipede. It was a high-wheeled, hard-rubber-tired thing, and must have jounced the stuffing out of him in those days before there were good automobile roads, but distances are never very long in England, and Dad could sort of follow the company in which his "Little Buttercup" was playing. Often he would ride twenty-five miles to see her, which was more than he would do for any other flower.

[1]"Little Buttercup" was written by William S. Gilbert and Arthur S. Sullivan, for the light opera *H. M. S. Pinafore* in 1878.

And Mother (she wasn't Mother then, of course) liked it.

But her father didn't. So, just as some of their ancestors' relatives had looked to America for freedom to worship, Mother and Dad looked in the same direction for freedom to love. Dad sold his velocipede and practically everything else he owned, and Mother turned whatever she could into hard cash. Then they set sail. Mother held out only two things which might have been sold: a diamond ring and a guitar. When she showed them to her newly made husband aboard the ship, he hesitantly brought out his own treasures to show her: a drawknife, a keyhole saw, a chisel, and a hammer.

"My father used these tools most of his life," he said. "I've used 'em as long as I can remember. I'd never be able to get tools like that in America. There's no steel like English steel."

They landed in New York in 1884, utterly penniless. They had no plans, no knowledge of what they would find here, no money—nothing but a devoted love for each other and a great courage. Mother took the lead at once and asked the Castle Garden[2] authorities where they would be likely to find jobs. They were advised to go to Brooklyn.

Shouldering their bundles they began to make

[2]Castle Garden, an immigrant receiving station in the nineteenth century, was built as a fort at New York's Battery in 1807. Its huge gallery was converted into a concert hall for the Swedish vocalist Jenny Lind.

their way along the freight-laden waterfront, finding a tortuous path between cases of goods, wagons, and cursing longshoremen, toward the imposing approaches of Brooklyn Bridge. It hadn't occurred to them that they wouldn't walk to Brooklyn. The bridges they knew in England were short.

Finding themselves finally at the bridge, wearied from the walk they had already taken, Mother took on at once the role of provider she had filled so many times during her life in the land of the free.

"You keep still, Sam, while I get carfare for us," she whispered.

Going up to a policeman whose face told her his origin, she assumed an Irish brogue, looking at him with eyes which melted with blue homesickness for the fields of County Cork, and asked him how a body fresh from the "ould sod" could get across the bridge without even carfare.

In a moment she came back to Dad with a silver dollar in her hand, their first American money, their total capital in a new world, and in state they rode to Brooklyn.

Here they obtained employment almost at once. Mother worked in a restaurant and later became wet nurse to Joseph Jefferson's[3] son Thomas, while Dad drove a mule car from the Brooklyn Bridge, out Flatbush Avenue to the car barns.

Neither of them knew, as they looked into my

[3] Joseph Jefferson (1829–1905) was a distinguished stage actor and producer.

Entrance to the Brooklyn Bridge, 1884
Courtesy New York City Public Library

crib in a Brooklyn flat, that they were looking at the son of one of the best showboat men America ever produced (you wouldn't have guessed it about Dad in those days), or that my bare feet would become more accustomed to the cooling waters of the inland streams of the Middle West and South than to the dusty streets of Brooklyn. Mother went on with her work in the restaurant and Dad went on driving his mule.

That is, he went on until the mule changed all that. One day, during a terrific electrical storm, lightning struck a tree and felled it across the track directly behind the car. It hit the street with a thunderous crash, and the mule, already full of fears and tremors from the lightning and thunder, decided that he would go away from there, fast.

He went, and if anyone thinks a mule is a slow-going animal, let him watch one in flight, or let him ask my Dad. There have been electric trolley cars on that line long since, but never one which covered the ten blocks from the place where the tree fell to the end of the mule's dash in the time that one covered them. Every time the car hit a joint in the rails with a bang and a rattle it increased the mule's panic, and Dad, sawing like mad on the reins and trying to talk mule language, probably seemed to be just one more thing the crazed beast wanted to get away from.

At a turn the car went over; Dad was thrown in front of it; the mule broke loose and scurried to whatever place he thought he could find peace. And Dad, when he picked himself up again, found that he had left one finger behind him.

In the hospital he talked it all over with Mother.

"I don't like mules," he said. "I'll take care of watercress, or turnips, or tulips, or buttercups, or cabbages, but I never want to see another mule."

So we went to Philadelphia, where Dad got himself a job with a florist.

But Mother wasn't satisfied. She longed for a return to the stage. The footlights, the heightened emotion which is the very air one breathes in any theater, the applause—they all kept tugging at her. In the evening she would bring out her guitar and, strumming those arrangements which she faked for herself, she would croon, "My name's Little Buttercup," or "When I was a lad I served a term,"[4] or some other song from the Gilbert and Sullivan operas in which she had played and which she loved. Sometimes she would vary this by singing, "Flow Gently Sweet Afton,"[5] or "Twickenham Ferry"[6] and then Dad knew that she was homesick.

Before long, though, her mind was again taken up by something more important to any woman than

[4]This song, written by William S. Gilbert and Arthur S. Sullivan, is sung by the comic admiral, Sir Joseph Porter, in *H. M. S. Pinafore.*

[5]"Flow Gently Sweet Afton," was written by Robert Burns. It was set to music by James E. Spillman in 1838.

[6]"Twickenham Ferry" was written and composed by Theophile Marzials in 1875.

the country she calls home—the birth of another child, my sister Florence. But as the novelty of the new baby wore off, Mother began again to have that lost-sheep look in her eyes which had worried Dad before. Between her singing of English songs she kept urging Dad to go into the show business with her—some way, any way at all.

So Dad, knowing that he would have to do something about her nostalgia, and knowing equally well that he could not take her back to England just then, took all of us to New York, where he bought a one-horse covered wagon, a horse, a tent, a book of magic tricks, five gallons of gasoline, several pounds of Cayenne pepper, some black oilcloth, some felt, rolls of copper and zinc wire, a Prince Albert coat, and a top hat. Here he had all the ingredients which, mixed later, produced a full-fledged medicine show of that Victorian era. With the gasoline and red pepper he made liniment; with the oilcloth, felt, and wire he made "electric belts"; with the book of magic, the top hat, and the Prince Albert he made people of the Middle West gasp and spend their money.

His strange outfit acquired, he drove around to the boarding house where he had left Mother, Florence, and me, and called us out into the street.

"There's your show business," he cried proudly to Mother. "Throw in your guitar and satchel and we'll get going."

I have often wondered what Mother must have

thought and felt when she saw that weird collection of things in front of her and heard that it was a "show business." What a sense of contrast and let-down must have flashed across her mind as she remembered the applause which had greeted her in England as "Buttercup," the warmth and color and friendliness of the theater, the praise of the press, the flowers in her dressing room, the after-theater suppers and the devotion of her friends.

What she thought I don't know, and if I heard what she said I don't remember. But I know Mother well enough to know that if there was any sadness or disappointment in her mind at the sight of this sorry-looking outfit, she gave no sign of it, and that all Dad heard was praise and encouragement.

Dad threw his precious tools and Mother's guitar in and we headed west, Florence and I often sleeping in the deep hay which half filled the back of the wagon as the horse slowly jogged over the rough roads toward Oklahoma, where the Cherokee Strip[7] was about to be opened to homesteaders.

At every town where it seemed as though we might do some business, we stopped and put on a show. If it was a small place, and looked as though it was worth only an hour or so, we would make a "high pitch," that is, we would stop at a street cor-

[7] The Cherokee Strip was a district in Oklahoma that was opened for settlement at noon on April 22, 1889. Within a few hours 100,000 people had moved in and 1,920,000 acres had been taken up. By nightfall on April 22, Oklahoma City had 10,000 tent dwellers and Guthrie perhaps 15,000.

ner where Mother would draw a crowd by playing her guitar and singing a few songs. After a few people were there, Dad would entertain them, and get others to come, by doing simple tricks of magic. His favorite was the old sucker-box trick, because it was so simple to do. The dice disappeared themselves without any skill on the part of the magician. It was inevitable that they should disappear. Nothing that he could have done would have prevented it.

If there were still not enough people there Mother would sing a few more songs. Then when there were enough in the crowd to look like some money, Dad would go into his real act, the spiel which the crowd had really been brought to hear.

"Now, folks," he'd begin, "come on up real close, because I'm going to let you into a secret. You, standing out there by the tree, come up here. I'm going to tell you something you'll thank me for the rest of your life."

Here he would pause a moment to let his words sink in. Then, with his voice solemn and low-pitched, and staring directly at the most haggard-looking individual, he would announce the nature of the great revelation he was about to deliver.

"I'm going to tell you how to get rid of pain."

Here he would pause again, for no one could be expected to absorb the full extent of such good fortune as this in a moment. And his impressive Prince Albert coat and tall top hat got in their best work when he was silent.

"It ain't right that you should suffer, folks, especially when it's so easy and costs so little to be free from pain."

No one there had said anything about suffering, but by this time there were nods of approval, and solemn eyes cast to the ground as Dad's listeners ruminated on the ills of the human frame and needless suffering, while the women looked with rapt attention at the serious, kindly face of the man they thought was about to offer them a salvation which not even Wine of Cardui or Peruna had ever really achieved for them.

"I want to tell you how I learned this great secret," Dad would go on. Pausing again, he would hold up his mutilated hand. "You can see I've got only three fingers on this hand. Neuralgic rheumatism got the other one before I learned what to do about it. I had such pain that I couldn't sleep at night, such pain that I would writhe and scream in torment, like a man in a madhouse. Finally the doctors, seeing that it was about to spread to my other fingers, and from there to the rest of my body, making a hopeless paralytic of me, cut off that finger, took one of the members from this body which the Good Book says thou shalt not mutilate! If they had known, or if I had known, then, what I know today, I'd have that finger now.

"A few weeks after I got out of the hospital I began to feel pain again in my hand. They hadn't got the finger off soon enough. Before they had begun to cut, the poison began to spread. I knew what that meant. I knew that if I didn't do something mighty quick I'd lose my hand.

"And then, by accident, I met a very wise man—a prince from India, a man whose people had known for centuries cures which English and American doctors haven't heard of yet. He told me about certain herbs and drugs with magical properties and about the mighty powers of electricity.

"And the results of the things he told me, folks, are in this bottle and this belt!"

Here he would stop again while he displayed impressively, one in each hand, an "electric belt" and a bottle filled with a slightly pinkish fluid labeled, "Dr. Bryant's Magic Liniment. For Soreness, Lameness, Neuralgic Rheumatism, Gout, Stiffness, and Congestion. KEEP AWAY FROM FIRE!" In the center of the label was a colored picture of a royal Hindu prince of the blood.

Putting the belt behind him for a moment, he would concentrate on the liniment.

"This liniment, which the prince helped me to make in my laboratories, cured me in exactly five applications. Before I started, my fingers were curled up like the claws of a chicken. I couldn't straighten them out. Now you can see for yourselves how supple and limber they are.

"How much do you suppose that was worth to me? I had spent hundreds of dollars on doctors and hospitals and they hadn't cured me. With about a

fourth as much liniment as there is in one of these
bottles, I was cured. How much would that be
worth to you? If I were to ask you five dollars for a
bottle of this magic fluid which will free you from
pain, would you say that it was too much?"

Invariably half a dozen heads would shake side-
ways. Dad would watch for the one which shook the
most vigorously and call that person up to the tail
of the wagon, to demonstrate the liniment and
make him a present of the first bottle.

"Feel it penetrate?" he would ask, and the victim, whose hand by now was burning like fire from
the vicious mixture of gasoline and Cayenne pepper
which Dad had rubbed on it, would nod a hearty
recommendation. Then Dad would cork up the
bottle and smilingly put it into the smarting hand.

"There you are, my boy," he would say. "Take it
home. Rub it on at night when you feel any pain.
It'll work wonders for you. Now, folks, here's the
big surprise. You've all agreed that five dollars
would be a reasonable price for this magic secret
medicine. But I'm not going to ask you to pay me
five dollars. I'm not going to ask you to pay me
three dollars. I'm not even going to ask you to pay
me a dollar. No, sir, I want this remedy in every
home in the land. I want its benefits to reach the
poor as well as the rich. Fifty cents, four bits, five
dimes, is all I want you to pay. Take three bottles
for a dollar, so you'll be sure to have it on hand
when you need it most!"

When he had sold as many bottles of "Dr. Bryant's Magic Liniment" as possible, Mother would sing another tune to her strumming guitar and Father would then launch a similar sales talk on the virtues of the electric belt, the magic properties of which extended from the ability to cure rheumatism to the conquest of sterility. The belt was "guaranteed to make you forget every ache and pain." And it probably did, for the chemical action set up by the zinc and copper wires which Father wove into them, and the felt pad soaked in vinegar, would produce a surface burning sensation which would make a man forget his name so long as it lasted.

In the evenings Dad worked on his electric belts while Mother filled bottles with gasoline and red pepper—the sole ingredients of Dr. Bryant's Magic Liniment—and pasted labels on them.

When we came to a larger town where we wanted to spend two nights, we would pitch a tent and put on a vaudeville show inside. The first night the show would be free and we would concentrate on the sale of soap, liniment, and electric belts. The second night we would charge ten cents admission and give the audience a more elaborate show, not neglecting sales during the intermissions.

By the time we got to Texas we had a little cash capital and added Frank L. Cutler, his daughter, Myra, and an Irish comedian named Joe Keaton to the company, enlarging our show. Myra turned out to be Joe's basket of watercress, his little buttercup, his do re mi fa sol la si do, and they were married. They had a son and named him Buster.[8] And thus a famous movie career was actually begun in the tent of a medicine show before there were any movies to receive it.

Finally, we reached the Cherokee Strip. On the day of the opening, April 22, 1889, our wagon was drawn up in Perry along with the rest and, at a signal given by a gun, the twelve-mile race started. The horses were white or roan or dappled at the outset, but so dry was the black dirt of the prairie that it was a gang of black men and black horses which finally arrived at the free land, where the men began driving their stakes.

Dad put his stakes in at a likely-looking spot and immediately set his tent up. Before dark Mother and he had a fine supply of liniment mixed and some handmade notices tacked on trees about the camp, announcing a show that night with twenty-five cent admission. His prices, along with those of everyone else who had anything to sell, had reacted to the standards of the frontier, and were up.

After the show, he immediately rearranged the inside of the tent and turned it into a hotel. He wrote little cardboard tickets out in pencil, each ticket allowing the holder to spend the night on the ground inside the tent, at a cost of twenty-five cents, and filled it from wall to wall.

[8]Buster Keaton (1895–1966) was a variety performer and an early successful film actor.

Water so muddy that after drinking it a man sneezed dust, was sold for ten cents a glass, and there was practically no food available. One day word went round that a carload of buns would arrive that afternoon at the railroad several miles away. All the homesteaders rushed to the railroad track. When the train arrived there were the buns, loaded loosely in a boxcar like so much coal. The conductor told the man who had bought them that he would have to unload them right away, since there was no siding there. When the bun merchant protested, the train crew simply pried open the side of the car which allowed the buns to fall out and scatter all over the ground.

Dad bought six at ten cents each. A few others bought some. Then there was an onslaught which the owner of the buns could do nothing to stop. Fifteen minutes later there was not a bun left, yet all the dealer had received was $3.10!

After awhile the surveyors came to lay out our new town. When the lines for the main street were run they went right through our tent, so we had to pull up the stakes and move on.

For several years we barnstormed through the West and South, and it was then that we learned the true value of Mother's guitar and diamond ring. At some time or other they were in hock for board and room in half of the towns in Texas.

At times like these, when we were penniless, Mother would canvass from house-to-house, selling liniment, corn salve, cocoanut-oil soap, and a cure-all patent medicine made from "barks, berries, roots, and herbs." If her customers said they didn't have any money she would take food or clothing in payment. Many an evening she came back to us with a pillowcase or sheet wrapped around a supply of beans, freshly baked bread, biscuits, home-churned butter, coffee—whatever she could get. And more often than I like to remember, it was only what she procured in this way that kept us from going to bed supperless.

When our tent finally wore out we were not able to replace it, so we let Frank Cutler and the Keaton family go, and Florence and I began our show career in the wagon. Sister played the guitar and I sang songs as we high-pitched our way. Often, when business was good, we would sell out our supply of bottled liniment and I then had to hold the crowd with songs and gags while Mother and Father moved to the other end of the wagon and mixed more gasoline and red pepper.

One of our major expenses was the cost of Dad's top hats. Often a crowd of rollicking cowboys would decide that the top hat was the most amusing target they had seen and it suddenly would become the recipient of stale eggs, tomatoes—even stones. Their accuracy was amazing! They could safely have called all their shots.

Finally, at an especially low ebb in our fortunes, we gave up the horse and wagon. We were playing

Raton, a small town on the Mexican border, when Dad was suddenly arrested for operating without a permit. Mother's guitar and diamond ring were then in pawn in Trinidad, Colorado, so we had to give up all the rest of our belongings as security for the fine.

The landlady at our boarding house was a kindly soul and stepped in to help us out. Her son was conductor on a freight train on the Santa Fe and she suggested that, if Dad wanted to deadhead with him to La Junta, Colorado, where there was a boom at the time, she would take care of Mother, Sister, and me until he could send for us.

What a picture Father must have made: immaculately dressed, as he always was, in his high silk hat, a form-fitting Prince Albert with velvet lapels, a white vest and puff tie to match, pinstriped trousers with gray spats, and his never-absent, gold-headed cane, as he rode in the red caboose behind the train rattling over the rails, bound for a destination he was never to reach.

He decided that it would be best for him to get off the train before arriving at La Junta, to avoid causing his host any embarrassing moments with the railroad officials. So at the water tank outside the city, he got down. As the train disappeared around the curve ahead of him, he picked up his suitcase loaded with electric belts and liniment, and started to follow it down the track.

At a short turn in the right-of-way he suddenly

came upon a number of men working on the road-bed. When they saw him, they immediately drew aside with a show of respect, while their foreman came running toward him. He shook hands heartily with Dad and then took his suitcase and started off through a field toward a large tent.

"You must be hungry," the genial foreman said. "How'd fried chicken sound to you?"

Dad thought that, instead of alighting peacefully from the caboose, he must have been killed in a wreck and gone to heaven. But he believed in never questioning the ways of providence, so he smiled with dignity and friendliness, and carried on as one should to a gracious host.

"I always did like fried chicken," he replied with enthusiasm.

"Well, we're all ready for you," the foreman assured him.

Now they were at the flap of the tent, from which came such delectable odors that Dad could hardly speak for the longing that was in his mouth. Chickens, mashed potatoes with yellow gravy, candied yams, delicious coffee, and two huge quarters of apple pie had gone to fill up the yawning chasm in Father's middle before any explanation was forthcoming. And, when it did, Dad knew again that he was alive, and face-to-face with reality.

It began when the foreman asked him what the railroad company's plans for a new spur were. Dad tried to look very wise as he answered.

"I really couldn't say," he replied slowly. So far, so good. It was a sage answer, in keeping with the important position of one who had weighty business secrets to guard. But when the foreman, accepting what must have sounded like a veiled reproof for his inquisitiveness, began asking by name about a number of people in the Kansas City office of the Santa Fe, Father knew that he was sunk.

"I don't know them," he said helplessly. "I've never been around railroad people much."

"Aren't you Mr. Benson from the Kansas City office, who was to arrive on that train?" the bewildered foreman asked.

"Not at all," Dad answered humbly. "I'm just a busted street fakir, trying to get to La Junta."

For a moment things looked bad. The foreman got red and white by turns and then, to complete a patriotic color scheme, turned the air blue with curses. But in a moment he stopped and proved his Irish descent by shaking with laughter. The joke was on him, but it was as good a joke as it would have been had it been on someone else.

"All right, Pop, you win," he laughed. "There's more chickens where those came from. Now let's see what's in that telescope you're carrying."

Again Father's heart sank. All of his stock in trade, everything with which he had hoped to replenish our fortunes, was in his suitcase, and he saw it all about to be confiscated to pay for his dinner.

But nothing of the kind was in the foreman's

mind. He was a good gambler. He had lost a bet and was about to pay. Led by him, his men crowded around and, in ten minutes, bought, at top prices, every bottle of liniment and every electric belt which Dad carried.

The next day he was back in Raton, with no electric belts and no liniment, but with more money than we had had at one time in years!

II

We Become "The Four Bryants"

MOTHER, who decided most matters of importance to us, pointed out that, with so much capital, we could break away from the horse and wagon and get into concert halls. Kansas City seemed the best place to start, and we headed for it—after going to Trinidad, where we bailed out Mother's guitar and diamond ring. We couldn't leave without them. Mother was too fond of them, and besides, who could tell when they might again be all there was between us and starvation?

In Kansas City we became "The Four Bryants" with a singing, dancing, and talking act which actually got an engagement, and our varied and rocky concert hall career began. It wasn't too hopeful, but we got by, working north and east until we finally reached Buffalo, which I shall always remember as the city that marked a dividing line between one life and another. Not that the new life was any easier, for a number of years, than the old. But it was from here, quite by accident, that we headed for the river which has dominated our life ever since.

Failing in Buffalo to get any better engagement, we went to work in Bonney's Comique on Canal Street, one of the toughest, roughest, dirtiest parts

of the city. This was now 1900, and the visitors to
the Pan-American Exposition didn't make the town
any quieter! They loved the honky-tonk shows Mrs.
Bonney put on and called for louder and rawer acts.

There was a small stage on which we put on our
act, and tables, instead of the usual theater seats,
where liquor was served. Instead of the regular theater balcony there was a series of booths, also with
tables, called "wine rooms." There were curtains
before these which were drawn when the parties
within became too intimate or too out of hand for
public view.

The management expected all the ladies of the
assembly to mingle with the patrons between their
acts, solicit drinks from drunken sailors, slumming
parties, or anyone else who had the price. On busy
nights, such as those when a freighter made port,
money was spent so freely that drinks came faster
than the ladies could consume them without passing out. So fake mixtures were served to the girls,
who secretly poured them down a trough built for
that purpose.

My mother was no exception to the rule, and had
to entertain undesirables along with the rest. Her
reward for this was a five-cent commission on every
drink and the assurance that Dad and I would be
kept working.

It was no disgrace to work in such an atmosphere
in those days. But Dad felt that it was humiliating
to have his wife hustling beer checks in order to

keep him in a job. Yet it was almost impossible for a man to obtain a position without a woman. The show world wanted girls. They were then, as now, the really important part of the show business.

Disgusted with his reputation as "Mrs. Bryant's husband," Dad longed for some practical method by which he could establish himself as the rightful head of the Bryant family. Since he couldn't sing or dance, he bravely set out to master the art of magic, then known as sleight-of-hand, with a view to becoming the world's greatest magician. He studied and worked for weeks to perfect the great mystic illusions he had in mind. Boxes of rabbits, guinea pigs, white mice, pigeons, and canary birds cluttered our furnished room until the sight, sound, and smell indicated that the place was a pet shop.

His routine of tricks included the breaking and cooking of an egg in a hat to be borrowed from some gentleman in the audience, and the apparent smashing up of a watch which he would obtain in a similar manner and return to its owner in its original condition. If he got that far, he intended to produce a few pigeons from the air. Then, to give the act a whirlwind finish, he was going to pull a rabbit out from under the collar of some gentleman in the audience.

Every night, after we got back to the room from Bonney's, he would set out to prove the plausibility of his plans by donning a misfit Hindu costume (which made him look more like a fourth-rate

nightclub doorman than a magician) and proceeded to put on his complete act in front of us to see
whether we could catch on to any of his manipula-
tions. But we could tell from the way he looked at
us, as he challenged us to explain how he did it,
that, if we knew, we had better not admit it.

After weeks of preparation and endless post-
ponements, he finally mustered enough courage to
go through with it. One Saturday night, in Bonney's
smoke-filled auditorium, the curtains slowly parted
on the eight-by-ten stage with Dad, Hindu costume
and all, right in the middle of it. The piano added
the sweet strains of the waltz "Over the Waves" to
the natural accompaniment of clinking glasses and
bawdy conversation as Dad, excited and unstrung,
struck an "Ajax defying the lightning" pose and
went into his act. His audience, which by now
seemed to be his accusers, greeted him with hoots
and mock cheers and applause which sent him higher than a kite. He immediately forgot all of the little
he had learned about magic.

Acting grimly and automatically, like a man in a
trance, he proceeded to break up quite irreparably a
perfectly good Elgin watch belonging to a gentleman in the audience, instead of a substitute which
he carried for that purpose. That finished, he ruined another kind patron's Stetson hat with a none-
too-good egg that he splattered all over it. While he
was doing this, all the pigeons got loose and Dad
completed the damage to the hat by dropping and

stepping on it as he tried to catch the birds. Completely out of touch with reality now, he nearly pulled the ears off a frightened, overfed rabbit as he tried to make it seem to emerge from under a drunken patron's vest. It was too much, at least for the beast, and the trick developed into what looked like a fist fight between Dad and the rabbit.

Mother finally led him gently away, a trembling wreck, and Sis and I carefully gathered up the debris—the remnants of his shattered dreams. At the little stage door in the alley Mother kissed him goodnight, whispering, "It's all right, Sam. You tried. That's all anyone can do." Still in his delapidated Hindu costume, she placed him in a cab and sent him home; then she went back to square things with the management and the audience.

It was nearing spring in Buffalo (showboat time) when Mrs. Bonney nailed a sign on her doors. It said, "Closed for Repairs." What it really meant was that business was rotten and we were out of a job again. The revenue from Mother's salary and beer check commissions soon ran out.

I built a shoeshine box and went hustling in the streets. My first customer was the eminent actor Thomas W. Ross[1] who was at that time starring in *Checkers*[2] at the Tech Theater. Mr. Ross was a

[1] Thomas W. Ross (1875-1959) was a popular American actor.

[2] *Checkers* was written by Henry M. Blossom, Jr., and first produced in September, 1903, at the American Theater in New York City.

conversational soul, and before I had finished pol-
ishing his first shoe I was telling him about my stage
ambitions. He then took me to the theater and got
me a job as a "super"[3] in the racetrack scene, at fifty
cents a performance. Mother had long started canvassing, as she always did when we became financially
embarrassed.

It was at about this time that we first ran into
George M. Cohan. We had been hearing about him
for months, all along the route from Kansas City to
Buffalo. The act which he did with his family—his
father, his mother, and his sister—was the sensation
of the season. They were known as "The Four Cohans," just as we had called ourselves "The Four
Bryants." From the first, I felt a prideful interest in
the Four Cohans and drew youthful comparisons
based on the similarity between their situation and
ours—a similarity which ended when relative success and failure were brought into the picture.

Secretly I admired George Cohan immensely,
with all of the intense admiration a boy in his early
'teens can bestow upon a man who is doing what
the boy wants to do. He was my idol and I was sure
that he was everything which my childish imagination said he was.

When Mrs. Bonney closed, the Four Cohans were
playing in an act called "Running for Office." We
had heard that Mr. Cohan had written acts for several other vaudeville troupes, the kind of acts that

[3]A super is an actor who does not have a speaking part.

The Four Cohans about 1900
left to right: George M., Josie (sister),
Jerry (father), Nellie (mother)
Courtesy New York City Public Library

41

eventually landed them on Broadway, so I conceived the idea that we would get him to write an act for us. God knows we needed one!

Father thought it would do no good to ask him, and Mother was skeptical too, but I was insistent.

"He likes to help people," I assured her. "He's one of the finest men in the world, and all we have to do is to ask him."

Finally, more to satisfy me, I think, than out of any conviction of her own, Mother consented to go to his hotel with me. She dressed me in my best clothes, which included a large, white embroidered Lord Fauntleroy collar that nearly covered my shoulders, and at two o'clock in the afternoon we entered the Statler Hotel and went up to Mr. Cohan's apartment.

Mother rapped timidly at the door and we waited breathlessly. After a second knock, we heard a gruff voice which froze all of my young enthusiasm.

"Who the hell is coming up here at this time of the morning?" it cried, and I thought we must have got the wrong door. I could not believe that this was the voice of the man I had idolized.

Mother knocked again, and the door finally opened just wide enough for Mrs. Cohan (Ethel Levy) to show her face and utter one short word which made both Mother and me feel as though we had wandered, by mistake, into a cold storage plant.

"Well?" Her tone told us clearly that our reply would be an unwelcome impertinence.

"I want to see Mr. Cohan on business," Mother announced.

"Well, you can't see him. He's in bed." The door was about to close, not only on Mrs. Cohan, but on all of the magnificent picture my hero worship had painted. An idol lay shattered at my feet and my heart was surging in bitter pain. I wanted suddenly to be sitting out in front of his act in the theater with a brick house which I could present to him one brick at a time. I wanted to hurt him as I was now being hurt—not just by his refusal, but by the sense of superiority his wife was exhibiting to Mother.

"He's all in from taking bows at the supper show, I suppose," I said, in a voice which I tried to give the high note of fine sarcasm.

Mother took me by the arm and pushed me behind her in the hall. She already had a feeling that this conversation wasn't going to last very long under any circumstances, and she did not propose to let me shorten it further.

"I am Mrs. Bryant of the Four Bryants," she went on, moving closer to the door as she realized that she was fighting a losing battle, "and we came to see if Mr. Cohan would consider writing a vaudeville act for us."

"Yes, and without any tambourines or bass drums like in his to cover up bad acting," I put in. It was sheer insanity, but I was aching with a terrible disappointment and, childlike, wanted to smash somebody. I think that, with any encouragement at all, I would have shouted through the door at Cohan, "Your act's lousy too!"

When Mrs. Cohan spoke, the thermometer had dropped several degrees more.

"I'm sure that Mr. Cohan would not take on any more writing obligations just now," she said, and the interview was closed. So was the door.

Faint from disappointment we started walking down the stairs, forgetting all about the elevator. I put my arm around Mother and attempted to provide some kind of consolation.

"Never mind, Mother," I said. "I'll write an act for us myself, and it'll be better than anything that guy could write!"

True to my promise, or at least partially true to it, I helped Mother and Dad lay out an act for the Four Bryants and, to our delight, we were allowed to open with it at Shea's two or three weeks later. I don't know to this day why I insisted on putting "The Green Grass Grew All Around"[4] in for me to sing. It is probably the greatest bore that was ever set to music. But, even in the first decade of the century, the amusement game in the big cities was too fast for me.

As I marched out before the footlights, swelling with pride, I thought that now I was going to show Georgie Cohan how an act should be put on. My

[4]"And The Green Grass Grew All Around" was published in 1912, with lyrics by William Jerome and music by Harry Von Tilzer.

heart was beating like a trip-hammer, to be sure, but it was from excitement, not from fear. I admitted that I had a good voice and I was about to lay them dead in the aisles.

Everything seemed all right as I sang the first verse:

> *Oh, there was a tree*
> *In the woods, in the ground,*
> *And the green grass grew all around,*
> *All around,*
> *And the green grass grew all around.*

Verse by verse I went on, putting a limb on the tree, and a twig on the limb, repeating, as that burdensome old song does all the long rigamarole of all the preceding verses every time I sang a new one, while the audience got more and more restless. During the fourth verse, in which a nest is built on the twig:

> *Prettiest little nest you ever did see.*
> *Oh, the nest on the twig,*
> *Twig on the branch,*
> *Branch on the tree,*
> *Tree in the woods*

and on and on, a man in the front row yawned and finally went to sleep. Even through my singing I seemed to be able to hear him snoring.

Inch by inch I fought my way, putting an egg in the nest, a bird in the egg, a wing on the bird, a feather on the wing (quite unmindful of the fact that unhatched birds do not have feathers), and at that point, in the ninth verse, which was, of course, longer than the eighth, which was longer than the seventh, since every verse contained all of every preceding verse, the sleeper in the front row woke up, gave one disgusted look at me, muttered "O, my God!" and promptly went back to sleep.

When I had finally got the fuzz on the feather in the tenth verse, and all the various elements of all the other verses assembled once more, and the green grass growing all around all around, I decided it was time to stop. I'd already given them enough for their money. If they thought I was going to stand there all night singing for the measly salary the Four Bryants were getting, they were mistaken. Now if they wanted to pay us a salary like that of the Four Cohans. . . .

I stopped and the orchestra stopped. I waited for the applause, so that I could take my bows. Brother, if you've ever fought your way to the top of the Alps, or even the Adirondacks, and stood there alone at midnight in winter, you'll know what I heard. Nothing. Absolutely nothing!

It was as quiet as Lonesome Hollow Creek. It was so quiet that I could hear my heart thumping under my loud checkered comedy vest.

Trembling from head to foot, I ran off the stage as fast as I could with tears streaming from my eyes. Somehow, senselessly, I blamed George M. Cohan for my humiliation, because he had refused to write an act for us. Between teeth clenched to keep back the sobs, I cried, "I'll get even with you some day!"

We never waited for our photos which were in the lobby, or the two sheets of music we had handed the ten-piece orchestra at rehearsal. All we wanted to do was to get out of sight of everyone we knew. By side streets and back alleys we shamefully made our way to our furnished room on Swan Street. Once there I began to rave about "the dirty trick 'the Yankee Doodle Boy'[5] had played on us." Mother humored me, for she realized that my sudden hatred for the famous comedian was born of pain and humiliation and was actually my first experience in professional jealousy, that cankering ulcer which attacks the soul of every actor at some time or other.

"How does he get away with it?" I screamed, as I moved chairs out of the way and prepared to give an imitation of his famous eccentric dance. "Here's all he does!"

With that I began hopping and skipping around the room like a maniac, shouting breathlessly.

"If my hair was just a little longer, there'd be nothing to it," I cried.

"If your hair was a little longer, someone would shoot you for a pheasant," my sister said.

Just then Dad came in with some doughnuts and

[5] A reference to George M. Cohan, who starred in the stage hit *Yankee Doodle Dandy.*

a copy of the New York *Clipper*,[6] a theatrical journal of the time. As he looked through the want ads, he stopped at one and read it aloud.

"Wanted: Stock girls ... sister teams ... also vaudeville acts ... must work the wine rooms ... Austin's Palm Gardens, Syracuse."

We all sat in silence, feeling ashamed, each waiting for someone else to pass judgment.

"What else is there?" Mother asked hopelessly.

Dad turned another page and then stopped.

"How does this sound?" he asked. "Wanted, for Price's Water Queen Showboat, vaudeville people in all lines, long pleasant engagement, no pets allowed. Tickets? Yes, if I know you. Captain E. A. Price, Evansville, Indiana."

"Showboat? What's that?" we all asked in one breath, as he finished reading.

Father didn't know any more about it than we did, but it was a prospect for a job which didn't include beer checks, and Mother was interested. She wrote Captain Price a long letter and we waited in suspense before we got the glorious telegram:

ALL O.K.

JOIN AT AUGUSTA, KENTUCKY, SATURDAY.

Not knowing us, he didn't send railroad fare, so the question of how we were going to get tickets

[6]New York *Clipper* originated as a sports paper but after the Civil War it paid increasing attention to the theater. It later merged with *Billboard* and ultimately with *Variety*. The leading touring companies and vaudeville companies advertised for performers in its pages.

immediately arose. Mother once more pawned her guitar and diamond ring, but we still needed several dollars. No one seemed to have any other ideas, so I slipped out and went to see my friend at the Tech Theater, telling him our story. Without any hesitation he dropped his work and went the rounds of the stage doors with me, telling everywhere, with enriching details of his own, the story I had told him. At every theater we got something.

Probably Billy B. Van[7] and Nellie O'Neil[8] have forgotten all about it, but I shall always remember the crisp five-dollar bill which Miss O'Neil slipped into my hand, and the sweet smile she gave me with it, and the adoration for her that I felt. It rounded out the amount we had to have for the trip.

One more thing was needed. Our rent and board bill hadn't been paid. So Mother made a deal with the landlady to do her week's washing, and Father gave her husband an electric belt, and we were free. We hurriedly packed up, sadly leaving behind the diamond ring and guitar, which we would send for later, and were soon on a train headed for the *Water Queen* and a completely changed life for all of us.

And the Four Cohans moved in another direction—to New York, and to success.

[7] Billy B. Van (1870–1950) was a popular performer in vaudeville houses.

[8] Nellie O'Neil may refer to Gertrude Lamson, known as Nance O'Neill (1874–1965). She was a famous touring company star at the turn of the century. She won fame in David Belasco's production of *The Lily* in 1909.

III

Here Comes the Showboat!

At Cincinnati we changed trains, and an old life for a new. As we crossed the bridge into Kentucky, we looked down for the first time on the still waters of the beautiful Ohio River. We were looking then, without knowing it, at what was to be our home for the rest of our lives—the river. We followed its winding course a stone's throw from the water's edge, nearly all the way to Augusta, strangely thrilled by the long, lazy, inviting stretch of water which continually lay before us. Sometimes it was so clear and shallow, at the islands and sandbars we passed, that we could see the blending of crystal gravel and sand beneath it. How I longed to take off my shoes and stockings and wade in!

All along the shore strange little boats, some of them seemingly no more than floating grocery cartons, were tied up, anchored, or beached out on the bank. They seemed especially to seek out the comparatively sheltered waters of the mouths of creeks. They formed a weird and varied fleet, scattered for miles over the face of the water. Wanting to know as much as possible about the strange land into which we were heading, I asked a fellow passenger what they were. He told me that they were houseboats, and that people ate, slept, and lived year around on these fragile-looking ramshackle craft. I could hardly believe my ears.

Just above Moscow we met the steamer *Queen City* coming down the river full steam ahead. What a majestic sight it was! It was the first stern wheel riverboat any of us had ever seen, and we watched it with something like awe. As if to please us with its tricks, it blew for a landing as we watched. I wanted to clap my hands with joy. It was my first river whistle and it made such a deep impression on me that I can still distinguish the voice of the *Queen City* easily among a dozen others, even though they are at some distance.

Spring was in the air and the willow-lined shores on both sides of the river were turning to a bright apple green. All along the way the farmers and their families were busy plowing and cultivating the hillside and river bottomlands for their annual crops of corn, potatoes, and tobacco. Now and then we would pass through some sleepy village where rolling stones had stopped to gather moss. Long since having lost the distinction of being listed on the train schedules as flag stops, they were now merely railroad crossings and their only connection with the outside world was the small mail pouch hurriedly tossed from a passing train once a day to a waiting, aged mail carrier, who conveyed it to the general store or across the river in a john boat to a waiting postmistress.

Ohio River Sternwheeler under Full Steam
Courtesy The Public Library of Cincinnati and Hamilton County

53

We particularly noticed how friendly everyone was. Apparently we were the only strangers among them, and we didn't remain strangers long. Even the usually cold and indifferent members of the train crew were agreeable and as talkative and inquisitive as a group of women at an old fashioned quilting bee. No one hesitated to ask who we were or where we were going or what we were going to do. By the time we reached Augusta we knew practically everybody on the train and bade each one goodby as if he were an old friend.

Now I began to worry a little, for I had a problem which had to be faced out with Captain Price. In Buffalo I had picked up a stray dog who had become so dear to me in a short time that I simply couldn't bear to leave it behind in spite of the warning note in Captain Price's ad. It had said "No Pets," but Prince was just a big yellow mongrel, as kind and gentle as a good woman. I didn't see how anyone could object to that dog, and if anyone did, I didn't see how I could leave my friend behind. So Prince was with me, for better or worse, and I became troubled about what Captain Price might say.

As we stepped to the platform with the grips and the dog, we heard the distant melody of "My Old Kentucky Home"[1] coming from a steam calliope on the river. I had never heard a calliope before and I didn't know what it was, but I thought it was lovely.

[1] "My Old Kentucky Home" was written and composed by Stephen Foster in 1853.

The town was alive with activity and excitement and there was a pronounced note of joy in the air. At first I was vain enough to believe that Captain Price had told the inhabitants to watch for the arrival of the Four Bryants, and that the celebration was no more than the reception we deserved. I was about to take a few of the bows of which I had been robbed in Buffalo, but Florence made a face at me which cooled my ardor.

"If you're going to pull that Georgie Cohan stuff again," she said, "let me get across the street first, so they won't think I'm with you."

Then I saw groups of children running aimlessly about the streets shouting, "Showboat! Showboat! Here come's the showboat!" while they danced and turned somersaults and the showboat calliope obligingly and gaily furnished them with the airs of "Turkey in the Straw,"[2] "Oh, Dem Golden Slippers,"[3] and "Way Down Upon the Swanee River."[4] It was then I knew that the excitement was over the showboat itself, which was just tying up.

[2]The melody of "Turkey in the Straw," or "Zip Coon" as it was often called, was probably derived from an Irish folk tune. The song itself was first published in Baltimore by G. Willig about 1834. It should not be associated with crude Jim Crow music, although it was popular with black-face minstrel performers.

[3]"Oh Dem Golden Slippers" or "Golden Slippers," published in 1879, was written and composed by James A. Bland.

[4]In 1851 Stephen Foster wrote and composed "Way Down Upon the Swanee River" or "Old Folks at Home."

An old darkey[5] who met all trains drove us down to the river landing in a squeaky surrey.

"Going to the showboat tonight, Uncle?" Dad asked him.

"Yes, suh!" he replied quickly, and his eyes gleamed with anticipatory pleasure. "Dat's one boat I'se nevah missed!"

"You seem to like it," Dad said.

"Dat's Captain Price's floatin' opera," the Negro said, and there was a note of pride in his voice, almost as though the boat were his own. "Me an' mah chillun and mah old woman an' her chillun by her fust husband always goes, because we're sure of gettin' our money's worth. De Captain's been comin' here for forty years an' ev'ybody likes him because he always gives a good show."

The way he emphasized the words "good show" rather frightened us. Dad was especially uneasy at the prospects. Seeing his nervousness, the rest of us began to wonder just where Dad was going to fit into the picture. As a devoted husband and loving father he had been a huge success, but he had blundered in all other departments of his life. He just couldn't seem to get his bearings. It was as though, every time there was a round hole to be filled, Dad whittled a square peg for it. At times his depressions and long melancholy silences indicated that

[5]Terms like "darkey" not only date the continued use of this pejorative term by whites, but also indicate how deeply ingrained was this mentality in the river community.

he realized his helpless position. As an actor he was really no worse than the rest of us. It was just that we had more galvanized gall than he had, and would stay out on the stage until someone gave us the hook, regardless of our reception, while he would become backward and timid and a victim of stage fright at the least sign of unfriendliness or ridicule in the audience.

On the way down the levee with our luggage we met Captain Price going uptown for groceries and other supplies. He was a short, wiry, little figure out of the past. He had mutton-chop whiskers and was dressed in a short, black alpaca coat and a straw hat which had seen better days. He was slightly bowlegged and taked excitely. As his excitement rose he would scratch his whiskers with one hand and the side of his leg with the other. This was the first impression I had of the man who was a nationally known river figure and one of the true founders of the modern floating theater.

As he greeted us, Mother apologized for my dog, which I was leading proudly, feeling that his leash added distinction to my general appearance.

"I hope you won't mind the dog, Captain," Mother said. "Prince isn't really like most pets, but more like a person."

Captain Price looked at the dog and raised his eyebrows.

"Prince?" he asked.

"Billy is responsible for the name," Mother

Captain E. A. Price's Showboat, Water Queen

Courtesy Kent State University Library, Kent, Ohio

explained, with a twinkle in her eyes. Then she leaned over and whispered something in the captain's ear which I couldn't understand, and they both laughed pleasantly. He looked at me tolerantly and smiled.

"Put the dog on the steamboat," he said, "and I'll see about it later."

There was a hitch when we got to the stage plank (gangplank to you, if you are used to ocean-going vessels). It was so steep and narrow, and the water made such a merry race beneath it, that Dad got dizzy and balked. It looked like a major difficulty until Florence stepped into the breech. Telling Dad to bend over, she bound a handkerchief around his eyes and, taking him firmly by the hand, led him aboard. She had once seen a horse taken out of a burning barn!

On the boat we again had a marvelous example of river folk's friendliness. We had all anticipated the possibility of coolness on the part of the rest of the company, such as that which we had often experienced from other vaudeville troupes. They would all be old river troupers, we expected, who might look down on such tyros as we were. To our delight we were provided a welcome which would have warmed anyone's heart. They seemed lonesome and delighted to see anyone from the big cities. They crowded around us, asking for news from Chicago, Detroit, Kansas City, Buffalo. In ten minutes we felt as though we were a part of the family.

We were shown about the boat, then taken to our tiny rooms which were bare as well as small. They were clean and tidy, and in each one a drygoods box, into which shelves had been nailed, served as both washstand and dresser. Beside it was placed a bucket with a rope attached. Since there was so much water all about us the lack of running water bothered no one. We had only to sling a bucket over the edge of the boat whenever we wanted to wash or bathe, and bring it up full of cool clear water. And for those chilly nights there was a little oil stove in each room.

Mother stood in the middle of her room and beamed.

"I think it's the loveliest room I've ever seen," she said softly. "Tomorrow I'll get some blue stuff for curtains at the window and in front of the dresser, and you'll see how pretty it'll look!"

While we were planning our rooms and arranging our things, rehearsal was called and we all went to the stage. I looked out the open door to the fascination of the water, while the orchestra, which was even worse than we were, fought its way through the music. And I hoped that we would stay a little while, at least, for I wanted to do some fancy swimming and fishing along those inviting shores.

Everybody was expected to double in brass, that is, to play some sort of instrument in the band during the noonday parade. Just before dinner Captain Price gave Dad and me each a band uniform, con-

sisting of a white sailor suit (or rather a suit which
had once been white) with a round sailor hat from
which ribbons hung down at the back. Dad's suit
was either too small for him or he got too far into it.
It didn't fit any part of him and he couldn't seem to
get his hat on his head so that the ribbons would
hang down his back. They kept flapping around his
ears and getting into his eyes, so that he was in constant warfare with them.

Worried about what Dad would do to the harmo-
ny, I took the band leader aside and told him there
was really no instrument that Dad could play. The
leader was a kindly soul and gave Dad an alto horn
with a cork in it so that, although Dad marched
along with the rest of us, and went through all the
motions, he just couldn't blow any sour notes.

Even when working, the alto or "peck" horn is
the easiest instrument in the band to play. It's the
horn that goes along on the after-beat, the player
using one finger only as he blows "um-twat, um-
twat, um-twat-twat-twat-twat," all up and down the
street, but Dad didn't even have to worry about getting his "um-twats" wrong.

I played the bass drum for the first time in my
life. The drum was practically as large as I was. As
we went up the hill with our instruments, followed
by a group of happy children, I looked the gang
over. It was positively the most suspicious-looking
eight-piece brass band (six musicians, a plugged alto
horn, and a bass drum) I ever saw.

We paraded around town at a lively clip and finally stopped, out of breath, in front of the post office, where we formed in a circle to play the free concert. For a finishing number we played a part of the *William Tell*[6] overture (the easy part), or I mean, we played at it. What we really did was to engage in a weird battle with its elusive notes. The leader stood in the middle of the circle keeping time with his cornet, to remind us that he was still with us and to keep us all from going stark mad.

During the overture there were several opportunities for the bass drummer to sit down. They were obviously put there to give me a break, but I sat none of them out. I kept right on beating time, for I knew that if I ever stopped, I'd never be able to get back into the swing of it again.

"William Tell" was one tune that we never did learn to finish all together on the last beat. Someone would invariably give an extra humiliating blast on his horn after we had all quit playing and were about to take a bow from the spectators.

Later I learned, to my surprise, that there were other bands just as bad. Most of the little towns in those days had local bands of their own who would play the free concert with us. We learned to distinguish their musicians from the rest of the group by looking at their positions. Their trombone player would stand back of our trombone player and their

[6]The opera *William Tell* was written by Gioacchino Rossini in 1829.

The Water Queen's *Band*

Courtesy Kent State University Library, Kent, Ohio

alto back of our alto and so on around the circle. They reinforced us marvelously. With their help the din we could make was something both terrible and grand.

When the curtain went up that first night with a packed audience out front, we were scared stiff and on the verge of a nervous breakdown. Much to our surprise and delight we were an instant hit, a riot! We "knocked them dead and laid them in the aisles." During the day Dad had purchased some chemicals at the local drug store and did the magic trick of turning water into wine and the wine back into water, and he was a panic! I thought they would never let him get off the stage. Their applause kept calling him back, again and again. He was so tickled and excited that, acting on an impulse of gratitude to his audience during his last curtain call, he drank a glass of the "wine" to prove that it was pure. He was sick for ten days afterward, but he said that it was worth it.

When my mother sang "The Fatal Rose of Red"[7] with illustrated lantern slides, the audience cried out loud. Florence followed with a song and dance number in which she sang "The Wedding of the Lily and the Rose"[8] which also went over with a bang. And, you can believe it or not, but my act was

[7]"The Fatal Rose of Red," published in 1900, was written and composed by J. Fred Helf and Edward Gardenier.

[8]"The Wedding of the Lily and the Rose" is probably "The Wedding of the Rose" which was written by Leon Jessel in 1911.

an absolute sensation. I simply wowed 'em with my mother-in-law gags, and took ten bows on "The Green Grass Grew All Around." I counted them as fast as I could get on the stage and off again. It was the first time in my life I had ever stopped a show!

What a glorious feeling the cheering applause sent through our veins! At last we had found an audience which really appreciated talent. They were perfect, as though made to order for us, and I wished that we could take them along with us and play to them every night. Dad was so enthusiastic and optimistic that the next day he repainted our trunks and ordered some new two-color letterheads.

Two days later I went back to the steamboat to see Prince, and was at first overcome with joy, and then suddenly amazed and frightened when I saw that instead of my dog alone there was Prince with a weakly wagging tail and a look of great pride and six small replicas of Prince! What would Captain Price say now! Instead of one pet I had brought seven without knowing it!

But my fears were soon allayed by the smiling face of the captain himself, who stood behind me.

"Better change that dog's name to Princess, Son," he said kindly. "A prince never did anything like that so far's I've ever heard. They sure are cute little devils, aren't they?"

"Can I keep her, Captain? And the pups, too?" I asked eagerly. His smile had been so reassuring, that I thought I'd better settle it right now.

"Sure," he said. "She's a mighty fine dog and the boys'd like those pups. Let's distribute them among the troupe. What say?"

I agreed eagerly. I didn't really feel up to the responsibility of seven dogs, and this solution would keep them all near me. But Prince stayed Prince. Once a dog gets a name that's her name, and no unpertinent discoveries as to sex changes it.

Several weeks later we left Prince, by mistake, on Manchester Island when we made a sudden jump with the boat. I wrote to the chief of police at Manchester about it, and six weeks later old Prince came along on a river packet, C.O.D. for $26. She had been on the packet two weeks and the captain said he had just missed catching us on three different occasions.

The whole family immediately fell in love with the river and we were all very happy. Although our salary was small, it included board and room, so that we could save practically everything we received. After our first week, Mother sent for the diamond ring and guitar, and we all felt better to have them with us again.

Every morning we woke in a strange town. There were new people to see, new boats, new houses, and a new throng waiting to cheer us. We brought them pleasure. Our visit was the high spot in their summer. We rode in perpetual carnival.

A day or so after our successful opening at Augusta, I swanked around among the other actors like a young cockerel. Nothing to it, I said. A river audience was a pushover. There was a veteran actor in the troupe who was a kindly and fatherly old soul, with an ever ready sense of humor and a friendly willingness to take on the instruction of the young.

"Don't let it go to your head, Son," he said kindly. "I've seen plenty of young actors come to grief that way. There was young Billy Bowes, for instance. It was mighty sad about Billy."

Immediately the rest of the actors looked solemn and shook their heads sadly. They all seemed deeply affected by the fate of poor Billy, whatever it was. I had a feeling that I was being kidded, and tried to seem uninterested, but curiosity got the best of me, and I demanded the story.

"Billy just naturally spent most of his life wanting to be in the glare of a spotlight," the old fellow began sadly. "But he wasn't so great as an actor, and there wasn't any real reason why the captain should buy a perfectly good spot just to please him. So Billy just pined and pined. One night, on the Monongahela River, he fell overboard and the captain, who was trying to save him, turned on the searchlight. As soon as it hit Billy, he thought that at last he was in the spotlight, and he took so many bows he drowned himself."

I laughed with as good grace as possible and tried to keep my bragging words to myself. Just the same I knew I was pretty good. This was only the beginning of the path to fame which would take me to

Broadway, where I would be accepted as the great actor I really was, to the thunder of Manhattan's applause, and the chagrin of Georgie Cohan who would regret, too late, that he had not seized the opportunity I once gave him to start me on my way. I was in no mood then to let a group of small-time river actors (even as friendly a group as this) put me in my place. It took a much more humiliating experience than that, years later, to make me realize that there were a few better men than I on the stage.

Florence and I attended school on the *Water Queen.* Mrs. Ralph Emerson Gaches was with the troupe that summer and every day she held school on the stage for the six children of the Conklins, an acrobatic pair, Florence, and me. It was very like a country school in which one teacher handles all subjects and all grades and frequently has a school population made up entirely from one or two families. At recess we would read the names written on the walls of the showboat and hunt for gum hidden under the seats. Often Captain Price would visit us during our classes, smiling with pleasure when one of us showed an unusual degree of brilliance by some miraculous feat such as remembering the names of the states the Mississippi bounds.

Our teacher's husband, Ralph Gaches[9] (who later

[9] Ralph Waldo Emerson Gaches had a distinguished career on the river. He was the captain of the *Argand*, which was used to tow E. A. Price's showboats, *Water Queen* and *New Sensation.* He also managed Price's boat *Floating Theater.* He retired to a more sedate life of farming in 1909.

became a famous showboat man) was advance agent for the *Water Queen*. He represented an innovation in showboat advertising. In the old days the captain used to mail his advertising matter ahead of him to the postmaster, along with plenty of free tickets, and the postmaster would see that it got around himself, distributing the handbills in the village and getting the rural mail carrier to bill the country-side. Under this system often two boats would play the same town on the same night. One would be coming up river, the other down, and each would mail advance notices ahead, unconscious of the other's presence.

The advance agent changed all this. He would use train, horse and buggy, boat, and often his own power, walking for miles in a frequently unsuccess-ful attempt to keep ahead of the boat. Some of the advance agents have become famous for their eccen-tric actions and exploits.

Ray Lambert, known as the "wildcat agent of the river," was one of these. He would come into a town, give a likely-looking lady two passes, and get from her in return a bucket of paste, lodging for the night, breakfast, and sometimes more intimate hos-pitality. During his bill posting career he walked the entire distance from Pittsburgh to New Orleans. At one time, on the Green River, announcing the arrival of the *Water Queen*, he found transportation facilities so bad that his greatest job was to keep ahead of the boat. He rode mules, rowed boats, and walked. Working night and day, he lost track of the time. At Cromwell, Kentucky, he was pasting a poster on a privy one morning when he heard the sweet strains of a calliope and looking down the river saw the *Water Queen* coming around the bend. Knowing Captain Price, he simply packed up his paste bucket and left town, deciding that he would rather quit than be fired.

Apparently he was less afraid of losing his job with Ralph Emerson,[10] another owner of a showboat. On one trip he went ahead of Emerson in a small motorboat. Progress was slow, though, for the motorboat was continually breaking down and being laid up for repairs. He ate and slept on the boat. He tied up one night, near Mount Vernon, his boat unable to proceed. During the night Emerson's showboat passed him, going down the river to another stand. In the morning Ray cast off with a stalled engine, thinking he could float down the river to Captain Emerson's stand and join him there. But just before he got there Emerson left. For a week this weird pursuit and flight continued. When Ray finally caught up with the boat at Paducah he explained why the towns hadn't been billed, and tried to soften the blow with a compliment.

"I can tell you one thing, though, Ralph," he said

---

[10]Ralph Waldo Emerson is also identified as Ralph Emerson Gaches. He dropped his surname because he insisted no one could pronounce it and because Emerson was a distinguished name.

to Captain Emerson, "the folks along those towns certainly liked your show, I talked to all of 'em right after you had showed."

"That's fine" Emerson answered, "but I never heard of any showboat before who paid an advance agent to trail along behind and find out how they liked the show."

Captain Price was a friendly and paternal man, easily excitable, but always kind, and the spirit of good fellowship which he felt permeated the entire boat. He never minded too much when the joke was on him—and there were several which became famous. One of them which I remember came about as the result of a storm which carried us out into the river without our power boat.

We were tied up at Friar's Point when wind and rain swept down on us with a fury which the lines could not withstand. They parted and we were cast helplessly adrift. One of the men was working furiously at the anchor, getting it ready to drop, when the captain saw him and yelled from the roof.

"Throw the anchor overboard. Quick! What are you waiting for?"

"There's no line tied to it, Cap," the man answered, still trying to get the rope attached.

But Captain Price was by that time quite beside himself as the boat, drifting farther and farther from shore, seemed in imminent danger. In a frenzy of excitement his right hand scratched furiously at his sideburns while his left kept digging at his leg.

"Throw it over anyway!" he shouted, and the deckhand, questioning no further, obeyed, thus dropping a perfectly good anchor onto the bed of the Mississippi River, from which it was never recovered. The story is still told along the river.

After we had been out a few weeks the captain asked me whether I would like to earn a little extra money by washing dishes. I thought of the lack of dignity in an actor who worked as a scullion, but I wanted the extra money and, thinking that Georgie Cohan need never know, I accepted gratefully. Before long I was helping the cook, too. We used canned milk diluted with river water. It never occurred to us that anyone might be ignorant of the use of river water as a beverage, let alone that one might object to it, until the night that we were accused of it by one of the actors, as though it were a heinous thing.

Apparently I had caught a minnow in drawing up a pail of water, but it escaped my notice even when I poured some of the water from the pail into the milk. But that night at supper one of the actors, in the middle of a drink of milk, stopped aghast, his lips closed over the head of a flopping minnow. It was only a second before he spat it out of his mouth, but in that time the vigorous little fellow, writhing madly to rid himself of this strange grip and get back into any liquid at all—even milk—had given the man a neat, cold slap on each cheek.

Choking with canned milk and rage, the actor

sprang furiously to his feet and fixed me with a baleful eye.

"You young devil! You've been putting river water in the milk!" he shouted.

I was frightened for a moment, not because I had done anything wrong by using river water—that was regular routine—but because I didn't want the enmity of any of the members of the troupe. I began stammering, trying to find a suitable answer, when Mac, the cook, appeared in the door.

"What's all the row in here?" he asked mildly.

"There was a fish in my milk," the outraged actor shouted.

"Imagine that!" Mac's round face was innocent of all but surprise. "Them darned cows must've been drinking out of the creek again." Turning, he went back to the galley, and by the time the laughter had subsided the wronged actor was grinning himself.

Thus passed one of the pleasantest summers of my life. We all loved it. When Captain Price hung up a closing sign backstage, telling us that we would disband at New Orleans about Christmas time, we were all heartsick. He looked uphappy too, when he bade us goodbye, and, as a final gesture of friendship, he paid our fare back to Cincinnati.

IV

Shanty-Boat Trash

Now we were "at liberty" again. Long before we reached Cincinnati we were missing the freedom of the river and wishing that, instead of traveling toward the poor prospects of the theaters and concert halls we could simply settle down and wait for another season on the *Water Queen*. And we felt it all the more strongly when we found that there were no engagements in Cincinnati save in the concert halls.

Mother and Father were determined not to take Florence and me into such an environment as that again, so they bought a span of mules, a wagon, five gallons of gasoline, a pound of Cayenne pepper, and proceeded to mix up a batch of liniment with the intention of high-pitching their way to Pittsburgh. Dad and Mother sat in the front seat and Florence and I jounced around on a bale of hay in the back. As we drove past Fountain Square on our way out of Cincinnati, someone started to laugh. Then everyone in the Square looked at us and began to laugh, and I felt as though I couldn't make myself small enough.

It seemed only a little time ago that our hopes had been borne high on the wings of our success on the *Water Queen* and I had been thinking that it wouldn't be long before I would make Georgie Cohan realize what a great showman I was. And now instead of a stage under me, I had a bale of hay; instead of a spotlight and applause, the ridicule of a street crowd. I was a long way from showing "the Yankee Doodle Boy" anything at that moment.

We had scarcely started when a cold snap hit us and we couldn't high-pitch any more, so we played the halls, schoolhouses, and churches. At Racine, Ohio, we showed in a large room over an undertaker's establishment. Our stage was built over rough boxes in which coffins had been shipped, and we pinned shrouds together for a curtain. There was a large brick chimney right in the middle of the hall which compelled the audience to sway from side to side as the action moved across the stage, in order to keep the actors in sight.

Here Dad cured a farmer of inflammatory rheumatism. That is, he rubbed the liniment so vigorously on the poor fellow's afflicted knee that the combination of red pepper and gasoline made the patient forget all about his rheumatism and he decided that he was cured. He was so grateful that he gave Dad five dollars.

We followed the river road nearly all the way to Pittsburgh. At one point Dad decided that we ought to go inland, so we turned off at Ravenswood, West Virginia, to go around by Ripley and Spencer, through the oil fields. But Mother deftly got us turned back. The summer on the *Water Queen* had made her fall completely in love with the river and she was not to be misled.

As the mules jogged on slowly toward the river towns, again Mother became silent and her face lit up with some inward stimulation, as though she were having a pleasant dream. Finally she let it out.

"It would be nice if we could have a boat of our own, Sam," she said softly.

Father looked a little startled, then became the voluble skeptic.

"Don't know where we'd get one," he said gruffly. A boat like the *Water Queen* costs thousands of dollars."

"Sure, I know," Mother answered quietly. "We couldn't start with one like that; but maybe we could get a little houseboat at first."

Bit by bit she worked on Father in the quiet way which always got what she wanted in the end. By the time we had reached the river, Dad was as enthusiastic as she. From then on, at every river town, Mother would ask if there was a houseboat that could be bought cheap. But it seemed that everyone who had a houseboat was living on it so there were none to be had.

At Little Hocking, Ohio, we passed a small deserted barn with one of the *Water Queen's* posters pasted on it. It was at least a year old, but it made us so homesick that we camped right there for the night, although it was scarcely two o'clock in the afternoon when we found it. The poster showed a picture of an Irish comedian, under which, in pencil, I printed: "BILLY BRYANT, THE GEORGE M. COHAN OF THE RIVER." Later in the afternoon I went to look at it and throw my chest out a bit, and found that Florence had changed the "B" in Billy to "S" and the "George M. Cohan" to "Blah Blah."

When we got to Pittsburgh it was spring. Here we turned up the Allegheny River to the little town of West Hickory, Pennsylvania. Looking back now I could be a bit sentimental about it and say that it was the hand of Providence which directed us to this spot at which our river career really started, but knowing Mother better than I do God, I suspect that she had learned of the shipyards there and had decided that her plans would be furthered by exposing Dad to a bit of shipbuilding.

Here the principal industry was the construction of wooden barges, to be floated down the river to Pittsburgh, loaded with coal, and towed to New Orleans by large stern wheeled steamboats such as the *J. B. Williams*, the *Raymond Horner*, the *Tom Dodsworth*, and many others.[1]

After the first day there, most of which Father spent time watching the shipwrights at work, the

---

[1] The *Williams*, *Horner*, and *Dodsworth* were powerful, stern wheeled, wooden hull steamers that moved immense tows of coal barges from Pittsburgh to Cincinnati during the 1880s and 90s.

gleam of ambition began to grow in his eyes. The second night at supper he suddenly sounded off, like the safety valve on a steamboat.

"I'm going to build a boat," he exploded, quite as though it were his own idea, looking around a little defiantly as though he would brain any one of us who opposed the idea or intimated that he was not a good carpenter.

"That's splendid, Sam," Mother said. "Isn't it fortunate that you've hung onto your tools?" There was no intimation in her words or voice that she had steered us to this spot with that very plan in mind, but there was a triumphant light in her eyes which spoke more forcefully than any words could have done.

The next day Father started to work on a flatboat ten feet wide and thirty feet long—just large enough to hold the Four Bryants, the mules, and the wagon. Hemlock lumber was cheap just then, so a hemlock boat we would have.

To our surprise and delight (and I think he was as surprised as we) Dad found that the work of a ship-wright came easily to him. He had only a few fundamental tools which he had brought with him from England, but he handled them with respect and affection and they did their work well, as good English tools do.

Just before the job was finished, we found that we absolutely had to have about twenty dollars' worth more of material and there was not a cent in the

Bryant treasury. By now, none of us liked to mention Mother's guitar and diamond ring. They had become the obvious last resort on so many occasions, and each time Father had said, "This will be the last time, Nell!" But as soon as Mother saw how things were, she took them out of the trunk and started to town with them, smiling, as she said, "They've never gone into anything I liked better."

Thus the personal treasures which both Father and Mother carried with them from the land of their birth into the land of their adoption went into the building of our first boat.

At last the great day of launching came. With all of us, including the mules, pushing and pulling and straining, we finally got the boat off its temporary supports, skidded it into the river, and set up a joyous shout. But even as we shouted, we all looked at each other strangely, and our shouts petered off into a wondering silence. It floated all right, but there was something wrong. It wasn't like any other boat we had ever seen. Low in the water, it seemed to be a sort of platform, with ends that sloped down to the water. Dad stood there scratching his head. Suddenly his face cleared.

"By golly!" he cried, "we've launched her upside down!"

During the process of construction the boat had rested bottom side up on its supports, and it hadn't occurred to any of us to turn it over before sliding it into the water.

THE ALLEGHENY, MONONGAHELA
AND UPPER OHIO RIVER AREA

LAKE ERIE

N

West
Hickory

Oil City • Tionesta

PENNSYLVANIA

Allegheny River

East Liverpool Georgetown
Wellsville Hookstown
The 5 Dike Cluster Sharpsburg New Kensington
Steubenville Davis Island Pittsburgh
Sixth Street
Bridge

OHIO

River

Wheeling Brownsville

Monongahela River

Muskingum

Clarington

MARYLAND

River Ohio Sistersville

Duck Creek
Government Light Marietta Raven Rock
Neal Island
Parkersburg Waverly Bull
Little Hocking Creek
Blennerhassett Fort Neal's Run
Island Boreman
Middleport Little Kanawha River
Point Racine
Pleasant Ravenswood WEST

Galli- Henderson
polis Raccoon Island VIRGINIA VIRGINIA

ALLEGHENY MOUNTAINS

Kanawha River ★ Charleston

0   25   50

Miles

The friendly local rivermen came to our rescue. In no time they had the craft out into midstream where, with our mules pulling it against the current, they soon flipped it right side up.

We hurriedly bailed the water out of it and loaded the wagon on one end, leaving just room enough for the mules to squeeze onto the other. Using the wagon tongue for a pike pole, with never a thought of a rope, skiff, side-sweeps, lantern, or any other aids to navigation, we proudly pushed our way out into the stream and waved a fond goodbye to the natives. In a very short time we had drifted out of sight of West Hickory, around the bend.

From West Hickory to Pittsburgh the Allegheny runs very much downhill all the way, as we discovered when we tried to land our little craft a few hours later at dusk. One end of the boat would hit the bank, and before we had time to take hold of anything, it would swing around in the current and the other end would take its turn. For the first time we realized that we were sadly in need of some means to make the boat go properly into shore and something with which to tie it up after we got it there.

Soon we were all thoroughly frightened—that is, all except Mother. She never has been really afraid of anything on the river. Through all of our efforts she kept humming "Silent Night," realizing that any suggestions from her for navigating the boat would have resulted in mutiny.

It seemed to get dark almost instantly, once it began, and nothing can get any darker than a deserted inland stream, flanked by mountains, on a starless night. Its inky blackness is indescribable. Standing at the head of the boat (which was swinging around so fast that it became the stern almost immediately), Dad lit a candle and held it above his head in an attempt to see the shore. A pleasing yellow glow spread about his pate and illumined his anxious face, but because of its glare the shadowy glimpses we had been able to make of the shoreline were now completely blotted out and there was just that little circle of light in a world of darkness.

We had equipped the boat with a gasoline cooking stove, but in our haste to get under way had forgotten to buy any gasoline for it. That didn't bother Mother, though. She simply went to Dad's suitcase and took out two bottles of liniment, which she poured into the tank. Then she lit the stove and put on a pot of coffee—standard first aid for Dad when he became extremely nervous.

Now and then, during the night, we could see a lamp-lit farmhouse in the distance, only to glide into utter darkness again. Once we drifted so close to the shore that we could hear the willows dragging alongside of the boat and catching in the spokes of the wagon wheels. We all rushed to that side of the boat and desperately grasped at the trees, but the weight of the flatboat in the swift current was too much for us. Our reward consisted of empty, smarting hands through which the sticky green willows had slipped mockingly.

Later that night Dad mistook the swishing tail of one of the mules for another clump of willows. Grasping it, he hung on for dear life and, when it didn't slip through his fingers, he was ecstatic.

"I've stopped her! I've stopped her!" he cried. "Come and help me hold her!"

But just then old Pete, wearying of the pull at his tail, backed up, nearly pushing Father off the boat.

It must have been nearly midnight when we felt a shock and realized that the boat listed a bit before righting itself.

"We must have run up on a log or something," Father said.

After that we took turns at watching, each getting some sleep, each standing watch against any eventuality. All through the night I kept hearing an occasional splashing about the boat, but couldn't decide what it was. In the morning we discovered that, ever since running onto "a log or something," we had been standing still, stuck on a little island near Tionesta. The strange splashing sound I had heard came from one of the mules, who had been jarred overboard at the impact and spent the rest of the night wandering around the island, coming down to the water occasionally for a drink.

Our next stop was at Henry's Bend, where we decided to land and obtain some feed for the mules, since they had been braying hungrily ever since we

had left Tionesta. Here there was a small ferry landing. As we drifted close to it, we noticed a girl in
her early teens hanging out washing on a line. As
she saw us, she dropped her clothespins in the
peach basket she carried and called her mother.

"Say, Ma, we'd better take in this washing, and
lock all the chickens up. Here comes some more of
them shanty-boat trash!"

Father knew that she was referring to us, and
laughed it off, but Mother couldn't sit there and
hear her home ridiculed, so she rose to battle.
Drawing herself up with the dignity of Sarah Bernhardt,[2] she stepped out of the wagon and onto the
whiffle tree.

"Listen you," she cried, pointing her finger at the
frightened girl, "I want you to understand that this
is not a shanty boat and that we are not shanty-boat
trash by any means, but the famous Four Bryants,
one of the greatest vaudeville acts that has ever
toured the Keith Circuit.[3] We have played the Pal-

[2]Born in Paris and trained for the stage at the *Comedie
Francaise*, Sarah Bernhardt (1844-1923) was perhaps the
most gifted actress of her era. She also achieved distinction
as a painter, sculptress, and author.

[3]Benjamin F. Keith was the czar of vaudeville. He began
his career with the circus and became a highly successful
booking agent. He later controlled a chain of vaudeville theaters where he introduced the idea of continuous rather than
single daily performances. He also contributed to making
the vaudeville palace a place where women could go unes-
corted. Shortly before the turn of the century he pioneered
the introduction of films into vaudeville houses.

ace in New York, the Hippodrome in Cleveland, and have appeared before most of the crowned heads of Europe."

It was completely wasted on this young backwoods girl, but Mother was mad.

"Why, you half-starved hayseed," she went on, "we have worked on the same bill with Josephine Sybil, Ezra Kendall,[4] George S. Primrose,[5] the Four Cohans, and Harry Lauder,[6] and we wouldn't have lowered our dignity by floating past your darned old clothesline if there had been any way to float around it." Here poor Mother flounced herself into the wagon.

It was Florence who really finished it off. Leaning out of the front of the wagon, she stuck her tongue out at the girl and shouted, "Go on home and blow your nose!"

Blankly the girl looked at us.

"What did you say, Ma'am?" she asked.

Dad, however, became friends with her father and traded an electric belt for a bale of hay and a piece of line with which to tie our boat up. My, what Dad couldn't do with an electric belt!

[4]Ezra Kendall (1861–1910) was an actor and playwright.
[5]George Primrose (1852–1919) was a Canadian-born performer who won distinction as a black-faced minstrel. He is said to have originated the "soft shoe" dance.
[6]Born as Hugh Maclennan in Scotland, Harry Lauder (1870–1950), became the most popular foreign-born vaudeville entertainer in America. He dressed in kilts, brandished a crooked walking stick, and regaled his audiences with English and Scottish music hall ditties.

After many hours of hazardous navigating we finally reached Oil City, where a large gospel boat was holding a series of evangelistic services. They had the wharf blocked off completely, so we had to land just above the religious aggregation. The old gentleman in charge of the program came out and looked us over suspiciously as we tied up.

"What's your business here, Brother?" he asked Father.

"We are just a vaudeville troupe taking a river trip," Dad answered carelessly. He was so relieved to have a rope to tie us up with, and to be able to look forward to a night of peace, that he didn't pay much attention to anything else. I thought he had understated the situation, so I chimed in.

"I can do a song and dance act like Georgie Cohan's," I said to the elder. "Want me to put it on tonight and get a lot of people down here for you?"

If looks could eternally blast anyone, I would have been blasted then. Fixing me with his eye, the old man uttered his words of doom.

"What ye sow, that also shall ye reap," he quoted. "Beware, young man, the gates of hell yawn wide!"

All that evening he kept coming to the edge of his boat and looking straight over at ours while he delivered one Bible quotation after another at us, all of which were calculated to make us see what a lot of rapscallions we were.

That night, with little warning, a tremendous

thunderstorm broke over us. It had evidently originated up the river and traveled down, for suddenly
a quick "pop" rise of the water bore down upon us,
piling driftwood at our stern in great quantities. By
morning the river had risen seriously and our boat
was tugging at its slender line, while the driftwood
kept increasing at our stern. About noon Mother
began to worry.

"Hadn't we better get out of all these logs and
trash, Sam?" she asked tentatively.

"They're the best thing that could happen to us,"
Father assured her. "They'll hold us right in against
the bank."

Just then our line parted in the middle with a
crack and we were helplessly adrift again. As we
passed the gospel boat at a rapid clip, the revivalist
who had spent most of the previous evening warning us about our doom rushed to the edge of his
boat and almost danced up and down in his triumphant excitement.

"What did I tell you?" he cried. "You are now
on your way straight to hell!"

"All right, Grandpa, we'll see you there," Florence shouted, while Mother took her arm and told
her to remember her manners.

Then we all began to look to the boat. With several large bridge piers looming up a short distance
ahead of us it looked a little as though the revivalist
had told the truth. However, contrary to the holy
man's belief, the Lord was still taking care of his

children and fools, and we passed safely through the narrow spans. Later, at New Kensington, we did hit a bridge pier, nearly upsetting the wagon, but our good ship righted itself and we went on without damage.

On a bright Sunday morning we passed through Sharpsburg, and a short time later saw the long rows of Pittsburgh's smokestacks. In the silence of a beautiful Sabbath morning, broken only by the ringing of church bells, we gently glided under the old Sixth Street bridge. Children on their way home from Sunday school waved their pamphlets at us from the bridges. Ahead we could see the famous point bridge where the Monongahela and Allegheny rivers meet to form the beautiful Ohio. The whole world looked peaceful and contented.

The river seemed so large and roomy to us that we thought we must be in a lake. It was not then the busy, smoky, traffic-jammed stream that it is today. Except for a few lazy-looking pleasure craft we had the river practically to ourselves. No one seemed in a hurry. Everyone was taking his time and seemed to enjoy being alive. Even the river was lazier. As soon as we drifted into the Ohio we found that the current was not nearly so swift as it had been in the Allegheny.

With head high, Dad surveyed his surroundings much as Christopher Columbus must have looked at the New World. He felt that he had done a big thing in building, with his own hands, a boat which he had successfully floated without power from the headwaters of the Allegheny all the way to Pittsburgh. Mother and Florence and I thought so too. I don't know what the mules thought.

"Well, folks," he said, as he lit his pipe for a comfortable smoke, "our troubles are over now."

Just then we saw some people on the bank waving and shouting at us. I thought, with a swell of pride, that they had probably seen us on the *Water Queen* the summer before, and waved back at them gaily, but they only gesticulated more furiously and waved the harder and shouted more loudly. But we were listening to what Father was saying.

"Yes sir," he went on. "This is what I call a river. Not a ripple in her!"

"There's a ripple just ahead of us, Dad," Florence said suddenly. When we looked ahead we saw that we were headed straight for a four-foot dam and about to go over it. Then I realized that the people on shore had been trying to warn us away from it.

It was the old Davis Island dam, as we learned later. Its purpose was to throw the water to one side to make a navigable channel. If you are on the right side of the island you go safely past, through the lock. But if you're on the wrong side, you're where we were that Sunday morning.

As soon as we saw what was happening, Dad and I began to pull frantically at the sweep, a long oar fixed at the stern of the boat. What we hoped to accomplish by this I don't know. What we actually did accomplish by it was simply to pull the boat around in circles, each of which brought us nearer to the crest of the dam. When we saw that we were doing no good, we stopped and waited for the drop. Mother hurriedly pushed Florence and me into the wagon, thinking we would be safer there, and we sat watching, fascinated, while the prow of the boat nosed gently over the dam.

Just then I happened to look at the mules and felt a tremor of guilt as I saw how completely peaceful and innocent they looked. Before the prospect of taking a four-foot drop with unpredictable results, they were entirely composed, munching hay with complete content in the glare of the noonday sun. Everyone knows how peaceful mules can look in warm sunlight!

But I hadn't long to contemplate our perfidy in letting the mules in for this without having told them the facts of life, for just then Dad shouted, "Here we go, Nell!" at Mother, and, looking ahead, I saw the bow of the boat descending in a sudden graceful dip. Sis and I stuck our heads under the straw. Under us the whole world was dropping away and I felt sick in the pit of my stomach. There was a scream from a woman on shore, and a sudden grinding thud under us.

The next moment—that moment in which I thought I might be walking the streets of Kingdom Come—we were floating peacefully down the river.

Owing to the lightness of the craft it had failed to turn over. To be sure it had dipped about a foot of water, but that was the worst that had happened. The mules, who long since had become used to wet feet, had, by the time I looked around, indulged in their brief expressions of surprise and were munching hay again as though nothing had happened.

As I began bailing water out, that insane unreasoned resentment toward George M. Cohan, which I felt whenever anything disastrous happened to us, swept over me again.

"Darn him," I muttered, "but for him we'd be playing Broadway today instead of bailing out an old tub!"

I'm sure that Dad wasn't thinking of Cohan just then, but his disgust with the boat and the river was even keener than mine. In spite of the enthusiasm with which he had begun to build the boat, his love for the river was chiefly a response to Mother's desire to be on it. I don't think he had ever really believed in it, and whatever fondness for it he had been able to work up had been pretty thoroughly blasted that first night when we had drifted helplessly in its current without any knowledge of what the next five minutes would bring to pass. All the way from West Hickory he had been holding his temper. Now he let it go with a rush like that of water through a suddenly burst dam. As a number of skiffs, john boats, and two or three small motor boats came out to help us, he suddenly exploded.

"Pack up your things!" he shouted at us. "We're going to get off this damned thing right now, and we're not going to get back on it!"

Although he said no word which indicated that he blamed Mother for the misfortunes which we had run into, the grim looks which he cast in her direction were as eloquent as if he had said, "I tried your darned idea and look where it got us."

I could not help feeling a little out of sorts with the river myself in my youthful way after what had just happened. If you have never gone over a dam in a flatboat, you've missed something. If you have, you know how unattractive water can be sometimes.

But my heart went out to Mother as she silently obeyed Dad's sharp orders, all of which were concentrated upon the idea of getting us, Mother, children, and mules, off the boat. There was not a word of protest from her, not a look of anger or irritation. I wondered a little that she would take it so casually, but I didn't say anything. I simply minded.

As we got ourselves unloaded, Father decided that we would camp right there for the night and sell the flatboat in the morning. Mother acquiesced without question. She was very quiet and gentle with Florence and me. When we suggested that it would be fun to cook our supper over an open fire instead of on the gasoline stove, she agreed and even helped us gather wood.

As the flames of the fire made a comforting circle of light and warmth, Dad began pacing up and down the bank, fighting against his own bad temper. From time to time he would stop and look at the three of us, and then, with a sudden impatient movement, be off again.

Some children gathered in the circle of our fire and we told them stories about our theatrical life. I sang "The Green Grass Grew All Around" for them and they loved it. Hungry for the companionship of other children, we suggested games, and played "Run, Sheep, Run" until, one by one, the children had all gone home.

By then Father's anger had seeped away, leaving only the dregs of despondency. He sat down by the almost expired fire and gazed sadly into the glowing embers.

Just as Florence and I were getting ready to go to bed, the steamer *Kanawha* came down the river and majestically threaded its calm way past the island on the right side. It was a lovely, cheerful sight with its lights, the smoke from its stacks, and the steam from its escapes.

"That's the side we should have come down," Mother said, as if to herself. Father said nothing.

Just then the captain turned his searchlight on and began playing it along the shore. It was like a huge spotlight against a magnificent drop of trees and bluffs, a stage set by nature for the delight of any who would look.

"Isn't that pretty, Sam?" Mother asked.

"I suppose so," Dad agreed half-heartedly.

"There's one thing about the river," Mother went on. "It's always so pretty. You won't see any sights like that in the cities. And no matter how hard the life is, you're independent. Nothing that could happen here could be so bad as the concert halls."

Now Florence and I knew that Mother had gone to work in earnest. Realizing that we would only be in her way if we hung around, we went to bed. Until we fell asleep we heard her gentle voice go on, talking about her favorite subject—the river.

V

Mister Charlie Poe

T HE NEXT morning I was wakened by the movement of the wagon under me. I supposed that
we were rolling down a dusty road, headed inland,
but, looking forward, I saw that no one was in the
seat. I looked out the back of the wagon and saw
that some strange men and Mother and Father were
pushing it onto the flat again. The mules were already in place, looking with only the mildest display of interest at the strangely inconsistent antics
of their masters.

Mother had won, as usual, and we were off on the
river again. All morning there was a happy gleam in
her eye and she was unusually pleasant to all of us.
How she had done it, I don't know, but between the
time the steamer *Kanawha* had passed us and she
and Dad had turned in, she had sold him the river
all over again, dams, floods, windstorms, and all.

Our next stop was Georgetown just a few miles
above East Liverpool, Ohio. It boasted a population
of three hundred. Sitting on the top of a hill, it
could only be reached by a long, winding road. It
was here we came in contact with one of the most
fascinating river characters we have ever met: Mr.
Charlie Poe. He owned and operated the hotel and

livery stable, was justice of the peace, postmaster, and owner of the largest store in the village. He controlled the ferry and all the land that flanked it on both sides of the river, and was wharfmaster and freight agent for all the river packets that landed there to pick up poultry and eggs for the Pittsburgh market. He was practically a one-man government and chamber of commerce. He was very fond of show people and the atmosphere of the stage.

Nearly every town and village has among its population at least one person who feels that he has missed his calling by not going on the stage. He may be a successful banker, or miller, or merchant, but somewhere in his early life he touched the fringes of the show business. Perhaps he only drove stakes for a visiting circus, or watered the elephants, or sold balloons at a county fair, or carried a spear in an amateur presentation of *Hamlet*, but he has cherished his memories of this experience all his life, and they have grown, as the years have passed, into a full-fledged conviction that he might have been a great actor. It is fortunate compensation, indeed, for the drabness of many lives. It is good that some may live glamorously in their imaginations. Charlie Poe was one of these.

He could not understand why we were floating two healthy mules and a wagon down the river, passing up all of the inland towns, when the mules and wagon could have taken us to them. He was itching to add a theatrical venture to his store, land-holding, ferry, and postmastering. Finally he insisted that we drive back to an inland settlement called Hookstown and give a show in their townhall. He said the town was show-hungry and we would pack them in. Dad knew that the mules needed exercise, so he consented.

Mr. Poe attended to all the preliminary matters such as advertising and renting the hall on the top floor of a three-story building. On the ground floor was a harness shop. The second floor housed the Knights of Pythias lodge rooms. On the third floor was the "Operé."

Mr. Poe put a table at the second-floor landing by the stairs which led up to the hall, and set himself up as ticket seller. Father stood downstairs on the wooden porch-like structure in front of the building, immaculately dressed in his Prince Albert and top hat, his gold-headed cane added a brave note of elegance to the ensemble. Father was adept at the ancient art of ballyhoo, and it was his job to pack them in.

The arrangements had all been made. We were ready for the crowd. I took advantage of the fifteen minutes which I knew would intervene before we got the crowd in to slip out and get myself a bite to eat from the lunch we carried in the wagon. As I started down the stairs I could hear Dad's voice doing its stuff.

"Ladies and gentlemen," he was shouting, "gather in closely, please, so that you may hear of the great theatrical opportunity that is knocking at the door of your beautiful city. You are now standing in the presence of one of the greatest theatrical producers in the world, who brings to you the famous Bryant comedy company direct from the Great White Way of New York City!"[1]

By the time I got to the first floor the people were already arriving. They were coming down the street in pairs, trios, and quartets. Dad's mellow voice seemed, on this night, to have the magic power of the Pied Piper's pipe.

"Listen, neighbors," and the very hills seemed to be listening, "on the third floor of this building at eight o'clock sharp we are going to present one of the greatest, most gigantic, most stupendous, performances ever witnessed in the long history of the American theater! You are going to see beautiful singing and dancing girls by the score, and Professor Sam Bryant, myself, will appear in person in the greatest, most baffling magic act ever known in the history of science.

"There will be funny clowns and funny jokes and a dozen other high-class vaudeville acts.

"Now we are not going to ask you to pay a dollar for this attraction, or three-quarters of a dollar, or a half-a-dollar. No, not even a quarter of a dollar! The price of admission for this day and date only has been reduced to the ridiculously small sum of a

[1] The Great White Way was the brilliantly-lighted theater district of New York City.

dime, ten cents. That takes you all the way in and brings you all the way back. Get your money ready, folks! Purchase your tickets upstairs. Step right in and get the thrill of a lifetime. Step right up, folks! Step right up! Hurry! Hurry!"

I looked back as I ran to the wagon, and paused to gaze in rapt admiration and gladness. The people were coming by the dozen, by the score—by the hundred! I had never imagined there were so many people in the village. Some of them might have come from the surrounding country, I decided; but how had they heard of us? Mr. Charlie Poe must have done a good job of press-agenting. Standing there I wished that Georgie Cohan could see what the mere mention of our name could do in the way of getting the population of a whole countryside to come to town!

When I got back Dad was about ready to go upstairs. He had a wild light in his eyes, the flush of success on his cheeks.

"I must have sent two hundred and fifty people up there," he said breathlessly. "Now we'll go up and wow 'em."

Together we raced up the stairs to start the show. On the second floor we looked in vain for Charlie Poe. We supposed that, with the hall full, he had gone about keeping the people interested until we came. We wondered whether there were enough seats for them all.

Dashing up the stairs, we threw open the doors

into the hall and gazed, horror-stricken and unbelieving, upon a completely empty room. Not a person was in it!

After a hunt we found Mr. Poe backstage, getting his things ready to leave, and Mother and Florence doing the same. Nobody was saying anything.

"Where are all the people?" Dad asked incredulously. There was a note of awe in his voice, as if he thought Charlie might have swallowed them, or, a better magician than himself, might have caused them to disintegrate.

"I didn't sell a single ticket," Mr. Poe answered wearily.

"But all those people I sent up here," Dad shouted. "There must have been five hundred of them! Think, man! They couldn't have disappeared into thin air!"

"Oh, them," Mr. Poe said, with complete disgust. "They all went to the Knights of Pythias doings on the second floor."

Our inland show career in that section ended right there. The next morning we shoved off again, headed for East Liverpool, Ohio.

Here we ran into what looked like a shanty-boat heaven, where all the good little shanty-boats from the distant past had come to bask in the peace of paradise. There were tiny craft of every description, their weird crooked stove pipes sticking out of their roofs and sides at all angles, their sides weatherbeaten or shining in the sun with the newness of

A Shanty Boat

Courtesy The Public Library of Cincinnati and Hamilton County

boards which had been used for recent repairs.
Many of the cabins were made from packing case
material, and stenciled names and addresses told of
their origin.

Hundreds of them had swarmed to the waters of
this friendly Ohio city until they were strung out
for nearly a mile, so closely tied to each other that it
was possible to take one's evening stroll stepping
from deck to deck all the way along.

The group was known as the "mosquito fleet" because of the diminutive size of the craft which comprised it. The owners found a wide range for fancy
in the selection of names for their boats. Many had
used small green willow branches from the bank to
twist into such appellations as "The Farm," "Oh
You Kid," "Skidoo," etc. But bacon and eggs fried
on any one of them smelled just as sweet, regardless
of the name or lack of one.

As we floated into the group, looking for a place
to tie, they gave us a warm welcome. The owners
were the embodiment of friendliness. Most of them
were employed in the Liverpool potteries and had
lived there for years. There were also carpenters,
bricklayers, and common laborers, who, with their
families, floated down the river following jobs of
public works.[2]

[2]Modern historians have not been able to identify this labor force, which is not evident in census records but is so
often mentioned in personal recollections. The ethnic and
racial origins and the community life of these people remains something of a mystery.

There was still another group of shanty boaters among them, the kind that idly drifted from one town to another, and not looking for work. They formed a sort of Sons-of-Rest organization, considering an offer of a job an insult. It was knowledge of this type that had caused the girl on the Allegheny River to warn her mother of our approach. Yet even these were a likeable crew. For one thing, they had perfected the art of avoiding loneliness. Each boat was well supplied with an abundance of children and long-eared coon dogs.

The farmers who cultivated their crops along the river usually planted three extra rows of corn on the river side for these arks that pass in the night. There was sort of a tacit agreement between them and the landowners that, so long as they limited themselves to these three rows, they would not be molested. They liked corn. And they liked watermelons and could snake them out from under the nose of a farmer awake all night in his melon patch.

It was a gay and easy life, drifting silently into a choice location well furnished with beans, corn, and tomatoes, stocking up to their hearts' content, and drifting on downstream as silently as they came. They were skillful in the matter of procuring chickens, too. Once in possession of a fat Plymouth Rock,[3] they would roll it in mud, feathers and all,

[3]The Plymouth Rock is an American variety of fowl that is raised for both meat and eggs. It has smooth yellow legs, a single comb, and gray-white plumage.

and then bake it in the ashes of a dying fire. When the mud was dry and removed, the feathers came with it, leaving a tempting golden brown fowl ready to serve. They seldom came into conflict with the enforcement of law. They almost never stole anything but food, and rivermen regarded them with tolerance as just another aspect of river life.

They were a clannish lot. Although family feuds might exist among them, they would, at the slightest indication of an invasion from outside, join in common cause, and pitch in against the enemy. Women and children fighting beside their men like pirates, using stones, pike poles, dishpans—anything which presented itself—as a weapon.

With the advent of modern times this colorful fleet has nearly vanished from the inland streams. The construction of the federal lock and dam system, which has made a nine-foot pool stage from Pittsburgh to Cairo, has robbed shanty boats of the freedom of floating undisturbed from one town to another. In addition to this, some of the towns have enacted houseboat license laws which have scattered these squatters of the river to the four winds.

This does not mean that the Ohio river and its tributaries are today entirely deserted by shanty-boats. There are still a number of them in existence. But now they are mostly used as summer homes or clubhouses, with bathing and fishing offered as fancy sports, instead of parts of the everyday routine of life. During prohibition there were a great many speakeasies on shanty boats, which could easily evade local laws by anchoring in midstream, or crossing, in a short time, from one state to another.

But the old-time, original pioneer, beautifully nondescript shanty boater of the past has joined the ranks of the vanishing American, and is a shadow which stalks no more.

VI

Fiddlin' Joe

IN MANY ways we prospered at East Liverpool. Mother did splendidly with her canvassing and was soon able to get her diamond ring and guitar out of pawn again. Dad was also busy. He traded the mules, wagon, and a gallon of liniment for enough lumber, nails, and roofing paper to build a crude cabin on the flatboat and we moved in with a sigh of relief. Sis and I indirectly contributed some dishes by doing our vaudeville skit at Thompson's party during the noon hour and were rewarded with a bushel-basket full of plates, platters, saucers, cups, and whatnots—all seconds.

On Easter Sunday morning we were startled by a tremendous commotion on shanty-boat row. Loud voices were calling to each other down the long expanse of the mosquito fleet, and a general note of joyful surprise was in the air. Looking up the river we saw a stranger craft than any of them floating toward us. From a distance it looked like a piano box sitting on top of the water. As a matter of fact it consisted of two piano boxes with a small hull built under them.

We learned that the new arrival was "Fiddlin' Joe," one of the most delightful, and in his quiet way, mysterious, characters that has ever floated the Mississippi basin. He was known and loved by all who were associated with the rivers from the headwaters of navigation to the Gulf of Mexico. He had floated the rivers for many years and boasted that he knew the age of every willow and the character of every path down which cows came to drink. No one seemed to know his origin. Every spring he showed up somewhere near Pittsburgh, where he would assemble a miniature flatboat, always using piano or dry goods boxes as a cabin in which to sleep. His meals he usually obtained from his many friends along the way.

The reception committee had now assembled in full force and was in the act of giving him a glorious and noisy welcome. Dishpans were beaten like drums, dogs barked, babies cried lustily. Joyous pandemonium had broken out throughout the area. Everyone seemed to understand that the coming of Fiddlin' Joe meant many happy hours of entertainment. Joe was a one-man vaudeville show.

As he came abreast of our boat he tossed us a shaggy piece of rope and smiled.

"Catch a line for me, partner?"

We willingly took his line and swung his boat in below ours, then the last in the fleet. Others rushed forward to help tie his boat and greet their idol, while Joe jumped up to his own roof and sat there grinning and swinging his bare legs and feet over the side. Then he took an ocarina from his pocket and began to play "A Hot Time in the Old Town Tonight."[1]

What a born showman he was! His audience was with him from the start. And what a head of hair and whiskers he possessed! His hair fell down over his eyes like that of an English sheep dog, and his whiskers came up to meet it. When he brushed it away from his twinkling eyes he looked like a mouse peering through a bale of oakum.[2]

Later that night, after he had made the rounds of his old friends, he paid us a social call. He had washed his face and attempted to comb his hair, but his efforts had not added much to his personal appearance. The wind and weather had had their way with him too long for one session over a washbasin to make much difference. He was pleased when he heard that we were troupers and asked us a great many questions about theatrical life, but failed to tell us much about himself except that he had been born at Hannibal, Missouri, the boyhood home of Mark Twain.

In many ways Fiddlin' Joe resembled Tom Sawyer and Huckleberry Finn. He lived the old adage, "laugh and the world laughs with you." But in spite

[1] Theodore Metz claimed authorship of "A Hot Time in the Old Town Tonight" but there is evidence that the song emerged from the famous Babe Conner's "House of Relaxation" in St. Louis, where it was sung by black women.

[2] Oakum is a term for loose fiber obtained by untwisting and picking apart old ropes. It is used for calking the seams of ships.

of his happy-go-lucky manner there were times when the twinkle of wit would fade from his strange little eyes and they would assume a far-away, unreadable expression as he sat and gazed across the water. It made us wonder what there had been in that obscure past of his to which he was now looking back, and whether, if one were able to see it, he would not also be able to explain Joe's tramp-like existence and his continuing avoidance of the ways of civilization.

He was known to be an expert in the many details of floating a boat down the river, so, when he announced his departure a few days later, we cast our lot in with his. With him we felt that our safe transportation to Cincinnati would be assured, and it was there that we were planning then to spend the winter. So, lashed together side by side, the famous Four Bryants and Fiddlin' Joe swung out into the stream, to drift for days idly with the current, often at the terrific speed of two miles an hour. That is, we went with the current if the wind didn't blow in the opposite direction; if it did, we went back up the river again.

What a pleasant, shiftless sort of life it was. To be at peace with the world! To be away from applause which could turn overnight to ridicule, away from the uncertain hazards of the theater, and, I found myself adding, the things which reminded me of Georgie Cohan.

We moved safely past the five dangerous dikes

known as "the clusters," just below Wellsville, Ohio, and on through smoky Steubenville, famous for its tin plate mills. Below Wheeling, near Clarington, we noticed that the air was heavy with the fragrance of newly ploughed land, and knew that we were entering the beautiful farming section of the Ohio valley.

Now and then we would stop at a fishing or mussel camp to visit some of Joe's old friends. There, just as at East Liverpool, he was always more than welcome. We could never tell whether it was Joe himself who made everyone want him to come, or his old banjo, his one-string fiddle, his ocarina, and his rusty baritone voice always ready to sing "Old Dan Tucker."[3]

I never tired of watching the mussel fishers. They worked in shallow water while floating with the current in a john boat, and caught the mussels with a contraption known as a "grab." It consisted of a piece of pipe perhaps six feet long from which little pieces of wire hung down about eight inches, dragging the bottom of the river. To these bits of wire the mussel would promptly clamp its shell as soon as disturbed and, in its completely dumb way, hold on for dear life. The catch—often as much as half a bushel at a time—was placed in boiling water to separate the meat from the shells. The pink shells

[3]"Old Dan Tucker," published in 1843, was written by Daniel D. Emmett, who performed in, and played a leading part in creating, the American minstrel show.

were thrown away and the white ones sold to facto-
ries along the river where buttons were made out
of them.

Fiddlin' Joe loved children and would often stop
for the sole purpose of singing and playing strange
tunes for them for hours while they climbed on his
back and sprawled on his lap, twisting his long handlebar mustache into question marks. Their parents
would always feed him, and after eating he would
stretch out in the shade of a tree and take a nap
while the children gathered around him with
branches of willows, brushing mosquitoes and flies
away. He loved to recite James Whitcomb Riley's
"Little Orphant Annie" with a deep sonorous voice
which echoed horror as he got to

> *An' the gobble-uns 'll git you*
> *Ef you*
> *Don't*
> *Watch*
> *Out!*

which would reflect itself in the clinging hands and
terror-stricken eyes of his small listeners.

He was something of a jack-of-all-trades, even including the show business in his repertoire. Often
he would stop at some obscure hamlet, when he felt
in an entertaining mood, to give a sleight-of-hand
performance in the schoolhouse, followed by an
old-fashioned square dance for which he did the
calling and furnished the music on his fiddle.

One Saturday morning we discovered that we were completely without money and provisions, so we landed at Sistersville, West Virginia,[4] which was then experiencing a bonanza oil boom. Weber's concert hall was thriving beyond all of the proprietor's dreams of avarice, so Mother volunteered to work for a few days, singing songs with illustrated slides.

But Fiddlin' Joe, bless his heart, wouldn't hear of it. He went up on a street corner and played his fiddle and passed the hat while Dad did a high-pitch with some song books. Between them they collected enough to send us on our way.

Joe had a friend who owned the general store at Raven Rock. He persuaded us to stay over one night and give a show in the schoolhouse, out in the middle of a field. After we had carried our wardrobe and other paraphernalia up to the building, a steady heavy rain set in. At eight o'clock that night there was no one there to witness our performance but Joe's friends, all of whom had come in free.

At eight-thirty Joe, in despair, rang the schoolhouse bell in an attempt to stir up some customers, but all to no avail. Just as we were about to pack up and go back to our boats two of the drunkest and wettest men I have ever seen staggered through the door and laid twenty cents each (the top price) on

[4]Sistersville, West Virginia, was founded in 1839 and named for two sisters, Sarah and Delilah Wells, who owned the land on which it was built.

the sugar barrel from which Dad was selling tickets and, with an "on-with-the-show" air, found their way to two front seats.

All of us were holding a consultation behind the sheet which we had tacked up as a dressing room shield to decide whether we wanted to give a show for just forty cents, when one of the audience—the drunkest one—crawled under the sheet as though it were a circus tent and engaged Dad in a whispered proposal.

"I'll give you five dollars," he said, "if you'll tell a good joke on my friend Tim Early out there."

He was like manna sent from heaven, and we put on the show with a will. At times it rained so hard on the tin roof above us that no one could hear a word anyone else said. It wouldn't have made any difference to them, anyway, but for the sake of our art, we put on a complete show.

There wasn't one round of applause, or the faintest ripple of a laugh throughout the entire performance. It was criminal. The audience sat stolidly out front as though waiting in a depot for a train. When it came time to pull the joke on Tim Early, Dad and I stepped off the stage and shouted it into their ears in order to make them hear it above the roar of the rain. It was a simple sort of gag, frayed and moth-eaten:

"I saw a man in an alley the other day pouring hot water down a chicken's neck trying to make it lay a hard-boiled egg."

"That's nothing. I saw Tim Early here, right in front of the Raven Rock Grocery, trying the same thing on a rooster."

The man who had paid the five dollars laughed harder than I had ever heard anyone laugh before. But Tim Early didn't laugh because he was snoring.

Thus we lazed along from town to town on our journey toward the sea. We forgot the days of the week, newspapers, and all the other unimportant details of civilization. We began to neglect our personal appearance until Mother started a campaign to snap us up. Her opening shot at me—one which never failed to bring results—was "How would you like George M. Cohan to see you looking like this?"

When there was no wind we floated all night with only a lantern as a signal to keep the passing steamers at a safe distance. There was a dream-like quality in those nights, an unreality in everything we saw and did.

I shall never forget the night we floated from the Duck Creek government light to Blennerhassett Island. Fiddlin' Joe had predicted that it would be an unusually beautiful and peaceful night.

"How do you know?" I asked.

"There's signs," he answered solemnly. "There was a flock of blackbirds on some drift back there sharing bugs and beetles with some swallows. Usually a blackbird is the most selfish bird alive, but he goes soft and generous that way when there's specially good weather ahead."

Although it sounded like nature-faking to me, Joe was completely serious. And whether the action of the blackbirds had any relation to the weather or not, the night turned out to be golden.

As we glided softly past Marietta, we gazed into the beautiful Muskingum River valley, past the weird shadows cast by the little iron bridge that spans that enchanted stream, catching it in moon-soaked splendor. The soft, almost inaudible sound of water trickling over the dam just above indicated that the water was low at that point, but not too low to prevent Old Man River from sending a welcome spray of moisture through the air on that dry summer night. We drifted on, until the city lights disappeared, one by one, behind us.

The night had even cast its spell on Florence, who had always thought that the beauties of nature were something they served on a Pullman dining car while she was compelled to eat an apple in the day coach. Now she sat in the cabin, eagerly bent over Charles Garvice's beautiful love story, *The Duchess*, reading by the light of a smoking lantern.[5]

Now and then we could distinguish the faint ringing of a cowbell in the hills. Farther down the river a midnight Romeo was crossing over with his only girl in mind. We could hear the rattle of his

[5]Charles Garvice was a highly popular English novelist and short story writer whose Gothic novels were sold in inexpensive editions and bought by thousands of readers in England and America.

oars in their locks keeping time to a voice which should never have tried to sing but which was now happily murdering "Will You Love Me in December as You Did in May?"[6] Mother, hearing the song, handed Joe her guitar, for she couldn't stand the sound of his one-string fiddle.

I have often wondered since what my mother's thoughts were like that night. She had traveled far from the applause of London audiences and the luxuries she had known. But she was not one to complain of hardships. When her course was chosen she stuck to it, and if she ever felt unhappy she kept that to herself.

With her fine soprano voice she began to sing "By the Light of the Silvery Moon."[7] We all joined in barbershop chords, Fiddlin' Joe contesting the melody with his indiscriminating baritone.

While we were singing I noticed a strange break in the water near our boat. Some small animal was swimming across the stream. Joe reached out and stunned it with his oar. As he fished it out of the water, we saw that it was a beautiful grey squirrel. I wrapped it in my corduroy jacket and held it close to me while I sang on. Later, fully recovered and

[6]"Will You Love Me in December as You Did in May?", published in 1905, was composed by Ernest Ball. The lyrics were by James J. Walker who later became famous as the Mayor of New York.
[7]"By the Light of the Silvery Moon," published in 1909, was composed by August "Gus" Edwards. The lyrics are by Edward Madden.

overcome with gratitude, he scratched my face and bit my hand before jumping into the water again to continue his interrupted journey.

Below James Island we flanked into a small eddy. I was lying face down on the deck with both hands dangling in the water. Suddenly they came in contact with a small floating jug, which I promptly lifted onto the boat, to find that it was attached to a trout line and acted as a buoy for a fisherman's net. Joe and I quickly hauled it on deck, much against Mother's protests, and helped ourselves to a choice mess of channel cats, green bass, and Ohio River perch. It wasn't quite an approved river custom, but it was done because we had just done it. After all I had found the fish in the river and they hadn't been branded!

We shaped out the channel of the river at Neal's Island and passed the Little (Muddy) Kanawha where it comes out at Parkersburg. There, just at dawn, Joe threw a line around a protruding willow and checked us in below Amme's Ripple on Blennerhassett Island, where Aaron Burr met with Harman Blennerhassett to discuss the formation of an empire that never materialized.

On the beach, in the glare of the rising sun, I wrote the words "Treasure Island" in the sand as Mother prepared a delicious breakfast of hot coffee, German-fried potatoes, buttered toast, and, of course, fish. Later, as a bold pirate, I explored the island and was broken-hearted to learn that it was inhabited by the white man and well-cultivated with an abundance of corn and potatoes.

A few days later we passed Point Pleasant, West Virginia. We didn't know, then, what an important part it was to play later in our lives.

When we reached Gallipolis, Ohio, the boyhood home of the famous columnist, O. O. McIntyre,[8] the river front was so crowded that we had to land just above the wharf boat.

In those days there were three large freight and passenger boats, commonly referred to as packets, plying between Pittsburgh and Cincinnati: The *Keystone State*,[9] the *Virginia*,[10] and the *Queen City*.

The *Keystone State* was on its up-river trip and had just landed at Gallipolis, which placed Joe's boat alongside the big boat's wheel. The colored[11]

[8]Oscar Odd "O. O." McIntyre (1884–1938) wrote a syndicated column entitled "New York Day by Day" that was carried in several hundred newspapers.

[9] *The Keystone State*, a stern wheel, wooden hull packet, was built at Hamar, Ohio, at the Knox Yard in 1890. The vessel hit an intake tower at Chain of Rocks on the Mississippi River above St. Louis and was lost in June 1914.

[10] *The Virginia*, a stern wheel, wooden hull packet, was built at Cincinnati, Ohio, by the Cincinnati Marine Railway Company in 1895. *The Virginia* was the first river vessel fitted out with a carbon-arc searchlight. Sold and renamed several times it was dismantled at St. Louis in the 1920s.

[11]The use of the word "colored" represents a step away from overt racial prejudice but still demonstrates the negative or patronizing attitude that many Americans of Bryant's generation had toward blacks. Billy Bryant both employed and knew black people, however there is only an occasional reference to them.

roustabouts were toting freight across the gang-plank and a crowd was gathered on the levee, when Joe, in a spirit of fun, called up to the captain.

"Hey, Captain, there are a couple of muskrats hanging on your rudders."

The crowd laughed gaily at the sally, which intimated that the *Keystone State* was so slow that muskrats could hang on without difficulty. The captain flushed angrily, but there was no trace of anger in his voice when he spoke.

"Thank you, Joe," he said quietly. "I'll try to get them off before I get back."

For several days we lay there and so it was that we were still there when the *Keystone State* returned on her down-trip, pulling in at midnight. The captain was at the wheel. At the proper moment for his purpose, he rang the bell for full steam ahead and drove the big *Keystone State* as close as possible to the shore, swinging the bow out into the river and the stern in on Joe's boat, throwing plenty of wheel waves at him. Any riverman can tell you what kind of results this sort of maneuvering will produce.

The first thing it did was to draw all the water out from under Joe's boat, leaving it cocked up on one side high and dry on the bank. Before he could get out of bed, the water returned and washed him fifty feet out on the shore. Then the dead swells began to roll in on him, with whitecaps three feet high breaking over his boat, literally washing his piano boxes off the hull.

Poor old Joe, in his ragged nightshirt, was running up and down the shore, cursing like a trooper. Later, when the captain had his boat rounded to, and landed at the wharf, he called down in a seemingly friendly voice.

"Say, Joe," he said, "I wish you would look around at my rudders for me and see whether those muskrats are still there."

But Joe wasn't in a mood for humor just then.

In the morning Fiddlin' Joe had disappeared. He had gone out of our lives as suddenly as he had come into them and we never saw or heard of him again. His abandoned battered little boat brought tears to our eyes. We felt alone without him and hoped then, as we do now, that it was through no fault of ours that our friendship ended so abruptly.

As we went down the river the next day we missed him terribly, not only as a friend, but also as a guide. Not knowing the river, we stuck on the sandbar at the head of Raccoon Island, just a few miles below Gallipolis, where the water, falling rapidly that night, left us high and dry for six weeks. We had no skiff or john boat with which to reach the mainland, and so, for a few days, until a friendly fellow came over to us in his boat, we had to "Robinson Crusoe" it.

It was here that I learned to eat turtle eggs and the tails of crayfish, which aren't so bad if you like turtle eggs and crayfish tails. Our boat had settled level on the sand so we could still cook on the stove and keep our dishes on the table all right. But it did make me sore to have to carry water out of the river to a boat that was on dry land.

After we had called "good morning" to someone on the Ohio side of the river, and "good night" to the West Virginia side for a week, we finally scared up a list of friendly neighbors who kept us supplied with butter, eggs, sweet milk, and always a chicken or guinea hen on Sunday. This was the only way I ever knew what day of the week it was.

It was here that I found my first note in a bottle. The bottle had been washed ashore in a little pile of drift. Breaking it, I pulled out a scrap of wrapping paper on which had been crudely written:

> *Roses are red, violets blue,*
> *Sugar is sweet, and so are you.*

It was signed with the name and address of a girl who lived close to Waverly, West Virginia, on Bull Creek.

Later I found several more of them, some simply with names and addresses. Sometimes the name would be preceded with the request to "write me a sweet letter" or "make a date." Sometimes the message was, to say the least, highly unconventional. I learned, as I went along, that it was a fad on the river just then. Many correspondences—and often more than that—began with a note in a bottle.

Day-by-day Dad became a little more irritable at our enforced idleness. The seemingly permanent

engagement we were playing on the island was beginning to tell on him, and we all saw that he was
about due for a blowup. He had worn a beaten path
from the boat to the water's edge, where he had a
mark to show if the river was rising or falling.

It had been an extremely dry summer. For the
first three weeks of our stay on the island the river
continued to be a little lower each day than it had
been the day before. Florence and I were having a
good time playing Indians and Buffalo Bill. Mother
went along from day-to-day with the patience she
always showed. But Father was slowly going nuts.

One afternoon, when Florence and I had been
getting on each other's nerves a little, she looked at
me with my long uncut hair hanging over my face.

"Why don't you invite George Cohan down for
the hunting season, and let him see how nicely your
hair is coming in," she said spitefully. "I'm sure
he'd enjoy a weekend with us!"

Father looked at both of us wildly as I told her to
shut up. Then, his eyes dark like the sky before a
thunderstorm, he stood up and dashed out of the
boat and down to the mark at the water's edge. In a
moment he came dashing back, gesticulating frantically and bellowing like a mad bull.

"I'm through!" he shouted. "This is a dog's life!
Look at my hands! Look at my face!"

I looked at his hands. They were dirty. But I
knew that I couldn't look at his face without laughing, so I didn't look. His bald head looked like a

whitewashed gourd and shone like a billiard ball. He was barefooted and had on a pair of trousers cut off at the knees, and wore a mildewed Prince Albert ripped up the back. He was, to put it briefly, a scream.

"I ask you," he shouted, "do I look like Dr. Sam Bryant or do I look like a bank robber? I can make a living easier than this. If you go to jail they at least feed you, and this place is worse than any man's jail ever thought of being. Just as soon as we get off of this God-forsaken island, I'm going back to civilization and stay there!"

With that he left us, and took out across the island almost at a run. Until long after he was out of sight we could hear him shouting that he was through, absolutely through! If we had been on the River Jordan instead of the Ohio he would probably have walked out on us right then, trusting to find the happy hunting grounds on the other side.

He had no sooner disappeared into the thickest of the willows than we heard a man calling from the West Virginia shore. The water was eight feet two at Kanawha Falls (the head of the Kanawha River) he said, and rising.

Before he had finished speaking, Mother was running across the island in hot pursuit of Dad, loudly calling to him.

"Sam! Oh Sam! Where are you? The river is rising, Sam!"

Sis and I ate our supper of black coffee, jowl

meat, and hoe cake in silence. We never attempted to seek our parents when Dad was blowing off, as we knew that Mother could handle him better alone. At dusk a flock of buzzards circled low over the foot of the island and we watched them in their slow, narrowing flight.

"Must be something dead over there," I ventured dolefully.

"Dad's hopes," Florence said.

But a few minutes later we saw Mother and Dad walking slowly along the beach, arm in arm. They stopped at the edge of the river where Dad had kept a record of the water's action. He bent down and examined his marks and discovered that the water was already rising. Then he put his arms about Mother and they kissed each other.

So Florence and I went to bed.

VII

We Winter on the Little Kanawha

Aꜰʟᴏᴀᴛ once more, Mother and Dad reconsidered their contemplated trip to Cincinnati and had the steamer *Darling*[1] tow us back up the river to Parkersburg, where we tied up for the winter in the mouth of Neal's Run, a small creek which came out about half a mile upstream in the Little Kanawha River. Here Florence and I went to a little red schoolhouse over the hill until the severest kind of poverty again caught up with us and made us quit school in order to do something about it.

Mother, as usual, had been for some time practically our sole support. While canvassing in the inclement weather she had contracted a lingering cold which kept her in bed for many weeks while Dad vainly tried to sell liniment and electric belts on the ice-covered, deserted street corners. So, one by one, we again pawned everything we had that was pawnable, including, of course, Mother's diamond ring and guitar.

Florence and I quit school and Dad and I carried firewood from the nearby mountainside of Fort Boreman to keep Mother warm. Sis spent her time

[1] Little is known about the *Darling* other than that the vessel was built at Parkersburg, West Virginia, in 1871.

131

in taking care of Mother and taking care, too, of the houseboat. It was an exceptionally cold winter. The Little Kanawha was frozen solid early, and the old swimming hole at the mouth of the creek was just one big icicle. All navigation was suspended. The ferrymen on the upper end of the stream who had previously furnished the only route across the river were frantic with rage as they watched the long lines of sheep, cattle, horses, cows, wagons, and human pedestrians crossing safely on twenty-inch-thick ice.

Hundreds of young people came many miles to this perfect natural ice skating rink. They would sit on the guards of our little boat, and Father, remembering his training as an English servant, would help them with their skates, and invite them onto the boat for coffee. There was one charming girl whose father was a doctor. Becoming interested in Mother, she persuaded her father to come out and attend her. He came daily for many days, and I have often thought that we may owe her recovery to him.

As Mother grew stronger, things seemed to take on a brighter aspect for us all. On Mondays my sister would help the neighbors with their weekly washing in return for her dinner and whatever else they could spare to send down to us on the boat. I had made the acquaintance of one of the bill posters at the Auditorium Theater and he gave me fifty cents a day to carry his paste bucket and brush around town and help him with the "paper."

Often the advance shipment of posters from show companies who were coming was more than we could put up. The leftover paper I would carefully save and bring home with me, regardless of the weather which often made me wrap the posters around my body under my coat, to keep them from being ruined, and stack them in one corner of our already crowded shanty boat. On them were beautifully lithographed pictures of Fiske O'Hara,[2] Porter J. White,[3] May Irwin,[4] and other current stage celebrities, in the parts in which they would appear. Finally, Florence grew disgusted at my rapidly growing pile.

"Couldn't you go in for stamps instead of show-bills, Billy?" she asked me one night. "They'd take up lots less room!"

"I'm saving them to use on our showboat someday," I answered indignantly. "We can just change the top and bottom. The middle will fit any show." I continued on enthusiastically, opening one of the posters, and pointing to the figures on it. "This could be me; this you; and here's Mother and Dad."

"Oh," Florence said drily, "I thought you were

---

[2] Fiske O'Hara (1880–1945), born George Fiske Brenen, was an actor and playwright.

[3] Porter J. White (?–1934) was an actor who is credited with being the first person to recite Hugh D'Arcy's poem, "The Face upon the Floor."

[4] May Irwin (1862–1938) was born in Canada and from almost her childhood achieved success in both vaudeville and the legitimate theater.

going to paste them into your memory book as a record of the most successful season the George M. Cohan of the rivers ever played."

The next day during a blinding snowstorm in a one-horse wagon we did a long country route for a special attraction that was coming to Parkersburg for one night only. As my boss covered the first barn, about a mile from town, with gaudy colored sheets, I built a fire along the side of the road to warm our hands and feet. Later, as I gathered up his equipment, my eyes were suddenly glued to the paper before me. Through the blur of falling snow I read with misty eyes and a lump in my throat: "Coming—the one and only George M. Cohan in his greatest comedy success, *The Governor's Son*."[5]

Trembling with excitement and jealousy, I continued on with my work but was silently thinking a multitude of confused angry thoughts. Here I was out in a snowstorm, cold and hungry, working for fifty cents a day to drum up an audience for a guy who wouldn't even give us a lift when we needed it, who was (I told myself) a no-better actor than I was, and who was pulling off one success after another while we starved.

For days, until the show reached town, I was silent and morose, without a decent word for anyone.

[5] *The Governor's Son* was written by George M. Cohan and produced in 1901 as a full-scale musical comedy starring the Four Cohans and Ethel Levy, who later married George M. Cohan.

Billy Bryant and George M. Cohan
as Young Entertainers about 1910
Courtesy New York City Public Library

Florence thought that I was still angry at her for the crack she had made about my posters and the "George M. Cohan of the rivers," and made a sisterly attempt to straighten it out. But I had forgotten all about that. I was obsessed with the idea that George Cohan was about to cross my path again, and that somehow I couldn't bear it. Yet what could I do about it?

The thing that I did, of course, was to go and see his show. It was only, I told myself, so that I could see how bad he really was and figure out how much better I would be able to do his act. My boss managed to slip me up into the fly loft and, for once in my life, I sat and looked directly down on George M. Cohan. Of course it was a marvelous show. Each of the Four Cohans had a part in it, and in place of each my envious imagination placed one of the Four Bryants, and the applause and laughter of the audience set my brain into a bitter whirl.

In the first act Mr. Cohan sang his famous song, "Then I Know that I'd be Satisfied with Life":

All I want is ten million dollars,
A sealskin to protect me from the cold,
Vanderbilt, waiting on the table,
And living in a mansion built of gold.
If Johnny Gates would let me spend his money,
If Hetty Green would only be my wife,
If I only owned the Pennsylvania Railroad,
Then I know that I'd be satisfied with life.

At that moment I would have been satisfied with much less—just the position the Cohans then occupied. As the show continued, I took a quick survey of the surroundings in general and recognized the aura of prosperity. It was noticeable in the newness and brightness of the scenery, the glare of the beautiful lighting effects, the smiling faces and general good humor of the cast, the reaction of a capacity house, and the sure, self-satisfied, fascinating manner of Cohan himself. As the contrast between the Cohans' position and ours burned into my mind, it was more than my childish eyes and brain could endure. I felt suddenly sick and faint and wanted to be at home.

As the laughing, praising audience made the theater thunder with applause at the end of Cohan's celebrated eccentric dance, I silently climbed down the ladder at the back of the stage and, with the sickening applause still ringing in my ears, rushed into the cold night air. In a blind fit of raging jealousy I ran all the way to the bridge that crossed the Little Kanawha. There, out of breath, I felt something burning and smarting on my cheek. I rubbed it off—it was a drop of ice, a frozen tear, and for the first time I realized that I was crying. Furious at myself, I ran across the bridge where I stumbled and fell against the iron structure, cutting my lip and breaking off a piece of one of my front teeth which is still noticeably missing.

In the glare of the light at the end of the bridge I

could see the blood from my mouth. Now I was scared. Although I was then wearing my first pair of long trousers, I was scared as a kid gets scared. In a bath of nervous perspiration, I shivered as the cold biting wind swept up the Kanawha from out in the Ohio. Then I ran with all my might again, along the lonely river road in the shadows of the hills of Fort Bowman. At last, completely exhausted, I stumbled aboard our snow covered boat. There, with my head in my mother's lap, I sobbed out the story of all that had happened to me that evening, including all that I felt.

Suddenly I jumped to my feet and began to pace the floor.

"Everybody in the show business seems to be getting ahead but us," I cried. "Here we are frozen up on a cracker box like a lot of Eskimos and waiting for what? We ought to get out of the show business or get into it! Oh Mother," I cried, "why can't we have a showboat like the *Water Queen*? I know we could make it go, because I was the biggest hit Captain Price ever had on his darned old boat!"

I shall always hold it against my father that he did not rise up at that moment and hit me on the top of the head with a piece of stove wood.

"The only thing that stands between the Four Bryants and a showboat is a little work," I shouted.

"The only thing that stands between the Four Bryants and a showboat is ten thousand dollars," Florence corrected me. Then she added, "And for

Heaven's sake, don't work yourself up into another George M. Cohan imitation!"

Dad had his chair tilted back against the wall of the boat, with his feet on the stove, as he surveyed us all critically.

"All right!" I cried. "All right! If you folks are satisfied to spend the rest of your lives on a shanty boat fighting mud and mosquitoes in the summer, and ice and starvation in the winter, listening to ice grinding against the hull and sitting down to a plate of muskrat soup for Christmas dinner while Georgie Cohan—"

"Oh Gawd," Florence groaned, "I knew that was coming!" Then she poured herself a cup of coffee and, taking up a newspaper, began to read it.

"Ain't I right, Dad?" I asked.

"I suppose so," he agreed, dispiritedly.

"Then why don't you do something about it?" I screamed at the top of my voice.

At that his chair came down on all four legs so hard that, had we not been locked in the ice, it would have made the boat rock, and he jumped to his feet faster than I had ever seen him move before. He broke from his chair with a snap like the parting of a spring line in the Marmet lock chamber on the Kanawha when the valve chambers are opened too suddenly.

"Do something?" he thundered. "What in hell do you suppose I've been going over dams for and living in the stone age on drift-covered islands?

Why do you suppose your mother has been ruining her health this winter by canvassing from door to door for a few paltry pennies if not to keep our heads above water until we can better ourselves in the way you so graciously suggest?"

"Now Sam, dear, don't lose your temper," said Mother softly.

"Don't Sam me!" he snapped back at her. "You seem to forget, young man, that showboats do cost money—real money, not stage money. You can't run one out of a hole with a ferret!"

After that he paced the floor in dour silence.

I could hear my mother softly sobbing now, and it made me feel utterly ashamed of myself for having spoken as I did. Dad finally broke the silence of an awkward pause by saying, "Now folks, let's hustle up and get to bed before the fire dies down and the room gets cold."

My sister and I slept on a straw tick on the kitchen floor, while Mother and Dad tried to rest in a folding iron bed with a thin pad on it, which was just about the same as sleeping on the floor, except that the word "bed" added prestige to it.

"I don't know," said Dad, as he put his shoes in the oven, hoping they would still be warm in the morning, "but I have a feeling that our luck is just about to change."

Just then there was a strange noise coming from up the river, a rumble and grinding sound which none of us seemed to recognize.

"I guess that's our changed luck sounding off now," Florence said, as she pulled the covers up to her chin.

She was absolutely right, though none of us, at that time, had enough knowledge to take from it the warning we should have heeded. For, as we turned in that night, we should all have been outside working madly, as our shanty-boat neighbors were doing, to save our home from destruction.

It was late in February. The weather had been cloudy and exceptionally warm for that time of year and the heavens suddenly opened their windows and poured torrents of rain upon the snow-blanketed mountains at the head of the little stream which housed us. Ditches, gullies, and ravines rapidly overflowed with a rush of snow, ice, and rain water that came roaring madly down over the mountain sides and poured funnel-like into Neal's Run and the Little Kanawha, then blocked off at the mouth by the ice-gorged Ohio. The river began to rise at the alarming rate of a foot and a half an hour, which is as fast as I have ever seen water come up any man's river bank.

Although it was our first experience in an ice break-up, we were not particularly worried, for we had out a new three-quarter-inch manila rope line which we considered sufficiently strong to hold our boat under any circumstances. Besides, we had been told that we would be perfectly safe in the mouth of Neal's Run.

At ten o'clock that night it was still raining. All up and down the river scores of rivermen were working with the aid of lanterns and torches, cursing and yelling orders to one another, trying to tie their gas boats, barges, sand flats, log rafts, shanty boats, and all that floated, safely. Many of them chopped or sawed the ice free around their boats in an attempt to hold their boats against the movement of the ice which they expected at any moment. Women carried their bedding, dishes, sewing machines, and other treasures to safety at the top of the river bank, where they carefully laid them in the mud and rain.

But we lay abed.

The water was now boiling wickedly over the ice in attempting to free itself from the grip of winter. One false alarm after another went the rounds to the effect that the ice had let go at the head of the river and was bringing everything with it.

It seems strange, but in all my years of river experience I have never known a flood to reach its full crest, an ice break-up to take place, or a terrific windstorm to go into action during the day. They will invariably make their appearance after night has fallen so as to add the horror of darkness to their own.

And, true to form, things began to happen about twelve o'clock that night. The rapidly rising water succeeded in cracking the ice near us. It broke with a sound like the report of a rifle, and our boat shook and trembled like an airplane passing through an air pocket. Neal's Run, the quiet haven which we had sought for safety, suddenly decided to be a battlefield, and broke up and came out first. And don't let anyone tell you that a tiny creek is safe just because in midsummer it makes a perfect setting for a watercolor pastoral, a calm trickle of water in which cows can scarcely get their feet wet.

What had seemed such a safe and calm and peaceful spot for us in early autumn quickly turned into hell in hip boots and on skis. After the ice broke up above and came roaring and grinding its mad way down the swollen creek, lashed and torn and tumbled by a fury of churning and growling water, it had no place to go except the place where we were first, and it had no respect for our priority. It piled up under our boat until we were propped up like a birdhouse on the end of a pole.

We scrambled, scantily clad, to the safety of the shore, and stood there shivering while we watched our home go to pieces. We had hardly cleared our boat when the Ohio River let go at Blennerhassett Island, leaving an opening for the Little Kanawha which, in turn, freed Neal's Run. The water, which had been the foundation of our home all winter, poured out as in a millrace, joining the raging torrent of the Little Kanawha, which bore along in its mad career a shattered assortment of shanty boats, barges, and john boats, and thousands of dollars worth of logs, frozen solid in a great mass of ice.

At the first squeeze of the break-up, the frenzied heavy ice shoved our boat from its pinnacle and turned it over on its side, where one large cake of ice after another quickly cut it down to splinters and carried it to complete destruction. With the exception of a few blankets, and Mother's diamond ring and guitar, which were still in pawn, we lost everything.

As I watched it go, piece by piece, I thought with an aching heart of my brave collection of posters, the beginnings of our showboat business. They would be dirty shapeless pulp now, ruined and lost, turned into the most insignificant details in piles of drift along the river. Where would I find another collection like them?

But my mind didn't dwell on them long when I saw the sadness of Mother's and Father's faces, and thought how they had struggled and fought for every piece of lumber in that grand little boat.

In the rain, and ankle deep in mud, we slowly made our way back to Parkersburg, where the kind hearts and hands of utter strangers furnished us with food and shelter.

VIII

We Find Our True Home

DOWN ON the wharf one day Dad happened to meet a steamboat captain name of Doggie Cross,[1] who was considered, in those parts, the best low-water pilot that ever rubbed the bottom of a river in the Pittsburgh and Parkersburg trade. At that time he was standing watch on the steamer *Katherine*,[2] a small stern wheel packet that plied between Parkersburg and Crescent on Little Kanawha. He offered Mother and Dad berths as cook and dishwasher at a joint salary of thirty dollars per month, and they accepted. So we all piled on board, glad to eat regular meals again and to have over our heads a roof which didn't leak. Mother had always been a good cook. Dad made a good dishwasher and a nice appearance too.

Doggie Cross was a great joker, and it is this quality in him that I remember best of all the things which happened during our life on the *Katherine*.

[1] Monroe "Doggie" Cross was a successful pilot and ship's master.

[2] *Katherine*, a stern wheel, wooden hull ferry, was built at Jeffersonville, Indiana, by Howard in 1889. Originally named *The New Idea*, the vessel was brought to Point Pleasant in 1907 and dismantled to make other vessels, including the *I.N. Flesher*.

He was also well known as a man who, like most rivermen, was fond of the ladies. On one trip we carried six round-trip, sightseeing Sunday school teachers, who spent most of their time in the pilothouse talking to the captain.

At Wells' Ripple lived an old crony of his with whom he had an arrangement for producing a faked echo for the edification of any passengers he might have on board. When he passed this point he would halloo loudly and his friend would repeat the call in a more subdued tone. The clear and accurate "echo" thus produced never failed to impress his guests. As we passed Wells' Ripple on this day he pulled the pilothouse sash open.

"Hello out there!" he called loudly.

"Hello out there!" the supposed echo came back.

"What you doin' out there?" the captain pursued, moved to further the demonstration by the expression of awed wonder on the ladies' faces.

But his collaborator was evidently in a dour mood for echo answered with painful distinctness:

"Rabbit hunting. Mind your own business, you bald headed so-and-so!"

When Captain Cross was moved to the larger steamer *Ben Hur*[3] on the Ohio, we went with him as far as Pittsburgh. Mother had saved practically every cent of the wages she and Father had received.

[3] *Ben Hur*, a stern wheel, wooden hull packet, was built at Hamar, Ohio, at the Knox Yard in 1887. The vessel sank at Duckport, Louisiana in March 1916.

Even after she had taken the guitar and diamond ring out of pawn she had nearly a hundred dollars left. It seemed a fortune to us!

We went to Brownsville on the Monongahela River, all united, at last, on a single plan. We would get jobs—any kind of jobs—and pool our earnings in a common fund with which to build a showboat.

Florence went to work as a waitress in a restaurant; Mother started out on a vigorous campaign of canvassing; Dad did a bit on street corners with liniment and electric belts; and I went to work driving a mule in the old Diamond coal mine.

In the evening I would hang around the stage door of the local opera house, and this, and my avid interest in everything which went on inside, finally got me another job. One night, when it was pouring cats and dogs, the property man saw me standing there drenched to the skin and called me inside in a gruff voice.

"Look here, youngster," he said, "we don't mind having you stand there on good nights, but on a night like this you've either got to go home or come inside. Which'll it be?"

There was no question in my mind and I grinned and took off my cap. The next night he gave me a job as assistant property man, to help with the "props" and take care of the "window work," that is, the posters which were put up around town— much the same sort of work, this last, as that which I had done in Parkersburg. It kept me scurrying to do that and keep my job as a muleteer, too, but I managed.

Whenever any paper would come in for a new show I'd hustle around and get the lithographs and cards up in the windows, and as soon as the show left town, I'd go around and pick them up again— not because the show wanted them, but because I did. Soon I had a much larger stack than that which had gone down with the shanty boat in the mouth of Neal's Run. Fearing Florence's ridicule, I didn't take my new collection home with me but stacked it up in the prop room at the theater.

When the property man saw what I was doing he began over-ordering on paper from the incoming shows and let me keep all the overs. He probably thought that I was mildly insane, but he was a genial and friendly soul. Seeing the pleasure which this mute stack of obsolete posters gave me, he contributed to it.

Often in the evening around the theater I would see some of the men from the mine where I drove the mule. Whenever I saw the beginning of a look of recognition on one of their faces, I would turn away, no sign of recognition on my own. And when I was asked at the mine whether I wasn't working at the opera house, I denied it. It was very silly, but I thought of myself as a showman and couldn't bring myself to admit that I was driving a mule in a mine. All of this, even the showboat itself toward which we were working now, seemed merely a prelude to

Colorful Showboat Posters,
the Kind Collected by Billy Bryant.
Courtesy The Public Library of Cincinnati and Hamilton County

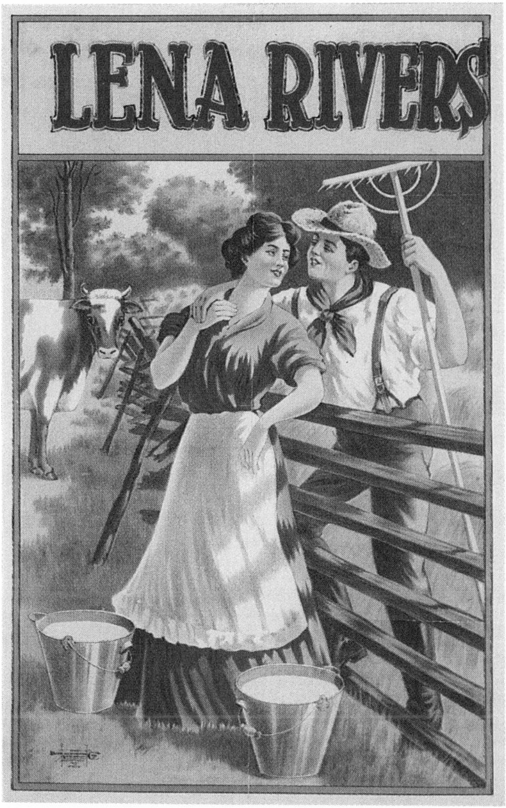
LENA RIVERS

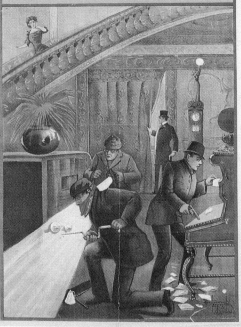

LITTLE NELL
OF THE OZARKS "

the day when, as a great and famous actor, I would see my name in lights on Broadway.

Meanwhile, Dad had got credit for most of the cost of a $700 gas engine and had built our first gas towboat, which he named the *Florence*, after my sister. It had been a long, hard, uphill pull, getting the money with which to do this. Often nails or lumber or both would run out in the middle of the week and all operations would have to cease until someone had a payday. But at last it was finished—the power end of our showboat outfit. There it was, like a horse without a cart to hitch it to.

Seeing how much money a showboat would cost and how hard money was to get, we all reluctantly gave up our idea for that year, and bought a small houseboat and a flatboat which we equipped with a tent. Hitching the *Florence* to it, we started a tour of the rivers with hopeful hearts, still looking forward to the time when we could own a showboat.

It was then that I had my moment of triumph over Florence. For several evenings I had worked late at the opera house, cutting off the tops of some of the posters I had saved and pasting strips of paper above the pictures on them. On the fresh, white space I had painted in large letters:

"BRYANT'S COMEDY COMPANY."

Below the pictures we lettered the place and date where we were to show. We used them all up and down the Monongahela River, where we would stop at each town, pitching our tent on a vacant lot for a week's engagement before we would move on again. We hadn't a showboat, but we had the next best thing. And it carried us along for several years.

Late in the autumn of 1906 we were tied up at Middleport, Ohio because the wheel shaft of the *Florence* was broken. Learning there was a machine shop at Point Pleasant, we cast off again and started to float down to it. But a high wind came up and blew us ashore about three miles above town. It was in the bend of the river and a bad place to lay up, but we had little choice, so we prepared to spend the night there, in spite of high water and the fact that the willows to which we tied were many feet from dry land.

Late that afternoon a large raft of logs, also more or less being beckoned by the wind, came drifting toward us, manned by three workmen with pike poles and side sweeps. As the raft passed, rubbing against the side of our boat, one of the men called to Dad.

"You're all right, Captain," he called, as Father looked alongside and failed to see any damage.

"I hope he's right," Florence said, who was eating a piece of sugared bread, as usual, "but if the Four Bryants have missed on any hard luck, surely that is news!"

Mother, noticing a worried look on Dad's face, quickly put on a pot of coffee and soon we all sat down to supper. During a pause in the none-too-brilliant conversation, we heard a gentle musical sound like that of a waterfall. It had nothing to do with the normal action of the river. At the same moment we became frightfully aware that the boat was listing.

Dad jumped up then, and quickly opened a trap in the floor that led to the hull of the boat. When he pulled his arm up again it was wet to the elbow. Florence screamed and, reaching for her canary bird, jumped off the shore side of the boat into water up to her waist. As the water began to find its way through the many cracks in the floor, and the boat began to sink more rapidly, Mother, with her guitar, and Dad and I, jumped into the john boat and rowed ashore.

Standing dismally together on the shore we saw a little jet of steam rising as the water covered the cook stove, and then, as we watched, our entire outfit settled to the bottom, with only the superstructure showing above water.

Sadly and in silence, save for the audible chattering of our teeth, we rowed the three miles down the river to Point Pleasant. At the wharf, we were met by the night policeman who, seeing our plight, took us to a famous old river hostelry, the Klein [or Kline] House. It had been closed for a long time, but a Mrs. Park was living in a few rooms with her family, and the policeman got her to take us in. She helped us to build a fire and we camped in one of the many abandoned rooms.

Then we began to learn about the almost inconceivable kindness of the people of Point Pleasant. Words fail me as I remember how that tiny town, to which we were then but complete strangers, rushed forward to lend us a helping hand, furnishing us with food, clothing and the other necessities of life. Coming to our aid as they did then, they were directly responsible for the prosperity which greeted us in later years. Since then we have proudly proclaimed that Point Pleasant would be our permanent home.

Long ago it was named by the Shawnee Indians "Tu Endie Wei," which means the mingling of the waters, because it is at the point where the Big Kanawha meets the Ohio. Later it was called "Shawneetown" by white men who decided the Indian name was too difficult. George Washington stopped there with a surveying party in the fall of 1770 and renamed it "Point Pleasant," by which name it has always been known since. Its natives will tell you that it is the oldest town on the Ohio River south of Pittsburgh, and that the first battle of the Revolutionary War was fought there.

Ever since there have been steamboats and showboats on the rivers, it has been one of the greatest of all ports on the inland streams. It is nationally known for its construction of marine equipment. Because of the fine workmanship of its plants, the United States Navy has awarded many contracts for Coast Guard cruisers to the Point Pleasant Machine

Works, the Kanawha and Enterprise Dock companies, and the Marietta Manufacturing Company.

It was here that we settled down for the moment and tried to find out just what had happened to us and what we could do about it. Our investigation up-river showed that the raft of 700 crossties which brushed against us had knocked a piece of the rake off our shanty boat, and that the shanty boat, in sinking, had pulled the *Florence* and flatboat down until the water had poured in through dry, and therefore open, seams.

We sued the Ironton Crosstie Company, but the men who manned the logs testified that Dad had told them that everything was all right. Dad testified that since he had not had time to investigate, he had made no complaint at the time of the collision, and, by a technicality of the law, this released them from responsibility, so we lost the case.

Then came an especially touching evidence of the hospitality of Point Pleasant people. A firm of lawyers named Summerville & Summerville had defended the crosstie company and won the verdict in their favor. After the trial was over, the Summervilles, seeing our predicament, offered, of their own volition, to lend us money with which to get on our feet again. They had done their duty to their clients. Now they were playing the human role of being friends to man.

But the man whom we shall always remember with the greatest gratitude was a banker—the late

Captain C. C. Bowyer.[4] He was a great riverman, a true lover of steamboats. If you went to him for a loan there were a couple of questions he would always ask: "What kind of security do you have?" and "Does it float?"

If you were unfortunate enough to have only a valuable farm or building somewhere, the loan would turn out to be just a routine matter of business. But if you had, or wanted to buy, any kind of a steamboat or river craft, his eyes would light up and he would immediately want to know all the details of construction—the size of the machinery, the age of the boilers, how much steam she was allowed, where she was built, and a thousand other details. This was not simply because he wanted to determine her value as security for a loan, but because he wanted to hear everything he could in connection with the river. And then he would take a personal interest and help you in more ways than in arranging a loan. He was like a fond mother of six lovely children talking to another mother who just had a new baby.

Any number of prominent rivermen of today, including showboat owners other than ourselves, are directly indebted to him for their present success.

[4]C. C. Bowyer, who was raised at Winfield, W. Va., near Red House Chute, was, indeed, a genuine river pilot and popular banker who invested heavily in the river fleet. He came from a family long associated with the river trade. His uncle was Captain E. P. Chancellor, a longtime resident of Parkersburg.

He was the ideal type of man for a bank on the river. Known and loved by every steamboat owner from the Allegheny to the sea, his reputation and his dealings were spotless. A steadfast friend and valiant opponent, he was never known to sound a backing bell on friend or foe.

He was one of the first to offer his help when he learned of our destitute condition. He went out of his way to do it, too, not waiting for us to come to him, but sending for us. Alive with excitement and hope, Mother and Dad made their way to his crowded little office in the Merchants' National Bank (the first bank on which either of my parents had ever called on business of their own), of which he was then president, and haltingly poured out the story of their ambition to own a showboat, hastening to explain that they hadn't a thing—save a diamond ring and guitar—in the way of means with which to build one.

"Building a showboat is a big proposition," he said slowly, and Mother doubtless felt like saying, "You're telling us!" How well she knew it! How far off that promised land had seemed to her for years! How often had its shores seemed almost in sight when some cataclysm had driven us farther than ever away from them. But we were nearer to them just then than any of us dreamed. Mother and Dad sat in silence while Captain Bowyer thought the matter out. Finally he spoke again.

"Suppose you just stay in town for a week or so

and see the sights," he said, "while I see what I can do about it. Have you got enough to eat?"

They assured him that they had and came back to our room in the almost abandoned Klein House, their faces alight with hope.

A week later the captain called Mother and Dad to his office again. He had found a condemned government dump scow then lying idle at one of the docks in the Kanawha River which could be bought for twenty-five dollars. It was sixteen feet wide and ninety feet long. Did they think it would do?

Without even looking at it, Mother and Dad agreed that it would be ideal. Captain Bowyer gave them the money with which to buy it, out of his personal account, and got the steamer *Cricket* to give us a hand in towing the scow across the river and raising our sunken gas boat for us.

I don't know whether you have ever seen an old-fashioned wooden dump scow or not, but I can tell you this, that it is about as unengaging a sight as anything you are likely to see. At least ours was that. It was humped up in the middle like an Arkansas razor-back hog. You couldn't tell which end was which. But to us it seemed the most beautiful vessel in the world. We scrambled over it, not missing any detail, and already we could see a stage on it, footlights, a seat-filled auditorium, and a throng of people gayly coming up the stage plank eager to see our show. That mud scow was a showboat the minute we laid eyes on her.

Florence began mucking around the deck, kicking at the thick incrustation of dried mud.

"Get a little of this off," she remarked, "and it'll be a good place to paint a picture of the George M. Cohan of the river. Good advertising!"

But I was much too happy then to resent her attacks, and we all set to with a will to clean up the scow and get ready to build.

"Boy, O boy!" I cried. "Sixteen by ninety! That's a big boat!"

"This boat will seat a hundred people when I get through with her," Dad promised, as he opened his precious set of tools and began to sharpen them.

"We'll paint her white and trim her green," Florence suggested.

"And cook our food with gasoline," I rhymed an ad-lib.

"Gasoline nothing! You mean liniment!"

That night we didn't sleep a wink until nearly daylight. All night long we sat around a table by the light of a coal-oil lamp laying plans for our showboat. Finally we all went to bed, and just as we were about to turn in Mother laid her hand on Dad's arm.

"Name her *Princess*, Sam," she said softly, "after me. Because that's the way I'll feel when she's finally built."

IX

Dad Actually Builds a Showboat

WHEN I look back on the winter that followed I wonder about the accuracy of my own memory. It seems a miracle to me now. We were engaged in a battle against circumstance, determined to build a showboat with nothing that anyone in the world could possibly believe would produce any kind of a boat at all. The one thing we really had to work with was the determination in all of us to have a showboat by spring.

Only the god of the river knows where the lumber came from. We picked it up from here and there—first some waste slabs from the sawmill with which to build a shanty on one end of the hull. As soon as this was up, we moved in. Then we started on the long task of collecting enough for the showboat proper. We bought a little—very little. When we needed a piece of quarter-round or moulding, Dad would set to work with his tools. I have seen him spend as much as a day whittling a piece of quarter-round out of a two-by-two.

At times there were many loose logs on the river, most of them branded with the owners' names. The custom of the river was for those who lived along the shores to pick up such strays and hold them for the owners, who would come along, claim them by the brands, and pay the finders from fifty cents to a dollar apiece. But we had gone too far, now, to be bothered by an old river custom like that.

During a rise in the river, Dad and I would row out in the swift current in a rickety john boat and search the mad rushing drift for odd bits of timber. Some of the miscellaneous flotsam that we caught was much too large and heavy for us to get into the boat, so we would rest one end of our prize on the stern seat, letting the rest of it drag in the water, while we would pull like mad for the shore, often drifting a mile or more downstream before being able to land. But wherever we touched shore, there were Mother and Florence waiting to help us pull our prey out onto the mud bank. When we were fortunate enough to catch a pine or poplar log, we would land it near the sawmill and, if it had been branded by its owner, we would hurriedly "deer-horn" it (that is, chop out the brand) and have it sawed into thin lumber for the roof of our boat.

By now we had many friends among the carpenters and calkers in the drydocks. These kept us as well supplied as they could with nails, scrap oakum, and discarded paint buckets which often contained enough paint to make salvage worthwhile. Yet even with the aid of these, and the river which floated so much of our lumber to us, we were constantly in need of money and borrowed from everyone in Point Pleasant, from a B. & O. track-walker to the

head bartender at the Last Chance Saloon, before
we were able to complete the naked four walls of
our showboat.

There was a tinker in Henderson who helped us
with some of the iron work, such as hog chains. His
name was Ernest King, but everyone called him
"Duckfoot," because he seemed more at home in
the river than out of it. His friendliness and cheeriness were almost as great a help as his tinkering. It
could never find expression in a mild voice. When
he talked to you, he shouted, as though you were
five miles away.

He owned an old-fashioned cylinder talking machine and had only one record for it, "Red Wing,"[1]
which he played over and over again. At almost any
time of the day or night, when you came near to
Duckfoot's shack, you would hear, "Oh, the moon
shines tonight on pretty Red Wing . . ." It was
Duckfoot's theme song.

Finally, early in the spring, just like we had
planned, we were ready for our opening. To be
sure, there was no paint on the auditorium, there
were no chairs, no glass in the windows, and no
lights but there *was* an auditorium, a stage, with a
roof over all, and we feverishly got ready for our
first show.

The town was feverish about it, too. They had

[1]The words to "Red Wing" were written by John Thur-
land Chattaway in 1907. The music was composed by Kerry
Mills.

taken a family interest in the project from the start. We were their foster children, left on their front porch on a night of chance. We had promised them a show in the spring, and they were not going to release us from our promise simply because we had no paint, lights, or window glass!

We hastily began to gather boxes of all sorts for people to sit on, tacked sheets and burlap over the empty eyes of the windows, and added to each handbill announcing the event the request that everyone bring a lantern and, if he wished to sit comfortably, his own chair.

What a first night it was! The Theater Guild's premières are impressive and quite the thing intellectually; the Ziegfeld Follies, in their balmiest days, were magnificent; the glamorous opening of the opera season at the Metropolitan in New York may be exhibit A for the Four Hundred, and for their sables and ermines—I know all these things. But not one of them could compare with the friendliness and joyous exhilaration shown at the grand opening of our palatial, mud-scow, floating theater, *The Princess.*

It's a truism that when any rural community decides to have a general turnout in order to put something across, you can bet your last four-and-a-quarter government bond that it will be a success. They will spend money like drunken sailors for the cause. At a church supper they will pay for the privilege of finishing a left-over platter of wings, neck,

The Bryant's First Showboat, Princess

Courtesy Kent State University Library, Kent, Ohio

and gizzard of the toughest old Dominic rooster[2]
who ever hopped a perch, all for the sake of the
Epworth League or Ladies' Aid Society. They will
swing their partners and grand right and left at a
platform square dance, paying ten cents a dance,
until the last fiddler is carried off the floor. They
will take an ice cream, strawberry festival the way a
Jack salmon takes a three-inch chub.

And that's the way those beautiful people of
Point Pleasant and Henderson took the opening of
the showboat which we had built in their front
yard.

Long before dark, the people from out on Crab
Creek Road, Red Mud, and Upper Five Mile had
begun to swarm into that little village as if they
were attending the New Orleans Mardi Gras. At
show time they came rushing over the river bank
like the Four Horsemen of Notre Dame.[3] I never
saw so many lanterns, rocking chairs, milking
stools, and nail kegs in all my life.

As fast as they came aboard Dad took their lanterns away from them and rushed them in to me,
where I was driving nails in the wall with a hammer
to hang them on. These were to furnish our sole
means of lighting the auditorium. (I don't know to

[2] The Dominick is an American fowl. A nondescript but
popular variety, it has yellow legs, a red comb, and gray
feathers.
[3] The "Four Horsemen of Notre Dame" is the name given
to that school's most famous football backfield: Elmer Lay-
den, James Crowley, Harry Stuhldreher, and Donald Miller.

this day how they identified their lanterns again after the show was over.) We didn't attempt to usher
them to any particular locations in the auditorium.
It would have been useless to try. They picked their
own places and considered the chairs or boxes they
had brought with them as two good seats on the
aisle. They almost packed and jammed that sixteen-
by-ninety boat to the point of suffocation.

Less than a third of them ever got as far as the
little box office on the front deck. They were lined
from the end of the gangplank all the way up over a
winding path and halfway back through a cornfield
that led to the main road. And still they came! As I
think back to the crowd my youthful eyes saw with
wonder that night, it seems to me that we turned
away enough people to fill Radio City Music Hall.
Any number of them just left their quarters at the
ticket window, wished us good luck, and went on
home. People were everywhere. They even lined
the upper and lower outside guards, where they ripped off our shutter sheets and pillowcases and had
their heads stuck in the windows, waiting for the
show to start.

The boat became so crowded that Dad pulled up
the front curtain and stacked them, three rows deep
on the stage, just leaving room enough for us to perform. Everyone kept seeing someone else that he
knew, and waved and shouted across the auditorium. Hat Stanley, mate on the *Robert P. Gilham*, told
me that he hadn't seen such excitement since the

Tom Dodsworth ran into the aft end of the *Val P. Collins*[4] at the head of the New Richmond Chute, knocking the *Collins's* wheel shaft right up into its recess and bringing all the crew of the afterwatch out of their bunks for a nightshirt parade.

Just as we began to wonder whether the old scow could take it, the ferryman arrived with a flatboat loaded with delegates from Point Pleasant on the other side of the river, bearing the key to the city, a four-piece string orchestra, and three jugs of hard cider. There simply wasn't room for them on the showboat, so they tied the flatboat up to us and tried to watch the show through the windows.

When it came time for the show to start, we couldn't seem to find each other. Mother had gone into the box office when we first opened our doors, and we never saw her again until the show was over. She kept selling tickets and wouldn't leave her job so long as there was a prospect of another quarter.

I don't remember what we gave them that night in the way of entertainment from the stage, but you can imagine. It didn't seem to me to be an evening at the theater at all, but more like a housewarming.

Near the middle of the last act, a heavy-set woman, sitting about where the third row should have been, who had been frantically fanning herself throughout

[4]The *Val P. Collins* was built in Charleston, W. Va. in 1901 for service as a coal towboat. She sank in a windstorm on the Ohio River in December 1914. Raised and rebuilt she was lost below Cincinnati during the big ice winter of 1917–18.

the entire evening, suddenly collapsed in the stif-
ling heat and rolled off her garden bench in a dead
faint. It looked for a time as if the audience would
push out the sides of the boat as they all tried to step
back and make it possible for her to get some fresh
air. Dad quickly suggested a glass of water and a wet
towel for the lady's head, but her husband thought
that something stronger would be better.

Immediately a valiant collection of bottles of all
sizes and shapes, filled with applejack,[5] peach brandy, and elderberry wine, were brought out. Even
the delegation out on the ferry flat gallantly sacri-
ficed one of their jugs of hard cider, passing it
through the window to the husband of the lady. It
wasn't very long before it was almost impossible to
distinguish which one of the family seemed to need
stimulation most.

Everyone was now sampling everyone else's special brand and seemed to have forgotten all about
the show. Dad tried to make an announcement explaining that the show was not quite over yet, but
he was too late. The applejack and peach brandy
had already begun to take effect and members of
the audience were clearing away the chairs and boxes, preparing to go into their dance, an old-time
country hoedown.

They put the string band from Point Pleasant up
on the stage and mustered out a big six-footer from
Salt Creek, with a voice that shook the rafters, to do

[5]Applejack is a brandy distilled from hard cider.

the calling. As he sprang up on the stage, he faced
the audience and yelled at the top of his voice.

"I'm a Salt Creek roarer, I can out-dance, out-
run, out-jump, throw down, drag out, and lick any
man twice my size. I love my licker an' women an'
I'm chockfull of fight. Let's go!"

With one whoop the dance was on and I never
saw such shindigging before in all my life. When
they would "do-ce-do-forward-and-back" across the
boat that poor old mud scow would weave up and
down in the middle like a jellyfish shaking with the
palsy.

It was impossible for us to continue on with the
show, so we just mixed with them and had a good
time, hoping and praying that they wouldn't suc-
ceed in shaking off the bottom of the boat.

Many of the men were rivermen employed on the
steamboats that operated in and out of that port.
We had begun to think that they were going to
dance all the night away when the steamers *J. T.
Hatfield*, *E. R. Andrews*, and *Florence Marmet*,[6] that
were getting ready to go down-river with tows of
coal, interceded for us by blowing their whistles,
calling the crews back to the boats.

As the last laughing patron went ashore, wishing
us a Merry Christmas and *bon voyage*, we heaved a

[6]The *J. T. Hatfield* and *Marmet* were built in Point Pleasant, W. Va. The former in 1904, the later in 1900. The
Andrews was built in Jeffersonville, Ind. in 1894. All were
used to tow coal barges on the Kanawha River to Cincinnati
and Louisville.

silent sigh of relief and all hurried eagerly into the tiny office to count up the night's receipts. They amounted to the grand total of forty-eight dollars and fifty cents, two rows of donated boxes and egg crates and four unclaimed lanterns.

With unbelieving eyes we sat and stared at the small fortune before us.

"At last we are in the big money," I whispered. "Forty-eight dollars and fifty cents! I'm wondering what George M. Cohan would think of that?"

And Dad, in a semi-conscious condition, stacked the coins in separate piles with trembling hands as he swallowed hard at his Adam's apple and moistened his dry lips with his tongue.

Mother sat silently thinking, without any outward show of enthusiasm. She was not one to wave her emotions on a flagpole, but there was a grateful light in her eyes which seemed to be thanking all of us, though we all knew that she was really responsible for the success of that night.

I sat constructing air castles much more rapidly than Dad had constructed the showboat.

"Gee," I cried. "A few nights like this and we'll surely have enough money to take the boat up the Hudson River."

From the point of view of navigation alone that would have been impossible, of course, for the boat could never have withstood a sea voyage, but I was seeing things: our ballyhoo band playing a concert in Times Square, myself handing out showbills in front of the George M. Cohan Theater, perhaps even loosening up with a few "Annie Oakleys," that is, professional courtesy tickets, for the great Georgie himself and *making* him come to our show to see how good and how successful we were.

It was nearly morning when we finally went to bed, planning to leave bright and early to go up the river. But nature in the raw, seldom mild, changed our plans before daybreak. We woke in a torrent of rain and wind on a river already rising in the disastrous flood of 1907.

A few days later we watched in fascination while the river surged over its banks and through the streets of Henderson and Point Pleasant. All day long a frantic populace rushed about the streets of its town in john boats, small flats, little gas boats—whatever would float, seeking higher ground for its families and their possessions.

It suddenly occurred to one of the helpless victims that our seatless showboat auditorium offered an excellent dry storage warehouse. Loading his piano and overstuffed davenport on a small flatboat, he worked his way over to us and asked if we would take care of them for him. Others followed him, and before nightfall our entire auditorium was packed from wall to wall with the oddest assortment of household belongings anyone ever saw.

All day long we watched the water spreading farther and farther over the surrounding country, lashing and tearing its way through all obstacles, always rising. From our vantage point we could see harried farmers driving their livestock to the hills, women and children being taken out of second-story windows onto boats, and, of course, the ever-increasing drift of wreckage from up the river—uprooted trees, barns, silos, the stored stock of whole lumber yards, empty barrels, boxes, household furniture, domestic and wild animals, many dead, some still living and fighting their way, madly bellowing or squealing their terror, the roofs of houses, and whole houses—anything which could float went racing by us on a furious tide which swept all before it.

One house, floating by on its side, exhibited a painted sign which read: "THIS VALUABLE PROPERTY FOR SALE." I wondered whether anyone had been contemplating buying it when the river had swept away all prospects of sale.

In the poor section of Point Pleasant, a woman bore a child while the water was creeping slowly to the second floor of her house in which she lay. Fortunately the delivery was a simple one and child and mother were doing well when she discovered that she could not nurse her baby daughter. What to do, with the river rising rapidly and cows either dying or driven to the hills? A neighbor solved the problem by getting a cow onto a flatboat and bringing it right up to the window of the lying-in room, out of which the child's father leaned to milk the beast.

Just as they decided that they would have to find

some way to move mother and child before the water swept over the bed, the house broke loose from its foundations and started off towards the river. With some little difficulty the woman's husband got her and the baby onto the roof, where they lay on a mattress. Eventually the roof of the house lodged against a telegraph pole and, a few hours later, its passengers were rescued and taken back to town.

The woman named the baby girl, Norah, because she had been born in a flood. She had taken as a feminine name the mispronunciation of the name "Noah" in the old Negro spiritual:

> *Norah built hisself an ark,*
> *Made it out of hickory bark,*
> *Animals came in two by two,*
> *Elephant and the kangaroo. . . .*

Liquor, as well as river water, was plentiful in town that day. Knowing the efficacy of good whiskey in the prevention of colds, flood-harassed people protect themselves against colds and low spirits at the same time. During the day a group of young boys equipped themselves with small-caliber rifles and rowed around town shooting rats which were trying frantically to climb anything including the plate glass windows of partially submerged stores, in their attempts to escape the water. One flood sufferer under the influence of liquor backed his boat through a plate glass window and fell into the store and water nine feet deep. When the police, cruising the town in a Red Cross boat, ordered him ashore, he swam to a telephone pole which, standing in deeper water, was almost covered, and, sitting on a cross bar, declared solemnly that he was now on dry land and they couldn't do anything about it.

A woman who ran a small grocery store sat in her rooms above it, terrified for fear the building which housed both her and the store would be carried away. Seeing an oak tree before the house swaying in the wind, she thought it was the house itself which was toppling, and sure that her hour had come, she fell in a dead faint from which she was revived only long after, when she had been taken, by boat, to the home of a neighbor.

We had tied up all winter to two cottonwood trees which were about seventy feet tall. Then their bases were high and dry on the bank. But in two days the shore had receded and they, like us, were in the river. By then we had learned enough of river lore to know how to proceed. Leaving our original tie at the base of the tree, we played out more lines as our boats rose on the flood, and took a new tie farther up with another line. Every day, for days, we had to move the new hitch farther up and let out more rope for the one tied at the base. Thus, no matter how high we went—even though the tops of the trees were finally submerged—we would not be cast utterly adrift because of the tie we still had at the base.

Before we had shifted our second lines for the last

time, they were practically at the tops of the trees, as the river made a fifty-five-foot rise in that flood before it finally began to recede. At its height, when the cottonwood trees would wave back and forth in the wind and current, we would be snapped from one place to another like the cracker on a whip.

The second night, with our auditorium blocked by our friends' furniture, and no sign that the river intended to do anything but go on up, we were all pretty lonesome and discouraged. We still felt that we knew too little about the river to come through a flood safely with our boats. We sat huddled about the stove, speculating on what might happen to our precious *Princess* before the water receded. After the hearty friendliness of our first audience we felt terribly helpless and isolated. None of us felt like sleeping.

About two o'clock in the morning we suddenly heard a familiar sound close by. Wheezing crazily, a cylinder phonograph was grinding out the strains of "Red Wing."

"It's Duckfoot!" I yelled, as I jumped up and started for the door with a lantern.

"And does he need those webbed toes tonight!" Florence added as we all rushed out and looked in the direction of the sound. There, just a short distance away, was a little shanty boat tied to the top of a tree. From its interior came the faint yellow gleam of a coal-oil hanging lamp and the crazy strains of the song. As we looked, Duckfoot saw us and, shutting off his phonograph, poked his head out of his tiny cabin and discussed the march of time with us.

"Well, we're going to get plenty of driftwood for our fires this time," he bellowed cheerfully. As near as I could make out, he was not at all depressed by the flood, but quite the contrary. It was some excitement to vary the monontony of his days. Never did anything cheer me quite so much as the presence of Duckfoot King that night.

After we had talked to him awhile—or rather bellowed at him and listened to him bellowing back, we went back inside and went to bed. Our fear of the flood itself was over now. Somehow Duckfoot's jovial cheeriness had taken care of that. There was only one thing which still worried us; the fact that we had almost no food on board and there were no stores in which more could be bought.

The next morning, at daybreak, we were awakened by the sweet notes of a crowing rooster. I rushed out on deck and there, lodged against the rake of the showboat, was a tremendous haystack, floating intact. Perched on the top of it, where they had climbed for safety, were nine chickens, two turkeys, a guinea hen, a kitten, and a small pig—almost a complete barnyard. But they seemed so forlorn, and were taken aboard so willingly and seemingly so grateful, that we hadn't the heart to do anything but put them in with the furniture and try to find a way to feed them as well as ourselves.

The river kept rising, forcing householders farther and farther from its normal shores to abandon their homes. To more than one of them our showboat suddenly loomed up as an excellent haven for their possessions, including their livestock. Before the flood reached its crest we had acquired, in addition to the animals who came floating down to us, the custody of six pigs, a cow, and a hundred or more chickens, who immediately took over the ceiling rafters and the top of the piano for roosting and other purposes. They never once tried to fly out of the auditorium, but remained perfectly still, day in and day out, as if they realized their helpless predicament. They were gracious enough to furnish us with an abundance of fresh eggs every morning, and the cow was a friendly guest too. She gave us plenty of milk twice a day.

There is one nice thing about a showboat during a flood. Its owner is never compelled to sing, "River, Stay 'Way from My Door."[7] He is just as much at home with sixty feet of water under him as he is when the river is at a normal nine-foot-pool stage.

He learns a lot about human nature, too. It's amazing to learn how friendly some of our uppish river neighbors can become when they find our gangplank resting on their front porch just about the time the rising waters are threatening to enter

[7]"River, Stay 'Way from My Door," composed by Harry Woods was published in 1931. The lyrics were written by Morton Dixon.

their homes to ruin the precious hollyhock wallpaper and down-payment grand piano. It is then that persons who have called us river rats become very sweet and democratic as they move all of their possessions aboard our boat for safety. Often they repay us for our hospitality by leaving their own brands of bedbugs and cockroaches. But that's all a part of owning a showboat.

It's an old story to us now—too old. We would like the river just as well if it would stay within its banks. During the great flood of the spring of 1936 (just past as I write this), when the rising Ohio exceeded all previous records, we were, by chance, tied up at Henderson to the same two cottonwood trees which held us all through the 1907 flood. Fortunately they had grown considerably in twenty-nine years, but even so, when the flood reached its crest, all of our lines were under water.

Duckfoot King was there near us too, tied up to the top of a sycamore tree with an abandoned bird's nest for his only companion. But he didn't seem lonesome. During the winter he had swapped his "Pretty Red Wing" record for a new one, so we listened to "Pony Boy"[8] all during the 1936 flood.

It was quite a relief.

[8]"My Pony Boy," published in 1909, was composed by Charles O'Donnell. The lyrics were written by Robert "Bobby" Heath.

X

Wheel Waves

As the river crept back into its banks again and life returned once more to its normal state, we began to make great preparations for our trip up the Kanawha. In spite of the fact that the river banks were a welter of mud left as the aftermath of the flood, we were still in high spirits, overjoyed at our successful opening at Henderson, and proud as peacocks of the showboat we had built ourselves at the cost of such infinite struggle. Early one morning, just at daybreak, we hauled in our lines and headed for Ambrosia, five miles away, where we intended to show that night.

It has been said that anticipation is always greater than realization, but when it comes to navigating a showboat up and down the rivers, anticipation doesn't picture the half of it. We had no sooner backed our boat out in the stream and come ahead with the *Florence* than we discovered that navigation was going to be half—and the most difficult half—of our river show business. A showboat acts on the water very much as a large wooden packing case would. It is high in structure and light in draft. Once out into the river, in any kind of a wind at all, it will skim over the water like a hydroplane and seems bent on going in any direction except the one you want it to. Although the *Princess* was not a large boat, it was as full of tricks as a six-weeks-old kitten. After turning around three times out in the middle of the stream, and hitting the bank on both sides of the river as many more, we finally arrived at Ambrosia that night about showtime exhausted and covered with mud from head to foot. Again we were greeted with a packed house.

Here we hired a young farmer lad to act as deckhand. He was even more ignorant (if possible) than we as to the navigation of river craft. He insisted on calling the wheel shaft of the *Florence* an axle and the wheel arms, spokes. He came very near drowning at Leon. It was a bright moonlight night with many tricky shadows upon the waters. During the show, a young girl accidentally dropped her feather boa into the river and he gallantly volunteered to save it. Rushing madly aft he looked over the side and, seeing the shadow of the skiff that was tied alongside of the *Florence*, he thought it was the boat itself and jumped in.

As he came to the surface, he grabbed hold of the outside of the skiff where, choking with water, he yelled, "Hey, Cap, come back here quick and help me out. Some darned fool has knocked the bottom out of this boat!" However, he didn't stay with us long. He complained that there weren't enough girls with the troupe, and besides, he got tired of watching the same show every night.

THE LOWER OHIO, KANAWHA, KENTUCKY AND WABASH RIVER AREA

LAKE MICHIGAN

LAKE ERIE

MICHIGAN

N

ILLINOIS

OHIO

INDIANA

Tippecanoe River

Grass Cr.

Grass Creek

River

Muskingum River

Little Kanawha R.

Bull Cr.

Neal's Run

Rising Sun

Cincinnati

Moscow

Vevay

Rabbit Hash

Georgetown

Point Pleasant

Ambrosia

Leon

Madison

Carrollton

Augusta

Ohio

Buffalo

Louisville Falls

Utica

Kenova

Winfield

Kanawha River

Tobacco Landing

Louisville

Louisa

Charleston

Montgomery

Smithers

Warehouse Landing

Frankfort

High Bridge

Boomer

Ohio River

Smithland

West Point

Ford

Kentucky R.

Dir R.

Big Sandy River

W.VA.

Uniontown

Caseyville

Gilberts Creek

Beattyville

River

Dog Island

Green River

KENTUCKY

Cumberland River

Tennessee River

TENNESSEE

Tennessee River

NORTH CAROLINA

0   50   100

Miles

We kept getting up earlier each morning trying to make our daily trip before the coming of the wind that usually rose with the sun. But we traveled so slowly that the wind would always overtake us before we reached our destination. One morning we were driven against the lock wall at Dam No. 9 with such force that it knocked Mother out of bed and upset all the cooking utensils on the stove.

Although it rained at Buffalo, West Virginia, as it has on every showboat night for the past twenty years, we had a very nice turnout. In spite of our usual request for the patrons to bring lanterns, there were only three that night, and they all belonged to one family—a girl, her father, and her husband. The old man became offended when we pulled the "hot water and hard-boiled egg" gag on him, and marched out with all three lanterns before the show was over, leaving us in total darkness. There was nothing that we could do except call off the show and refund the money.

We never allowed that particular misfortune to occur again, however, for we quickly reduced the grocery allowance and bought several large Rochester coal-oil lamps.

At Winfield we encountered the famous Red House Chute, lying in wait to undo us on our next jump up the river. It is one of the swiftest spots on the inland waters. With a current like that of a mill-race, it is almost impossible to navigate with as scant power as the *Florence* gave us. Dad looked at it with a countenance which seemed to say that All Was Ended, and began to talk about abandoning the rest of our trip.

When it was time for supper I missed my sister. I looked about for her and at last discovered her aboard the steamer *Evergreen*,[1] a small stern wheel packet which was lying over at Winfield that night and was tied up just above us. She was in tow of the woman cook and chambermaid, and both were surrounded by the crew, who were urging her to stay to supper.

She stayed, and, as I learned afterward, came away with the entire life story of practically everyone on the boat. The woman told her all about the difficulties of cooking and cleaning up for a lot of men, how she had been driven to this pass by the faithlessness of a worthless lover, and how she still hoped to meet, somewhere along the river, the man who would take her to a vine-covered cottage. The captain showed her a picture of his late mother-in-law who had been accidentally drowned on her honeymoon; and the youngest of the deckhands, on his first trip, talked to her about his mother.

After we had eaten our supper and it was getting near to showtime, I began to worry for fear she would not be back in time for the curtain and went

[1]The *Evergreen*, a stern wheel, wooden hull packet, was built at Parkersburg, West Virginia, in 1902. The vessel hit a canal lock wall on the Kanawha River during the winter of 1912–13 and was ultimately dismantled at Point Pleasant in 1916.

outside to look for her. I could see her standing at
the cookhouse door on the steamboat, still listening
to the troubles of the chambermaid hostess. Every
few minutes the conversation would be punctuated
by Florence's high pitched exclamation, "For God
sake!" It was a habit of hers, when listening sympa-
thetically to others, to inject this critical comment
at the top of her voice, after which her tones would
drop to normal again.

Showtime came and I saw Florence leave the
Evergreen with its entire personnel following her.
In single file they trooped up the stage plank of the
Princess—chambermaid, captain, night watchman,
fireman, dishwasher, deckhands and all. "What a
good press agent she turned out to be," I thought, as
I hastily counted them and got ready to sell them
eleven tickets. But when she marched past the ticket office, her head in the air, explaining that they
were her friends, and seated them without the for-
mality of tickets, it was I who, in her own tone of
voice, said, "For God sake!"

The next morning, however, I felt somewhat
friendlier about the whole affair. We were about
ready to go, but none of us seemed to have any idea
how we were going to get through that formidable
millrace ahead of us, when Florence quietly left the
boat. In a moment she was on the *Evergreen* explaining our difficulty to her woman friend there,
and soon the captain was listening in. Still feeling
friendly over "the elegant show," as he called it,

that he had seen the night before, he brought the
Evergreen over and gave us a shove. With our own
towboat, the *Florence*, and the *Evergreen* shoving as
hard as they could against the swift current, the bow
of the *Princess* started to go under water, whereupon the passengers and spare members of the
Evergreen's crew all piled onto the *Princess* and
stood with our actors on the back end, pushing her
nose up, and we went merrily up Red House Chute.

This was the beginning of Florence's wide circle
of friends on the rivers. More and more, as she approached womanhood, she developed into a neigh-
borly person who wanted to get acquainted with
people wherever we stopped. At every village she
would go ashore and make friends. Today, wherever
we stop, the first thing Florence does is to go uptown to greet her friends there, and often they are
at the wharf to greet her.

A few days later we passed Charleston, the capital of West Virginia, and soon were in the mining
country. Here we discovered that we had a new
type of audience to deal with. The miners demanded a good show from every showboat which came
their way, and had very fixed ideas of what consti-
tuted entertainment. They preferred old-fashioned
melodramas with plenty of hokum comedy to any
other kind of show. They insisted on vaudeville between the acts. They would not tolerate intermissions, and if the whole show lasted less than two
hours they felt cheated.

Contrary to the legend that has sprung up, the river audiences do not, as a rule, cheer the hero and hiss the villain. They take their shows seriously. And the miners, those hardy and vigorous patrons of all showboats along the river, were perhaps the most serious of all. When thoroughly enthused they would whistle and stamp their feet. Otherwise they were pretty stingy with applause and other demonstrations of approval.

They had a more definite way of their own of telling us whether they liked the show or not. If they were satisfied they would go their way in peace and friendliness when the show was over. If they were not, they would get out on the bank and bombard the side of the boat with rocks. They usually aimed at the pilot house, which was 90 per cent window. Many a pilot house has been turned into a shambles of broken glass by a dissatisfied showboat audience. But we were lucky. We hadn't bought any glass yet and all they could knock out of our pilot house windows was a lot of cardboard.

At Crown Hill they went so far as to pile up their rocks in advance, which, in its way, was a kindness, since after the show we didn't have to wait for them to collect the rocks before we knew that they hadn't approved of our entertainment.

At Boomer we became acquainted with another of their outdoor sports. During the afternoon I had slapped the face of a young ruffian who had indulged in the spirit of pure fun to the extent of breaking the glass in the ticket office windows in an attempt to get the money and tickets out of the cash drawer, and who had later carved his initials in the piano. That night we all went to bed as usual after the show and slept soundly. The next morning we were all awakened by a frantic ferryman at Smithers, a mile or so down the river, who pointed out that we were about to go over Dam No. 2, then in sight, where we all, no doubt, would be drowned. The friends of the young hoodlum at Boomer had come back with him, long after we were all asleep, untied our lines, and set us adrift. It was just a variation of the rock-throwing habit and, like that, was an old river custom.

When we got to Mt. Carbon, Dad went up to Montgomery and bought a small wildcat whistle from an old dismantled ice plant. He mounted it on the air tank of our gas boat, intending to use it instead of a calliope to let people know we were in town. He got it all fixed up late that afternoon and, like a child wanting to try a new toy, blew it that night just as the show started. As its musical notes penetrated the air with unearthly sound, falling and rising like the voice of a mountain cat, there was a riot in the auditorium. The next thing we knew everyone on board was jumping from the windows, crowding out the front door, scrambling up the bank, and rushing madly over the hill. There wasn't a soul left to whom we could play the rest of the show.

We were dumbfounded; but when, a few minutes later, we learned that the town had a fire siren that sounded almost exactly like our new whistle, we knew that Father's blast had made everyone there think that his home was on fire. We didn't wait for them to come back and express their feelings about the trick they must have thought we played on them. We just untied and left.

At Kenova, so named because Kentucky, Ohio, and West Virginia all meet at that point, we turned up the Big Sandy as far as Louisa, Kentucky, for a show that night. But I scarcely remember the show for the battle we had with willow bugs, two-winged insects which look like mosquitoes, except that they are much larger. They don't sting or bite, but they don't have to. They arrive in such numbers that, while they are there about all you can do is try to fight your way through them for air. They are attracted by a light and the only defense against them on the river is a torch hung over the water. They swarm around it, burn their wings, and fall into the water. But even with a torch out they were literally four inches deep on the stage.

Just as we were wondering how we were going to put on a show, Dad came back from the front of the boat where he had been scooping them off with a shovel. Out front there was a big crowd waiting to be entertained. Like us, they were fighting the bugs with waving hands and fans, taking the visitation, which they had learned to face once each year, with good-natured tolerance. Dad gave one look at them and started for the stage with his shovel.

"Dad-burned plague of Egypt!" he grunted, looking at our expensive oil lamps, the lights of which were noticeably dimmed by the swarming cloud of willow bugs around them. Florence tried to jolly him out of his rage.

"How'd you like to have a quarter admission from every one of them, Dad?" she asked brightly.

Just then a bug got in Father's eye, and with a roar of rage he swung his shovel at the swarm which was buzzing around the nearest lamp, smashed the lamp with a jangling crash, nearly setting the boat on fire. At that point Mother led him away for a cup of coffee and we just went on from there the best way we could.

The next morning the willow bugs were all dead and the only signs left of them were their carcasses, which cluttered the boat, and the unusual display of early morning fish coming to the surface to get them. Willow-bug day (for they live only twenty-four hours) is apparently the high spot in the life of any fish on the Big Sandy.

Now back on the Ohio, we headed downstream to Carrollton, where we turned up the Kentucky River. We passed the twin chimneys, two giant pillars of rock standing side by side on such slender foundations that one might think the slightest push would topple them over. But they have not toppled through the centuries during which they have stood there. The old covered bridge at Brooklyn was plastered with old-fashioned posters advertising Old Virginia Cheroots, Sweet Caporal Cigarettes, and a country fair. The fair had been held a year before and the poster was faded and tattered, but its gaiety still clung to it.

After a tiresome all night run from Gilbert's Creek we decided to stop for supplies in the restful cove made by the Dix River where it puts out at High Bridge. As the boys ran a headline up the shore I rested my weary arms on the pilot wheel and gazed spellbound at the magnificent spectacle before me.

Small streaks of gray could be seen forming on the eastern horizon as a bright full moon fought a losing battle with daybreak. The crickets and katydids had ceased their midnight serenades and the liquid throated mockingbird, the songsmith of the South, along with a brown thrasher with his alarm notes of a rich and loud melody, were singing their praises to another dawn. In its peaceful slumber, this heavenly stream was clear as crystal and its glassy surface was disturbed only by the rolling of dead swells from the now quiet wheel of the *Florence* and the splashing of many frightened frogs that were plunging to safety at the bottom of the river as croppies, mountain bass, and bluegills had come to the surface in search of smaller fish for their breakfast. The small fields at the foot of the ridge were strewn with white daisies and yellow

buttercups that stood up in startling vividness, and
hogs could be seen rooting holes in the hillside in a
meadow above a nearby orchard of maidenblush
apple trees in full bloom.

A heavy morning dew was fast disappearing before the glare of a rising sun as wild honey bees and
butterflies gathered on the sticky mud shores for
their morning capers. A sleepy-eyed turtle with
great effort crawled out upon a water-soaked log for
a nap in the sun; a herd of Holstein cattle came
down to drink from the refreshing stream on the
opposite shore. At that moment I felt a complete
sense of ownership. The river was mine!

I love all the inland streams, but the Kentucky
seems to me to be the American Rhine, the most
beautiful of them all, and I have boated on nearly
every navigable stream in the Middle West and
South. In midsummer, when its waters turn to a
moss green and the high mountain tops and per-
pendicular overhanging rock cliffs are strewn with
many strange green, brown, and yellow foliages, its
beauty surpasses any sight that I know.

Only one thing marred my enjoyment of the perfect beauty before me that day—the thought of
Broadway, and the success which George M. Cohan
had achieved there while I had been fighting for
recognition and a bare financial security among river audiences. What would New York audiences be
like? I kept asking to myself. Deep at my vitals
gnawed the worm of ambition. Some day I would

get off of the river. Some day I would play the big time—match my ability against that of Georgie Cohan's in the setting of the bright lights of Times Square.

Kentucky has long been noted for its famous blue grass sections. On its almost vertical mountain sides that come down to the water's edge can be seen many energetic farmers cultivating small crops of corn and tobacco where it is so steep they tell you how the mules, when plowing, often wear the hair off their sides from rubbing against the mountain. One day at Palsgrove Landing, a farmer, covered with Spanish needles, came tumbling down over a hill and landed at the foot of our stage plank where, while brushing himself off, he discouragingly announced, "That's the third time I've fallen out of that darned cornfield today."

At an isolated landing just over the border of "Bloody Breathitt" County, near Beattyville, we encountered our first shooting scrape. Just as the show began, a young raw-boned intoxicated mountaineer came aboard the boat looking for his sweetheart, Annie. He was a rough-and-ready type of lad and so tough he wore rawhide shoestrings. We could see that he had been drinking and would make trouble before the night was over so we told him Annie wasn't on the boat. But he refused to go, insisting that she was attending our show with a rival suitor. Finally, he made such a disturbance that it interfered with the performance and we decided to throw him out on the bank. We had to call on the assistance of the entire crew, but we finally got rid of him.

Swearing revenge on the whole shebang for this sort of humiliation, he mounted his mule and rode away. Just as the audience was filing out after the show, he returned with a double-barreled shotgun. Firing point-blank at his sweetheart and her escort, he rushed madly aboard the boat to take his revenge on us.

The girl escaped with slight injuries, but the lad fell back on our stage plank bleeding and seriously wounded. As his friends rushed him to medical aid, the crazed fellow with the gun dashed inside the showboat, blazing away at us actors. We jumped behind set-rocks, trees, prop trunks, and floor lamps to safety like a lot of Texas jack rabbits. The way he chased us around the showboat would have done credit to the "Ben Hur" chariot race. We were all running in so many different directions that, without any plan to do so, we surrounded him. Since he had run out of ammunition by then, we immediately proceeded to throw him out on the bank again.

We were unable to learn whether the injured youth ever fully recovered or not, as we were so scared that we never stopped running with our outfit until we reached the Ohio River and ran our showboat halfway out on the Indiana shore opposite Carrollton, Kentucky.

Thus we journeyed on, gradually becoming more

enlightened in the ways of river life. Business was tremendous. Practically every town we had played since our opening in the spring had been a sell-out. By the time we arrived at Cincinnati, I had become nigger rich[2] and couldn't buy a hat big enough to fit my head. I had also made many enemies along the way by reason of the overbearing sarcastic attitude I had assumed.

We had shipped up another deckhand at Rabbit Hash, a small settlement across the river from Rising Sun, Indiana, who was so tall that I nicknamed him "Centerpole." And did I boss him around? I had a white cap with a flour mill advertisement on it that I covered with the word "captain" and insisted that he address me thus at all times. Sometime later, when I got my license as pilot and captain, I correctly gained the right to that title, but at that time I had no more right to it than he had.

I bought a three-carat, canary-yellow diamond stud with a two-carat flaw, that succeeded in making me more vain than ever. I wore spats and carried a cane (which was strictly against all river traditions) and walked with a Broadway swing. I had a one hundred-dollar bill that I would ostentatiously drop on the counter of every little grocery store that I entered to make a five-cent purchase, and I would

[2]Bryant's use of the expression "nigger rich" is an example of the racial stereotyping so characteristic of American society during this period. It refers, of course, to a foolish, ostentatious, and vulgar display of wealth on the part of someone who lacks it.

loudly demand, "What's the matter with this burg?" when they were unable to change it for me.

Mother and Dad had cautioned me several times about my actions, but they couldn't kid me. I was following the same course that Georgie Cohan had pursued when he first discovered that his income was too large to keep under the mattress any longer and would stand on the corner of Forty-second Street and Broadway and say to the gang, "Mention my name, boys, mention my name."

However, Mr. Cohan was quick to realize his mistake, and soon turned his gaudy neckties, yellow-top suede shoes, and other bizarre wearing apparel into comedy wardrobe and considered the incident closed.

But I was not so fortunate as he in mastering or breaking the spell. What I needed was just what I got—a nice baseball bat draped over my head. The ideal location was near Utica, just a short distance above Louisville on the Indiana side, where the populace was considered so tough that all the steamboat pilots ran by there on a slow bell.

It was on Sunday and a friend had driven me out in the country to see a ball game. Somewhere during the game a dispute arose over the umpire's decision on a certain play. Just as the argument was about to develop into a free-for-all, I stepped down and out of the grandstand and strolled out on the diamond, with a straw hat tilted over on one side of my head, and contemptuously twirling a bamboo cane through my fingers, with all the stupid assurance of an Emperor penguin.

"You're all wrong, boys," I said as I edged my way into the center of the group and proceeded to take sides with the visiting team. Poking some big gorilla in his hairy chest with the head of my cane, I shouted, "I'll bet you a hundred dollars that you never touched second base," and with that I drew the bill from my pocket and waved it on high so the spectators in the grandstand could obtain a good clear view of it.

I don't know just how long the discussion continued, but the last thing I remember saying was, "It's a foul, and you can't make anything else out of it."

It must have been nearing sundown when my friend finally delivered me back to the showboat again. Both my eyes were blackened and my clothes were in rags. The ballplayers had also relieved me of my diamond stud and precious hundred-dollar bill. It was most humiliating for me at the time, but I realize now that the experience was a cheap buy, for out of it grew a new point of view toward myself and my place in the world.

XI

The Play's the Thing

IT WAS late autumn. Fall blossoms were being nipped by early white frosts and already leaves of many beautiful colors were dotting the green surface of the waters. The nights were chilly and we had no way to heat our auditorium. We had succeeded in saving enough money to pay off all our debts in Point Pleasant and carry us through the winter. Mentally and physically tired, we decided to close for the season. We then shoved back up into the Kentucky River again, where we wintered just above the ferry at the little lumber town of Ford, Kentucky. There, throughout the long winter months, we listened to the hoot owls and lonesome winds whistling through the heavily timbered mountain sides as we enthusiastically made our plans for another season.

We all agreed that it was high time for us to branch out with a larger company so we would be in a position to replace our former "variety" type of show with high-class drama that would touch the hearts of all. The principal of the high school in that vicinity, with whom we had become acquainted, suggested that Shakespeare's *Hamlet* might make an interesting play for the river. He told us that such prominent actors as Walter Hampden, Fritz Lieber,[1] and Ben Greet[2] were then appearing with great success doing the part of the Melancholy Dane, so naturally we thought if it was good enough for actors of their caliber, it should certainly be good enough for our ham opera, and we immediately began preparation for bringing the immortal bard to those who lived along the inland streams.

We obtained a volume containing the complete works of Shakespeare, but it all seemed pretty foreign to us and we went about it with a great many misgivings. As I read it, I began to wonder how we were going to stage it with our one set of scenery that represented a cornfield. However, after the schoolmaster had separated *Hamlet* from *King Lear* and *Richard the Third* for us, we finally succeeded in reducing it to the size of our cast by omitting the king and queen, and you may not believe it but we never missed them.

I doubled four parts: Polonius, Grave Digger No. 1, Bernardo, and the Ghost. Dad played Laertes, and he and I got the only laugh in the show. That was when I, as his father Polonius, attired in Santa Claus whiskers, took his hand and affectionately

[1] Fritz Lieber (1883–1949) was a distinguished actor who performed Shakespeare with Walter Hampden and also had his own company.

[2] London born, Sir Philip "Ben" Greet (1857–1936) was a famous actor, director, and producer who is best known for the Shakespearean revivals he produced during his stay in America, 1902–14.

said, "Goodbye my son, my blessings season this in thee," at which time he would drop his eyes in deep meditation, his shiny bald head turned toward the audience. The chap we had in the part of Hamlet was an east side New Yorker who took strange liberties with the English language. Shakespeare would never have recognized his own lines when our Hamlet declared solemnly, "All de woild's a stage."

It's an awful thing to have to stand out on the platform and talk for two hours and not know the true meaning of one blessed thing you have said.

My sister Florence played a lady in waiting and spent most of the evening waiting for proper cues which she never received. Mother did Ophelia. In the burial scene, we had no room to carry her in on a slab, so we brought her on sitting up dead in a wheelchair. In Shakespeare's version (he had a good one, too), he just buried Ophelia in the grave, but in our version, we buried the whole cast in the same grave, as that was the only way we had of letting the audience know when the show was over.

It was pitiful to watch the confused expressions on the faces out front. They tried so hard to follow the story of the play and to figure out what it was all about. We couldn't blame the audience for not being able to, as we didn't know what it was all about ourselves. It was the biggest mess we ever got into in all our lives.

Before the last act had begun I donned a bathrobe to obstruct the view of my union suit tights and stepped before the curtain to thank them for coming down to see our little offering. I emphasized the fact that we were the first showboat people to bring Shakespeare to the rivers and they looked at me as if they would have been overjoyed had we drowned him on his arrival. When they left the boat that night, the line resembled a funeral procession. The audience seemed to be in a stupor, as if they had been gassed or something.

The next morning as we were preparing to leave, Dad asked the ferryman how he had liked the show the night before. "Say, Cap," he answered, seeming to ignore the question, "we got a fellow up here in our town you ought to have on the stage. He'd make you a Jim-dandy. He ain't got a lick o' sense."

It has been said by many Shakespearean societies that a man by the name of Bacon[3] wrote *Hamlet* and Shakespeare lifted his stuff. But I'll wager that Bacon would have been more than willing to give Shakespeare full credit for our river production of his famous play.

Hamlet, to my way of thinking, is like the measles. You have to go through with it some time in life, either as a study in school, or in amateur theatricals, or as we did. But I'll say this: that anyone who has been unfortunate enough to sit through our

[3]Francis Bacon (1561–1626), Baron Verulam and Viscount St. Albans, was an English philosopher and essayist. He is at times thought to be the author of Shakespeare's works because of his wide knowledge of law, history, and politics.

performance of this Shakespearean classic will admit to the world that he was so thoroughly vaccinated before the fall of the final curtain that he will never catch it again.

By the time we had arrived at Madison, Indiana, on the Ohio River, we were all on the verge of a nervous breakdown. The actors had begun to take their parts seriously and became temperamental and high strung over mere trifles. Hamlet himself absolutely refused to eat margarine any longer and, in a fit of anger, deliberately threw a can of condensed milk overboard and demanded that he have pure cream for his coffee. He had let his hair grow until it hung about his ears. He walked with a stride and admitted to us all that he was the greatest Shakespearean tragedian that the river had ever known. One night when he insisted that we hold a first act curtain for fifteen minutes until he could get into the proper atmosphere for the Melancholy Dane, Dad flew into a rage and threw the grave effect into the river, burnt up the spears and swords, and told the whole shebang to pack their suitcases and go over the top—meaning the river bank. Hamlet's "To be or not to be" was not to be for us any more.

Ten days later, with a new cast, we again opened our show. This time we presented the grand old English drama *East Lynne*,[4] which was going from

[4] *East Lynne* was adapted from Ellen Price Woods' novel by T. A. Palmer in 1874.

bad to worse as far as securing a play that would meet with the river audience's liking was concerned. Mother played Lady Isobel, and I, shaving from my upper lip the fuzz that had been conspicuously accumulating for the past few months, lay in a cot with my legs folded under me covered with a sheet, and died as her little son, Willie. That scene alone should have discouraged the idea.

Anyone familiar with the original story of *East Lynne* is aware that several deaths and murders take place throughout the presentation. It is strictly suffering and dying entertainment. In the short cast version that we had adopted, the characters died and were murdered so fast that there wasn't anyone left to finish the show. In order to tell a complete story and not contradict the book from which the play was dramatized, just as soon as one of us passed to the great beyond he or she would immediately don a black mustache or another dress and rush back on the stage again as another character.

At Tobacco Landing, below the Louisville Falls, we were thoroughly convinced for all time to come that *East Lynne* would never be accepted by the river people. It came about in an amusing way. It looked like rain just before showtime, so all the natives brought along their umbrellas, as they had learned from past experience that showboat roofs always leak somewhere.

Everything went smoothly until the third act when it started to rain in torrents. I was lying in the cot as little Willie getting ready to die, and Mother, as Lady Isobel, was kneeling at my side ranting and raving as if her heart would break. Everyone out front had his umbrella up by this time and was seriously watching the play.

All of a sudden the showboat roof sprang a new leak right over the cot where I was dying. I tried to move over and dodge the stream of water without attracting any attention, but I couldn't make it. An old Negro lady, who had been sitting down in the first row on the side under an umbrella, became so interested in the play that without any thought of strangeness she walked up in the box and onto the stage saying, "Yo' pore chile, ole' Aunt Emma ain't goin' to let little Willie die in no puddle o' water like dat." And she held her umbrella over me until I had finished dying.

As she left the boat that night, Dad met her at the front door.

"How did you like the show tonight, Auntie?" he asked.

She looked up at him through great tears.

"It was all right, Cap'n, I guess," she sobbed, "but it sho' was an ol' folks' show."

What she meant was that that type of play was much too sad for the people of that community. We were forced to agree with her, so *East Lynne* was immediately shelved and a round-table discussion was held back in the kitchen to ascertain just what type of play would be the best for our next offering.

One of the performers in the group suggested that he had a sure-fire script in his trunk, a play called *Jesse James, the Missouri Outlaw.*[5] He told us that it contained plenty of exciting situations and good comedy and would be a wow on the river. All he needed to produce it was two thirty-eight revolvers, a gross of blanks, and a set-rock.

It sounded good, so we started rehearsals and put it on the following night. Much to our surprise and delight, it was a sensation—a knockout! It was full of knock-down and drag-out stuff and the audience ate it up. I loved it because every time I forgot my lines, all I had to do was to pull out my gun and keep shooting until I could think of them again. However, to the discouragement of us all, we were again compelled to change our show as the incessant shooting throughout the play awakened the mothers' sleeping babies and their crying interfered with the performance. They often yelled so loudly that we had to call the show off for the night.

The character man with our troupe then suggested that we try out *Dr. Jekyll and Mr. Hyde.*[6] All his life he had a secret ambition to star in that particular role. Naturally he loved the idea of playing the part and volunteered to work for nothing as he

[5] *Jesse James, the Missouri Outlaw*, may be any of several melodramas popular at this time that used the James narrative for a lively plot.

[6] *Dr. Jekyll and Mr. Hyde* was obviously adapted from Robert Louis Stevenson's work of the same name, which was published in 1886.

considered that it would be the finest event of his theatrical career.

In due time we rang up the curtain on *Dr. Jekyll and Mr. Hyde*. Oh how that poor thespian worked throughout the show. His hideous deathbed scene in the last act, where, with a green spotlight on him, he blew (bromo-seltzer) froth through the tusks (he had cut out from a celluloid collar) that he held in his mouth while (carmine) blood trickled down his head and onto his white-bosom shirt front, was the most atrocious piece of acting that has ever been seen since the days of Coarse Payton.[7]

My one hope was that George Cohan would never drop in on us at that embarrassing moment. During that terrific scene Hyde would jump up and down like a monkey and scream like a hyena as he smashed bottles, mirrors, and tore up a Sears Roebuck catalogue that we substituted for a Bible. Finally, out of breath and exhausted, he would roll on the floor in bloodcurdling agony and die covered with a sheet under which his trembling form could be plainly seen. At the final curtain we would all rush out on the stage and pick him up from the floor where he had fallen into a strange coma, and carry him to the back deck where we would revive him. That is, we did this until we played Caseyville,

[7]More correctly "Corse" Payton (1867–1934). He was notorious as the self-advertised "World's Best Bad Actor." He toured the Middle West and later founded a stock company in Brooklyn, New York, that became a training ground for Lillian Gish and Fay Bainter.

Kentucky, where a large section of the high clay bank caved in with a sickening thud creating a miniature avalanche just at the time of Hyde's death. It frightened him so that he jumped up and ran off the stage without any assistance. After that he did his own reviving.

He became so enthused over the part that during the day he would dress up as Dr. Jekyll in a long black fur-collared coat, plug hat, and cane and then stroll through the village gazing hollow-eyed at the frightened natives who would draw back from him and hoarsely whisper, "That's the man who plays Dr. Jekyll and Mr. Hyde." And did he love to hear that! He frightened the Negroes so that they were afraid to go home after the show was over. They fully expected Hyde to spring viciously upon them from behind every bale of cotton that they passed.

Mandy White, at a cowpath landing below Florence, Alabama, on the Tennessee River, who had always done the show people's washing every year was so scared after Hyde's terrific death that she ran home screaming. Early the next morning she gave birth to a bouncing baby boy. To this day, when asked how old her son is, she will date his birth from "showboat time."

As a final resort, we presented good old *Ten Nights in a Bar Room*[8] which was a howling success and has been our masterpiece ever since.

[8] *Ten Nights in a Bar Room*, an American temperance play, was written by T. S. Arthur in 1855.

During the two years that we had been out with the *Princess*, our greatest drawback had been music. Although we had had a piano aboard nearly all that time, we could never seem to get anyone to play it for any length of time at the salary we offered. The salaries pianists often asked were outrageous, but we firmly held out that six dollars a week with board and room was enough for any actor or musician. Although my sister Florence could pick out "A Hot Time in the Old Town Tonight" with one finger, it didn't seem to fit in very well with a wedding or deathbed scene.

I had often said that if ever I married, the girl would have to meet with two requirements: First, she must live along the river, and second, she must be able to play piano. Strange to say, she did both. I came to know her in the most unusual manner. It all came about on Dog Island at "Old Maid" crossing just above the mouth of the Cumberland River where we were blown in early one morning. On the head of the island, near Smithland, Kentucky, stranded high and dry, was a large drift pile. Now to the rivermen of our type there is nothing that affords such keen delight as the process of foraging through a pile of drift because one can expect to find anything from a corpse to a ten-dollar bill wrapped neatly around a dry willow branch. After an hour or so of poking around in this one I had salvaged a gallon of black walnuts, a cork life preserver stenciled "Str. Helen White," a baby's high

chair, and, away down at the bottom of the drift a
bottle with a note in it which read:

Into the shallow waters of the Wabash blue,
I cast this note as a message to you,
It comes from a lonesome girl yet in her teens,
Who has been cast aside by the man of her dreams.
If it should drift unobserved from here to the sea,
What difference would it make to you and to me?

LONESOME
1228 Wright Street
Logansport, Indiana

I carefully unfolded the damp piece of paper and
slowly read its contents again. I checked the course
it had taken. "Lonesome" had set the bottle adrift
at the headwaters of the Wabash River and it had
drifted to Warehouse Landing, and out into the
Ohio where the two rivers meet, a few miles below
Uniontown, Kentucky.

I had been too busy all my life keeping mud off
the forw'd end of the boat and stores on the aft end
to entertain many love affairs. Just the same, I was
interested in the lonesome little girl who, at a low
ebb, had written the note, and I began to wonder
what she was like and particularly whether or not
she played the piano.

The next day at Cave-In-Rock, Illinois, I had a
tintype taken of myself as I sucked a milk shake
through a straw and enclosed the picture with a

note written on pink paper highly scented with sachet powder. This is what I wrote:

I am the pirate that discovered your note,
On the head of Dog Island and that's no joke.
But you can save your stamps for other beaus,
If you can't play a piano, read, fake and transpose.

In spite of the impudence of my letter and the idiotic picture I had enclosed, a correspondence sprang up between us that lasted for several months during which time she never once disclosed her true identity.

That fall we began an overhaul of both boats and I was so busy scrubbing and painting that I neglected to write and completely forgot her for the time being, so I heard from her no more.

Spring came along with the usual hustle and bustle and on our opening day, still minus a piano player, we received a telegram from an ad we had inserted in the *Billboard* which read, "At Liberty— Experienced Pianist—Salary your limit—Can join at once without ticket. Address Joe Costello, Grass Creek, Indiana."

"An Italian," Dad remarked, a note of doubt in his voice as he again read the message aloud.

"Oh, you can't tell, Sam," Mother replied. "He may not be an Italian at all."

"Don't fool yourself," I interrupted. "With a name like that what else could he be?"

"Well, what if he is?" Mother replied. "You see

what his message says. Salary your limit—Can join without ticket. Lots of good musicians are Italians, and we do need a piano player."

"You're right, Mother," Dad said. "Run up and send him a wire to join at once," he told me.

"Yes" my sister added as I went out the door, "and bring back a sack full of garlic and a large bale of spaghetti."

The next day I met all the incoming trains and stopped each man that alighted with a grip, but none of them answered to the name of Costello. Tired and disgusted, I returned to the boat, where Mother came running to meet me.

"The piano player is here and she's a dear," she exclaimed.

"She?" I cried in surprise.

"Yes, the he's a she. Her name's Josephine," she went on with a twinkling eye, "and not an Italian either but as Irish as Paddy's pig. And she's beautiful, Son," she whispered.

Later, when I was introduced to her she looked at me in a peculiar way, as if she were inspecting a marked-down garment on a bargain counter, and I agreed that Mother was right. She was as pretty as a picture and there was an air of refinement about her which made me wonder whether she would ever be able to adapt herself to the crude and strange life of the river.

She was good humored, energetic and talented, and she soon set my doubts at rest on that point.

Jo Bryant Playing the Steam Calliope
Courtesy Kent State University Library, Kent, Ohio

After each meal, she would quietly roll up her sleeves and never leave the kitchen until the last dish was dried. She scrubbed and redecorated her room all by herself as if she had settled down for the rest of her life. She was a wizard at the piano, and her marvelous playing and feminine charm often created more interest than the show. As the people left the boat each night, she would entertain them with a medley of Irish songs which she played and sang in her own delightful way. When my sister took sick, she jumped into the leading role on short notice and with complete success. She also played the piano before and after the show and between the acts. The entire crew, including myself, fell madly in love with her, but she gave us all a wide berth and attended strictly to her own business.

She was an expert swimmer. One day at Vevay, Indiana, as she finished a swim, she asked me to hand her her bathrobe from under the shelf back of the door in her room. In doing so, I accidentally upset her scrapbook, which came tumbling to the floor and lay open before me. There I saw a familiar sheet of pink writing paper and I read:

I am the pirate that discovered your note,
On the head of Dog Island and that's no joke.
But you can save your stamps for other beaus,
If you can't play a piano, read, fake and transpose.

With my cheeks flaming with embarrassment and pleasure, I dashed out to her, the open scrapbook in my hand. A few minutes later, with my arms about her—wet bathing suit and all—she told me that she had read the ad while visiting friends near Grass Creek, and, piqued because I had not written to her, had wired us from their address.

Three weeks later I proposed to her and we were married at Christmas time in Cincinnati. Since she had been born and raised on the banks of the Wabash and was an accomplished pianist, I had fulfilled my early vows about my marriage.

The Famous Four Bryants now were five and, as time proved, were later to become six—all the additions the strange result of a note in a bottle!

XII

When Dreams Come True

WE CARRIED on with the *Princess* with continued success until 1917. At this time some of the larger boats were beginning to stop at the smaller towns along the route of our once virgin territory, furnishing a competition which we found increasingly difficult to meet. Although showboats have frequently been spoken of as just one big happy family, in the days when such towns as Augusta, Kentucky; Vevay, Indiana; Rose Clare, Illinois; and Cape Girardeau, Missouri were in their prime, that old river tradition was only a sweet thought. The rule was "every showboat captain for himself." Our competitors often went so far as to play day and date with us, and, of course, invariably stole our audiences with their big boats, calliopes, brass bands, and orchestras. As a last humiliating taunt to the rest of us smaller outfits, the *Goldenrod*,[1] then the largest showboat on the river, headed all its gaudy advertising posters with the belittling words, "After the Minnows, then comes the Whale."

The first time we clashed with the *Cotton Blossom*,

[1]The *Goldenrod* was built in 1909 and in 1950, its hull encased in steel, was tied up at St. Louis and is still in use as a showboat. It has a seating capacity of about 1000.

Florence took up the cudgels in her own way and nearly ruined us both. The bigger boat had rounded to at the local wharf early that morning and the captain selfishly rammed the head of his big boat up against our little craft, making us look like a gnat on an elephant's back. All day long the actors and musicians took a keen delight in baiting my sister by asking her such questions as, "Where did you get that double-decked cigar box?" (referring to our showboat). "Do you expect a big turnout tonight?" "Are you the leading lady on the boat or the night watchman in the kitchen?"

That afternoon she took her revenge. She was on shore with one of her many village friends. This one happened to be the daughter of the constable.

"I hear the *Cotton Blossom* played last night in a town where there's smallpox," Florence whispered.

Her companion's eyes widened with excitement and fear.

"Honest?" she asked. "Do you think they have brought any with them?"

"Well, you never can tell," Florence answered sagely. "I hear one of their actors is in bed on the boat right now and they say he's got smallpox!"

That was enough for any constable's daughter. Rushing off to her father she told him the whole tale and the village was instantly into a furor. The constable, backed by a crowd of frightened citizens, their fear transformed into enmity, marched on us. None of them would come onto either boat, but

Showboat Goldenrod

Showboat Cotton Blossom

Courtesy Kent State University Library, Kent, Ohio

shouting from the bank in no uncertain terms they told us that neither of us would be allowed to show that night and that we were both under quarantine. For ten days we lay there idly, unable to leave the boat or to receive anyone on it. Now and then the captain of the *Cotton Blossom* would glare at us, muttering under his breath. I think he suspected the source of the constable's false information. When they finally let us go we had to jump a hundred miles to get ahead of the propaganda which had preceded us down the river.

But wherever we went the bigger boats had just been or were billed to be there soon. We were caught in the trap which at some time or other catches every small enterprise. We were learning that, in the showboat business as well as any other, the little fellow has small chance against the competition of the larger ones. The public is queer that way.

For years we had dreamed that we would own one of the greatest showboats on the river, or at least one equal to those of our competitors who seemed determined to put us out of business. Now it looked as if we had to have a bigger boat or quit. So we sold the dear little *Princess* and the *Florence* to a showman at Parkersburg for a pitifully small amount and began figuring the cost of a new boat. But the amount we had received for our old outfit was scarcely a beginning.

I have never yet got far enough in the science of

mathematics to figure what happens to a boat's value as soon as its bottom gets wet. You may build any type of watercraft you desire and invest any amount of money in it, but if you try to sell it ten minutes after it has been launched you will find that it has decreased in value from 25 to 50 percent.

We added up the amount we had saved and the pittance we had received for our first outfit, and looked at the total in dismay. Then Mother and Dad went to see Mr. Bowyer again. Before they could talk about money he had to hear of all that had happened to the converted mud scow he had bought for us—the *Princess*—and all the plans we had made for a new boat. As they talked he would suggest details of construction for the new boat, his eyes alight with interest. Without any difficulty Mother and Dad negotiated a loan of several thousand dollars and our grand project was under way.

In a fever of excitement we laid our plans, and soon lumber, nails, roofing paper, doors, windows, paint, scenery, opera chairs, etc., came rolling in C.O.D. from all points. In no time, the pounding of hammers and clinking of steel calking irons could be heard all over town. The army of carpenters and laborers, all personal friends of ours, worked with as much energy and pride as if it had been their own boat they were building. Every night after quitting time, Mother and Dad would take a lantern, go through the boat, and lay out their plans for another day.

We spent borrowed money as though we were the New Deal[2] and wondered whether we were ever going to be able to pay it all back again. Then, after weeks of laborious efforts during which Dad sawed off another inch of his already crippled finger, and I nearly drowned when I fell overboard with a keg of nails, the boat was finally completed. And what a boat it was!

The auditorium was the fulfillment of all our beautiful dreams. It was painted white and trimmed in gold, with red plush curtains and black tassels draped over the boxes and around the orchestra pit. It had a balcony, and seated nearly seven hundred people. Steam pipes and electric fans were installed along the walls to make it comfortable in early spring and mid-summer, and down each aisle was a strip of green-striped coconut matting. The stage had only an eighteen-foot opening, but to me it looked like the New York Hippodrome. There was

[2]President Franklin Delano Roosevelt pledged a New Deal to the American people in his effort to overcome the effects of the Great Depression. He believed that through government spending the economy could be stimulated, and as a result, his administration undertook a program of road construction, work relief, public housing, heavy farm subsidies, and increased low-cost loans to business and to industry. The national debt rose because the President did not wish to stifle economic growth with taxes. Conservative Americans argued that the nation could not spend its way out of the Depression and denounced Roosevelt's New Deal as deficit spending. It is not surprising that Bryant, a comedian, would lampoon the President when he borrowed money and spent it so freely.

a spotlight in the balcony, in the bright beam of which I planned to sing and do my sand jig.

The boat was so large that we had to find a steamboat to handle it properly. So we put an ad in that riverman's Bible, the *Waterways Journal* of St. Louis, where you will find everything from the design of the latest steel barges to news of where the best fishing is, and obtained the steamer *E. F. Jackson*[3] from Pittsburgh. We quickly found the *Jackson* insufficient, and about that time we met John F. Klein, known as "the little giant broker," the most prolific and versatile trader of watercraft on the inland streams.

When, in telling this story, I think of a man like "the little giant broker," I wish that books could be four times as long as they are and that I had at my command as many words as Hervey Allen put into *Anthony Adverse*.[4] It would take that many to describe all of the river characters we have met.

"The little giant broker" is one who deserves a long discourse. Constantly roving up and down the rivers, a friend of every man, he will buy and sell anything which has any connection with the inland

[3]The towboat *E. F. Jackson*, built in 1894, was originally named *Dewing & Sons*. After towing the Bryant showboat, she was purchased by the Lyons Coal Co. of Fairmont, West Virginia. She sank in 1926.

[4]Hervey Allen's *Anthony Adverse* (1933) was a huge—1227 page—novel that captured a vast popular audience. There were at least twenty-two editions and it was made into a successful film.

Bryant's New Showboat

Courtesy The Public Library of Cincinnati and Hamilton County

streams, and he is always cheerful. If you are down-hearted, all you have to do to get over it is to spend half an hour with the always smiling John F. Klein.

Through him we sold the *E. F. Jackson* and bought the *Valley Belle*,[5] our family river horse which furnishes us with power to this day.

Years ago, when the *Valley Belle* was a packet, running between Marietta and Middleport, she was so fast and handled so much freight that the roust-abouts had little or no time to sleep between land-ings. She would leave Middleport, Ohio, at five in the evening, make the seventy-mile run to Marietta by the next day, load up, and come right back again. Consequently she was considered a hard boat to work on, and the rousters made a song about it. As they loaded cargo they would sing, letting their voices drop to a mumble when they came to the line about the captain and the mate:

Oh the old Valley Belle she runs by steam and never gives us rousters no time to dream, Oh she calls us early and she works us late, the captain is a son of a bitch and so's the mate!

[5]Billy Bryant secured the vessel in 1919. *Valley Belle*, a stern wheel, wooden hull packet, was built at the Knox Yard at Hamar, Ohio, in 1883. The vessel sank at Kanauga in 1943 and was raised and dismantled.

However, we had no intention of crowding our crew, thus having the traditional song of the *Valley Belle* turned against us, so we started out with her joyfully and we soon made her a member of the family, to be loved, sworn at, and depended upon.

On the first of April, with flags flying and banners waving, we nosed the head of our new showboat into the Point Pleasant wharf, where we had landed in 1906 homeless and destitute, our entire earthly belongings piled in a leaky john boat. But how different everything was now! High-powered searchlights playing on the heavens created the effect of a Hollywood picture première. My wife Josephine, back on the steamboat at the calliope, made a musical proclamation of our joy, and a brass band on the head of the showboat played snappy tunes at intervals while hundreds of patrons gaily swarmed up the gangplank at twenty-five and fifty cents a head to help us open our season in a blaze of glory.

Dad, attired in a Prince Albert, and Mother in a black spangled gown with a rhinestone necklace, stood at the front door and greeted their many friends, who had once fed and clothed us, as they came aboard bringing flowers and other beautiful presents as tokens of their wishes for our success. Their kindness was extremely touching to Mother and Dad, who, with tears of gratitude filling their eyes, could only mumble the word "thanks" as the audience passed through the door and on into the crowded auditorium.

Packet Valley Belle
Before Becoming the Tug for Bryant's Showboat
Courtesy The Public Library of Cincinnati and Hamilton County

Dear old Henderson, across the river from the place where we had built the boat, also came through with a bang. Its townsmen had bought out half the boat in advance, and the first one to come aboard was the large fat lady who had fainted at the opening of the *Princess*. I immediately seated her near one of the new electric fans and surreptitiously tried it out to see that it would play directly on her if necessary so that she wouldn't throw anymore fits like the one that had broken up our first opening.

Mr. Bowyer and a group of Point Pleasant's leading citizens attended with opera glasses and in full evening dress. The sight of them thus accoutered made Dad so nervous that he tore off the wrong end of their reserved seat tickets, and later, when they weren't sure which their seats were since there were no numbers on their stubs, he blamed it on the ushers who, he said, were working an audition.

As I flew around that night, I felt more important than I had ever felt before in all my life. I nodded and smiled at everyone at the slightest indication of recognition until my face and neck hurt. Later as I stood in the balcony and watched the ushers on the floor below, dressed in blue sailor suits, rushing up and down the aisles, seating the hundreds of people as the boat rapidly filled to its capacity, I wanted to weep with joy, for I realized that all our efforts were now bearing fruit and that our dreams had surely come true.

The orchestra, that doubled as our band, began

the opening overture costumed in black sateen shirts, white duck trousers, and white bow ties. And did they cut their stuff that night! They played part of the "Poet and Peasant"[6] waltz, and then went into "A Hot Time in the Old Town Tonight," and not one blew an extra note at the ending. They all finished together!

As a play, we presented *Over the Hill to the Poorhouse*.[7] Mother, in the famous mother role, had them crying from the outset. Even Max, our hard-hearted orchestra leader, was crying. But after the show he told us that his tears had been brought on by the odor of turpentine from the freshly painted auditorium. After my specialty, which, I later acknowledged to the entire company, was the hit of the show, the mayor came up onto the stage and introduced me to the audience as one of the greatest showboat comedians that the river had ever known and then he presented me with a key to the city with a bow of pink ribbon on one end. As I acknowledged the thundering ovation, I thought to myself, "My God, if George M. Cohan would only step in the front door now!"

At the close of the performance we all rushed out on the stage and forced a curtain call with Mother standing in the center of the group, waving and

[6]The "Poet and Peasant Overture" or "Dichter und Bauer" was written by Franz von Suppe in 1854.

[7]*Over the Hill to the Poorhouse* was composed by David Braham in 1874. The lyrics were added later by George L. Catlin.

throwing kisses to that grand audience. And so our gala opening night, that had been a sensational success, came to an end.

After the lights were extinguished and things again simmered down to normal, we all eagerly gathered at the front of the boat to count up the night's receipts, just as we had done on that other night, years before, when we opened the *Princess*. Spellbound with joy, we found that we had taken in nearly three hundred dollars!

We went up the Kanawha River for two weeks, where at every landing our loyal friends from the *Princess* days gave us a glorious welcome and heartily congratulated us on our new boat. On our return to Point Pleasant, we paid off one of the many thousand-dollar notes that the bank was holding against us. Then we headed for Pittsburgh, still packing and jamming them at every stand. At Marietta we purchased January, a bucking mule, from Jerry Mugivan, of the American Circus Corporation, as an added attraction. We offered a ten-dollar reward for anyone who would come up on the stage and ride him. The country boys always landed in the third or fourth row as soon as they attempted to get on his back. But up on the Monongahela River, in the coal fields, we had to omit the reward, for those black-eyed miners who knew their mules would stick on old January's back like porous plasters; and often when he would be making a special effort to free himself from some conquering hero, he would get too far offstage and kick all the bulk-heading off the side of the boat.

One afternoon at Warsaw, Ky., we were in re-hearsal and I was trying to get a little feeling into the scene. All the actors seemed to be overflowing with lead.

"All right, boys," I said impatiently, "we'll do that scene over again. Think of your art, think of your public, think of lunch—think of anything! I want that scene done with finesse, boys. It's the Belasco[8] in me!"

There was a snicker behind me and I looked back to see one of the town boys who had come aboard laughing at us from the doorway.

That night we staged, without intending to, a thrilling rescue scene. We had arranged quarters for January, the mule, on the steamboat, and had taught him to go unaided from the showboat to his quar-ters, stepping with ease from one boat to the other. Although he knew the way, he would take his time in getting to his stall, usually stopping to scratch his rump against one of the hog chain braces.

On this night he started back all right and we left him to his own devices. Suddenly we heard a terrific splashing in the river and, rushing back, we saw Jan-uary plunging and leaping about in the water like a

[8]David Belasco (1859–1931) was an actor, writer, and pro-ducer. He is best known for his New York theater where he stressed realism in staging his productions, even to the point of brewing real coffee during a scene in a restaurant.

suddenly awkward and frightened porpoise, looking up at us with terrified eyes. There was nothing to do but go to his rescue, so I plunged in. This seemed to frighten January more than ever, and he headed for the middle of the stream, with me after him. When I called to him he hesitated and then turned around and headed straight for me. Now I was frightened, for his front hoofs were working ahead of him like a pair of flails and I knew that one blow from them would make me the one who had to be rescued, so I turned and used the most furious dog paddling I have ever known to get out of his way. Just then I heard the voice of the boy who had snickered at rehearsal that afternoon.

"Better keep that Belasco inside of you, Cap," he called, "or it's going to get wet."

Meanwhile a large crowd had gathered on the bank. Someone had called out the fire department, which arrived and swelled the audience, until January and I were playing to the largest crowd we had ever faced.

I'll never know how far I swam that night or how far January swam. We chased each other over half an acre of water. First I would chase January and then January would chase me. Finally we compromised by swimming in a circle so that no one could say which was pursuing and which pursued.

At last, exhausted, I abandoned the argument and made for shore, whereupon January decided to take control of the show without assistance and tried to climb aboard the boat. He chose the paddle wheel for his attempted ascent, and in half a minute it was a tangle of legs and hoofs and splintering wood. If the engineer had rolled the wheel ahead at that moment, he would have thrown old January up onto the roof of the steamboat. It was a sight to make strong women weep.

At last we got him ashore and, with coaxing and pushing, tried to get him up the stage plank. But it was not until Florence, remembering how she had taken Dad aboard the *Water Queen*, arrived with a large handkerchief to tie over his eyes, that we finally succeeded.

After that he could not be made to go along the boat on the river side. He would always choose the side nearest the shore and nothing could change his determination. Even on that side he stuck so close to the cabin that he wore a streak of hair off his ribs and rump.

There are two very awkward things that I know of. One is to carry an intoxicated woman up a flight of stairs. The other is to get a frightened mule onto a boat out of ten feet of water.

XIII

The Showboat Goes
'Round and 'Round

THE RIVER was high when we reached Louisville, which enabled us to go over the falls there and down to West Point along one of the most beautiful stretches of water I have ever seen. Sometimes, as I stood in the pilothouse with little to do save keep my hand on the wheel, I would watch the magnificent spectacle slipping gently past us on both banks and wonder whether we were in business or taking a pleasure cruise.

Bit by bit we were gathering the traditions of the river and learning to recognize its spots of interest. There is the bluff where a steamboat captain is buried, in accordance with his dying request, standing up and facing the river, so that from his tomb he can curse all of his river enemies as they float past him. For the first time we picked the place out on this trip.

At Paducah we turned off up the Tennessee River and found, to our delight, that with our new outfit we could climb without difficulty the famous Duck River Sucks, one of the most worrisome stretches of swift water in the south for those with low-powered boats.

At a crossroad landing near Savannah, a spot at

which General Grant was lodged for a time during
the Civil War, my wife bought "the bed that General Grant slept in." She was filled with excitement
and I, eyeing suspiciously the rickety thing, which
was held together with haywire and string, saved
myself from an argument by agreeing that it was a
priceless find. Later, in the village, I happened to
go into a secondhand furniture store where I found
prowling around, half drunk with corn liquor, the
antique dealer from whom she had bought the bed.
He was pawing over several old beds and he
grinned drunkenly at me.

"Got to get another General Grant bed," he said.
"Sold my last one this morning. Fast as I sell 'em I
buy more. They all look the same to the women
when I tell 'em Grant slept in 'em!"

It was August and too early to go South—not because of the climate, but because of the crops. A
showboat usually plays the North in the spring because of road conditions. In the mining country, on
the Kanawha and Monongahela rivers, the miners
live in little rows of houses which are always collec-
tively known as "the patch" and are always just a
short distance from the river, so bad roads or inclement weather does not hinder them from attending the showboat, particularly if it arrives around
payday. A coal miner is a great spender and will
demand the best of everything as long as his cash
holds out. The boats go south in October and November to be on time for the cotton and cane har-

vest, since the most prosperous territory is on the sugar coast between Baton Rouge and New Orleans. Lent, which usually comes in February or March, sends the boats farther North, as that section of Louisiana is a strong Catholic center and its population does not go to shows during that period.

For this reason we decided to put in some time on the Illinois River, which puts out at Grafton on the upper Mississippi. Early one morning just at daybreak we swung around the famous Cairo point at Cairo, Illinois, out of the peaceful emerald-green Ohio and into the roaring, muddy Mississippi with its terrific current nearly rolling over the front deck of our showboat, while the old *Valley Belle*, with every ounce of steam that it was allowed, trembled from stem to stern. Its faithful old slide-valve machinery with California cut-offs made the paddle wheel literally fan the air in an effort to keep up with the mad rush of water.

It finally succeeded in shoving us past Byrd's Point at the pace of two miles an hour, landing us in Thebes, Illinois, at ten o'clock that night, two hours behind our regular showtime schedule. It was a distance of only forty-odd miles, but the slipperiest forty I ever traveled. Since then, we always figure when starting up the upper Mississippi from Cairo to St. Louis (a distance of some two hundred miles) that we will average three or four miles an hour going upstream, and ninety-nine miles an hour coming down.

It seemed as if we burned up at least three coal mines on that trip. We took on fuel at every possible landing. We finally made it into St. Louis and on past the Alton slough and the wide mouth of the Missouri River, after which the current eased a bit. A short time later we were safely anchored in the dead mucky waters of the Illinois.

The Illinois River has long been conceded to be the greatest showboat river of them all. Such towns as Kampesville, Pearl, Browning, Pekin, Henry, and others have never been equalled for their persistently show-going people. They naturally love all types of entertainment and have been known to follow a showboat for miles in order to see the same performance over and over again.

When we stopped at Browning the river was up and it was impossible for us, owing to trees and other obstructions, to get our showboat any closer than seventy feet from shore. We thought we would have to give up our plan to show that night, but the natives wouldn't have it. Jumping in to solve the problem themselves, they helped us build a freakish pontoon walk by turning shanty boats, john boats, rafts, and floating gunnels end-to-end until they finally reached from the shore to our boat. Over this shaky, improvised bridge eager amusement seekers often stepped ankle deep into the muck and mire. One young mother tossed her baby from one pair of outstretched arms to another, as if it had been a watermelon they were loading into a cart.

This section of the state, particularly around Beardstown, is known as great duck and fish country and is famous for its fish fries. Mack Franks, our leading man, who loved to fish and always had a throw line cast out from the steamboat somewhere, was in paradise here. At Montezuma, during the last act of the show, he was late for his entrance cue and no one could find him, so we kept on ad-libbing until he finally came rushing onto the stage out of breath. When I had a chance I whispered to him, "What was the matter? Where were you?"

While still shaking with excitement, he silently mumbled, "I just caught the biggest damn catfish you ever saw!"

Late that fall, on our way down the lower Mississippi, we had our first experience with a hysterical, panicked audience. We were tied up to "dead men" (that is, buried logs) at Bayou Sara, Louisiana. At about nine o'clock, in the middle of our show, we were suddenly struck by a typical southern tornado, which parted the lines holding the showboat, but not those of the *Valley Belle*. As we swung out into the river, driven by the terrific wind, our light connections with the *Valley Belle* were also severed, and in total darkness, unable to control the boat, we drifted helplessly to what we did not know. In the auditorium a screaming, pushing audience fought for the doorways, determined to jump overboard. Fortunately there were some river-wise men among them who immediately joined with us to calm them.

But that which we couldn't do, Nature suddenly did for us. The screaming of the women and children was suddenly hushed by a terrific clap of thunder and an instantaneous torrent of rain through which forked lightning furnished intermittent illumination. The water came down in sheets, in rivers. The thunder roared and the lightning flashed all about us. It was the most dramatic spectacle I have ever seen and it succeeded in cowing the audience so thoroughly that they were robbed of the power of action and simply waited, their faces ghastly white in the blue light of the recurring lightning flashes, for whatever might happen.

Then the crash came! All of us, audience and actors, were thrown onto the floor in a heap, and again the screaming began. I took a lantern and, jumping onto the stage, pleaded with them to be calm while I found out what had happened.

Going to a window I waited for a flash of lightning, wondering why I could feel no motion. As soon as the lightning came I saw to my delight that we had been blown clear across the Mississippi River and had skidded several feet out onto shore, where we were stuck securely in the mud. Then we all settled down, by the light of a lantern, and told stories and jokes until daylight, when the *Valley Belle*, which had been looking for us all night, found us, pulled us off, and took us in tow again.

It was also on this trip that we witnessed another unusual event. We were at the junction of the Mississippi and the Red River of the North, where the current is swift and the river several miles wide. On the river bank is the famous Angola prison farm. As we travelled along one night, I saw forms swimming in the river toward the boat. Rushing to the side of the deck, I soon discovered that they were men fully clothed in working garments and fighting hard against the current. I called one of the boys and we quickly gave them a hand aboard, where they sank exhausted to the deck.

They obviously didn't want to talk much. One of them told us a rambling story about having capsized in a john boat in midstream. I offered to land them on shore, but they said not to bother. After resting ten or fifteen minutes, they suddenly got up and, without another word, plunged into the river again. Later we learned that two prisoners had escaped from Angola by swimming across the river. Everyone commented on the feat of endurance which it represented and we held our own counsel, knowing that, through making it possible by giving them a rest halfway across, we had unwittingly aided and abetted their escape.

Turning off the Mississippi we followed the Red River of the North to the Achafalaya, down which we headed at a lively clip, passing through one of the most weird and isolated stretches of wilderness I have ever encountered. From Mellville, Louisiana, to Grand Lake we traveled for miles between brush-tangled shores and under the overhanging branches of dead trees without seeing a human being or any sign of one. Alligators, ugly-looking water moccasins, long-billed sea gulls, and barred owls were there by the hundred. And I think to this day that we could have scared up a few monkeys in those trees if we had tried. The name "Achafalaya" means "lost river," and I, for one, am quite content now to have it remain lost.

In the evening, when muskrats boldly swam in the open and swallows darted crazily over the surface of the stream in pursuit of insects, when we heard the distant monotonous rumble of frogs, and the occasional high-pitched and unpleasant voice of an awakening bat in some red or white cypress tree, or the mournful call of wild geese overhead, the night seemed to stretch ahead of us like a horrible dream from which we could not escape, and we longed for the more populous northern waters.

Yet the natives themselves, whenever we found any, were intelligent and friendly people who gave us a hearty welcome. They seemed content in their hideout, isolated from the rest of the world. But when, among them, we would meet one wearing a full beard halfway down to his knees, yet who spoke with a cultured accent and showed that he had good manners, I always wondered what bank he had robbed in the East. Certainly if I were ever fleeing from the law there is no place where I would feel safer from pursuit than along the shores of the Achafalaya.

XIV

Two Song and Dance Men

TIME ROLLED on with the river and the Famous
Four Bryants, who had fought public indiffer-
ence, hunger, and floods, were at last well beyond
the fears which poverty breeds. And there were now
two new Bryants—my wife, Jo, and our daughter,
Betty. Year after year Bryant's Showboat continued
to grow in popularity. Season after season we
packed the river audiences into our new boat.
When a town heard our calliope it was the signal
for a holiday like that which we had witnessed the
day we joined the *Water Queen* in that far-off time
when we had been living from hand-to-mouth.

We were all happy, yet there were times when I
found myself restless and ill at ease, overcome by
nameless regrets—like a child who goes to bed wor-
rying over the lie he told his mother during the day.

One night, when we had played opposite a sugar
plantation, I took stock of myself. It was cotton-
picking time; there had been a good harvest and
money was plentiful. Though the show had long
since been over and we were all in bed, a number of
the Negroes from the balcony audience still hung
about the levee talking, singing, and dancing. One
of them had a banjo which furnished the music.

From time to time he would strike up a spiritual and the Negroes would sing.

I lay in my bunk with wide-open eyes, unable to find that moment of pleasant relaxation, that point of conscious letting go of awareness, which tells the tired person he is about to sleep. As I lay there a rising golden moon found my window and suddenly illuminated my stateroom with bright magic. Of course, it only added to my restlessness. It seemed so near that I thought, by leaning out of the window, I could thrust my arm into its liquid gold.

The Negroes were singing:

> *Yo' say yo' headed fo' de skies,*
> *Yo' mus' be a lovin' at God's command!*
> *Why don' yo' stop yo' tellin' lies,*
> *Yo' mus' be a lovin' at God's command!*

Unable to sleep I went out on deck and looked down the path of gold the moon made on the river. As I watched, the steamer *Boaz*, with a tremendous tow of loaded coal barges, passed by on its way to New Orleans, leaving a long foamy wake in the path of its mammoth paddle wheel. In daylight it would have seemed nothing unusual—just another boat passing on the river. Now, with its blinking side lights and red and green signals, the foam of its wake turning to gold in the moonlight, the harsh lines of its coal barges merged into the soft shadows of the night, it seemed to be a beautiful thing from another world.

From the shore side the strong voice of a Negress was beginning another song.

> *Let us break bread together,*
> *On our knees, yes on our knees;*
> *Let us break bread together,*
> *On our knees, yes on our knees.*
> *When I fall on my knees*
> *With my face to the rising sun,*
> *O Lord, have mercy on me!*

I strode about the deck, turning my face away from the *Boaz*, my heart filled with a nameless ache. The night was bewitched. There was something that I wanted and couldn't name, something which I had missed, and I didn't even know what it was. I felt a strange sense of brotherhood with all the world, yet at the same time I wanted to be alone.

I suddenly felt small and mean, as though I had been involved in some unworthy affair which I should have left alone. I found myself thinking of a time when I had gathered dynamited fish that had come, stunned, to the surface at Manchester Island. I remembered a cheap trick we had played to get an audience by telling them that moving pictures would be taken of them, and how we had used a phony camera made of a cracker box; but remembering these things and regretting them didn't seem to do any good.

Down the river an all-night fisherman suddenly began to whistle "Yankee-Doodle-Doo," and then I thought of George M. Cohan—of my childish resentment of him, of the bitter thoughts I had had of him, the bitter words I had spoken of him, the senseless blame I had cast upon him simply because he had refused to write a sketch for us once and had gone on from one success to another while we were tasting the bitter dregs of failure.

Suddenly I saw clearly, in the spell of this revealing night, how insane it had been, how my bitter jealousy for a better actor and showman than myself had corroded my soul and cast a shadow over my life for all these years. Obviously it hadn't hurt Cohan any—I had simply been hurting myself.

And I realized then that this feeling of shame, which had come to me so strongly on this magic night, had begun long before when I had read of the death of Cohan's sister Josephine, and then of his father and mother. And suddenly I felt the compensating hand of fortune in the thought that the Four Bryants, who had suffered so many hardships together, were still together. With other four-person vaudeville teams we had weathered the old-time concert hall days, but unlike the Four Mortons,[1] the Ford Family,[2] and the Four Cohans, all of whom were now broken up, we were still a happy family.

I stepped off the boat and sat on a log, brooding

[1] The Four Mortons was a turn-of-the-century popular vaudeville act. It had a very Irish flavor.

[2] The Ford Family, like the Bryants, operated a family-style showboat.

and watching the lights of the big *Boaz* disappear around the bend of the river. Behind me the Negroes were singing another song which seemed a direct suggestion.

> *Goin' to lay down my burdens,*
> *Down by the riverside,*
> *Down by the riverside,*
> *Down by the riverside,*
> *Lay down my burdens,*
> *Down by the riverside,*
> *An' study war no more!*

For years I had been at war—not with George Cohan, for he knew nothing about it and could not possibly be worried if he did—but with myself, with my littleness and conceit and lack of understanding. This was behind me now, for I had known for a long time what base nonsense it had been and had felt ashamed of it, but I had never done anything about it. Now, with the magnetism of that great southern moon upon me, the softness and silence of the night about me, the murmur of the swift current as it passed under the rake of our boat and the sound of the Negroes' voices in my ears, I felt a sense of kinship with and sympathy for George M. Cohan. I wondered what he was doing at that moment in the great city of New York and how his Broadway would compare scenically with my river. I wondered what he was like as a man and I wanted to meet him and shake his hand. And above all I wanted to unload the burden of my silly conflict about him.

Would he read a letter if I were to write it to him, or would it only find its way unopened to the nearest wastebasket? But what did that matter if, by writing, I could unload through confession the terrific pressure of jealousy I had felt?

Going back on the boat and seizing a lantern from between the legs of the night watchman who was sprawled on a tarpaulin fast asleep, I went up to the kitchen and sat down to write. The Negroes had deserted the levee now and the shore was haunted with silence. But here on the boat a multitude of little sounds violated the night—the snores of the tired crew, the thumping of the boat's rudder stocks in the swift current, the creaking of timbers.

Taking my lantern and writing materials I went out onto the levee where, seated on a bale of cotton with a pencil, a paper, and a dingy lantern, I rapidly wrote a long letter to the man who had been torturing my mind. I told him the whole story of my bitterness without missing any details, from his refusal to write an act for us in Buffalo to the night in Parkersburg when I had watched from the fly loft of the Parkersburg Auditorium and would gladly have dropped a sandbag on his head while he went through his magnificent performance of *The Governor's Son*. And I told him how, in my thoughts, I had wronged him and that I needed to offer him this apology in order to free my own mind.

When I had finished I felt a sense of release and peace which I had not known for years. It was nearly five o'clock in the morning. As I approached the boat, I could see that Father was hauling in the stern lines getting ready to move. As I went aboard he was stamping through the dawn-lit passageway above deck, pounding at the doors of the crew's quarters.

"Gol damn!" he grumbled, as I passed him, "They're sleepin' their lives away!"

Poor Dad! He never could believe that anyone but a wastrel would lie abed after four in the morning. While the crew arose noisily there were groans from the actors on the other side of the boat who were still trying to sleep. There is a constant feud between actors and crew on a showboat. At night, when the members of the crew are trying to sleep, the actors keep them awake; in the morning the crew, arising early, disturbs the actors who are trying to catch up on sleep.

Father was splitting kindling for the kitchen stove now, and getting the fire started for the early morning coffee, stopping only long enough to make another trip above to the room of a member of the crew who always had to be called several times.

"Goin' to sleep your head off?" he shouted, while the actors, who could hear his irate voice as well as the man for whom it was intended, groaned and turned over again. There was no point in going to bed now, so I stayed in the kitchen with Dad and

Harry, the cook, and in a few moments sat down to a smoking breakfast of bacon and flap-jacks.

At our next stand up the river I walked five miles in the country to a fork in the road where I waited several hours for the arrival of the rural route postman to whom I gave my letter. I don't think I expected an answer. The letter had served its purpose as soon as I had written it and told Cohan what a complete fool I had been about him. I turned and walked back to the boat whistling, my mind and heart relieved.

Several weeks later, though, the answer came in one of the most gracious and kindly letters ever written—written in Cohan's own hand—a shaggy scrawl—and telling me to forget it. It was an unusually gracious thing for a man as busy as he was to do, and it completed the release which that night of moonlight had begun.

I was filled with gratitude and admiration and almost immediately my mind conceived a daring and enthusiastic plan to pay a tribute along the rivers to this great showman. I would bring a Cohan play to my entertainment-starved, play-loving audiences of the inland streams! We had been prosperous. We could afford at last to pay for our shows, and our river friends deserved a good Cohan comedy as much as any Broadway audience did.

I talked it over with Mother and Father and good old Dad said simply, as he has said so many times since, "Whatever you think, Billy." So when we tied up at Pittsburgh that fall I put some banknotes in my bag and started for New York, determined to do whatever was necessary to bring a Cohan comedy back with me.

I'll never forget my delight at my first view of Broadway—and the confusion which I felt as I tried to find my way about New York. Day-by-day I felt more out of place. A feeling of strangeness gradually gave way to one of fright. I felt ridiculously small and out of place in the bustle and hurry, and I found myself speaking in an apologetic tone of voice, as though I had something to conceal. But I swallowed my desire to run back to the rivers and set out to find the proper person to talk to about buying a George M. Cohan play.

Then came a series of shocks. Wherever I went I met curt rebuffs, outright refusals, and even sneers and scornful laughter. Secretaries stopped me in outer offices and told me that they were quite sure that Mr. Cohan would never consider such a ridiculous idea as to have his plays butchered on a showboat down along the rivers. I then tried the play brokers, who told me the same story. I went to see Dennis O'Brien, Mr. Cohan's attorney and personal adviser, who roared like a Monongahela River steamboat whistle when I suggested that I buy *Forty-Five Minutes from Broadway*.[3] As he backed me around his mammoth office, I thought what a

[3] *Forty-Five Minutes from Broadway* was written by George M. Cohan in 1905.

great traffic cop he would make with just a few brass buttons.

Then, as a last resort, I made my final appeal to the late Eddie Dunn, Cohan's veteran representative and one of the grandest men in the theatrical world. I was nervous and the palms of my hands were wet with perspiration as I twisted my hat into a pulp. My lips and tongue were ash dry as I recited my story, fearing the almost certain result.

At long last Mr. Dunn's interest began to fan a smouldering spark of hope in my heart and the details came from my tightened throat more easily.

"And here I am," I concluded.

"Great God, what a history you've had!" he exclaimed. "Meet me tonight at eleven o'clock in front of the Erlanger Theater and I'll take you to see Cohan himself."

At first I wanted to crumble right down on the floor, then I wanted to run to the window and scream the news to the world. It was only a step, only a promise of a hearing, but it was the climax of twenty long years of mental stress.

The audience was just leaving the theater where Mr. Cohan was starring in *The Merry Malones*,[4] when I walked into the lobby. I saw Mr. Dunn standing at the box office and, frightened, I ran out into the street toward Eighth Avenue. I was pale and trembling when he finally caught up with me.

[4] *The Merry Malones* was written and produced by George M. Cohan in 1927.

"What's happened to you, Son?" he asked.

"I can't do it, Mister," I said. "I just can't face him after all these years. Let's drop it."

But he succeeded in pulling me backstage where I came face-to-face with the famous George M. Cohan for the first time. As I was presented to him, he put an arm about my shoulders and led me into his dressing room where he introduced me to a host of friends who had been waiting for him. Then Mike, his Japanese servant, served coffee.

During the next hour or so I had a splendid opportunity to study this famous figure. He had aged considerably since I had last seen him, but he was still as energetic and as high-strung as one of the whirligig beetles which throng the rivers by the hundreds, darting frantically here and there and tracing graceful curves on the surface of the stream. He had the most piercing eyes I have ever seen and he thought so fast that I was afraid to speak for fear he would say just what I had been about to say. He offered me a cup of coffee. Although I needed it just then, I declined because as nervous as I was at that moment, I knew I would never be able to get it safely to my mouth. Bill Bryant, the big shot of the rivers, the guy who had been criticizing and belittling this marvelous man for years, was so flushed with shame that he felt like ten-cents-a-dance as he tried hard to act at ease among such a gathering of notables.

Mr. Cohan finally turned to me and opened our

real conversation. "I understand that I've been on your mind for twenty years, Billy. Is that right?" His voice was friendly and he never once referred to our correspondence.

"Why—uh—yes—something like that," I stammered in a weak voice.

"Well, now that we're real friends and pals, what can I do for you?" he asked. The hum of voices ceased and all eyes were turned upon me as I sat helplessly staring at him.

"Take your time now, Bill, and tell me slowly," he said. "No one is going to shoot you."

"Well, you see, Mr. Cohan," I began, "I mean— that is—I'd like to—Oh hell, you wouldn't understand," I said, and turned to go.

"Out with it, showman," he cried. "Out with it. What's on your mind?"

"Well, I came to New York to see if you would lease us one of your plays to do on our boat," I began stoutly. "I can pay any price you ask. I want to give those river folks a classic piece. Your kind of piece. And we've got a big boat now, you know. I wouldn't think of asking for your newest ones, but I thought maybe one of your old ones, you know. The ones the public has forgotten here."

He stared at me a moment and then beamed with enthusiasm.

"It's a great idea. Make your choice out of that script trunk. I have written twenty-nine plays," he went on. "I'm going to give you the whole twenty-nine and they won't cost you a dime, now or ever. Play them any way you want to, with any kind of cast. Cut and piece them to suit yourself. They're yours to play with and there are no strings on them. Help yourself, kid, and God bless you!"

I was speechless. Great tears of gratitude rolled down my cheeks. I could only whisper one little word—"Thanks." Only the fact that I was a grown man and in the presence of that group of celebrities kept me from breaking down completely and crying like a child.

"Cut it out, kid, all of us are show folks here," Cohan said softly. "I remember your act. You're my kind of guy. Get the scripts and forget it. And say," he added, as a thought struck him, "here's something else. Let me have your routing list for next August so I'll know where you are and maybe I'll come down on that old showboat of yours and play *Broadway Jones* for you for a couple of weeks. How's that?"

It was unbelievable—unthinkable—yet there it was direct from the lips of the great composer, producer, and actor himself. So I selected *Broadway Jones* and streaked for Pittsburgh, walking on air.

In the spring we took that Cohan piece, divided it into half, threw in a half-dozen song numbers, taught a chorus of six to dance to the melodies, and surged down the rivers with *Broadway Jones* transformed into a musical comedy.

Other things intervened for Cohan and he never

got around to fulfilling his suggestion that he play the part of Jones on our showboat, but there is another sequel to the story which is almost as good as that would have been.

Broadway Jones is, as everyone knows, a straight play. Cohan had never intended that it should be played as a musical comedy. That was our idea for the river audiences, and we made the play over, as he had told me we might do, for that purpose. One day during the next summer Cohan happened to pick up, in his office in New York, one of our handbills that I had mailed him, and read, "Through the kindness of George M. Cohan, Bryant's Showboat presents *Broadway Jones* with Music and Girls . . . This is the Boat that Spreads Happiness to Thousands . . . the Hen that Lays a Good Egg Has a Perfect Right to Cackle."

That afternoon Mr. Cohan sat down and composed a song which he called "Happy." He handed it to an assistant who played it while Cohan listened. Then he suddenly said, "I'm going to cackle! Send out a call for girls and cast me *Broadway Jones* as a musical comedy."

Rehearsals proceeded, and the show was ready for an out-of-town tryout. But it had no title. One day Cohan, searching for a title, thought of the embarrassed river showman who wept upon receipt of such a magnificent gift and then had done, in a small way, that which had suggested what Cohan himself was now doing in a big way.

Bryant's Showboat *Poster*
Courtesy The Public Library of Cincinnati and Hamilton County

"We'll call it 'Billy,'" he said. "No, the girl is the star of this version. Feminize it and let it ride. The title of the show is 'Billie.'"[5]

And thus it was given to the world and ran for many months as a smash hit on Broadway.

And thus George M. Cohan cast a play upon the waters to have it come back to him as a musical comedy.

[5]"Billie" was produced by George M. Cohan in 1928.

XV

"To Be a Ham and Admit It"

THE SUMMER of 1929 started off very poorly for us. There seemed to be plenty of money in the country but we didn't find much of it scattered down along the river, so we decided to find out, at last, what a city audience was like. Cincinnati was our first big city adventure. For years we had run by this port considering it much too large for our kind of entertainment. We had been afraid even to stop there for our mail or to have a suit pressed; so naturally, when we landed there for a three-day engagement, we were nervous and made great preparations to make our opening night a huge success.

We had the piano tuned and purchased a new portière for our parlor-door set. The actors got fresh haircuts and purchased new wardrobes and make-up for the special occasion. Then, to give the show a citified atmosphere, we presented a smart Cohan comedy with no vaudeville so there would be long, tiresome waits between the acts, just as there are in the first-class opera houses. But all of our efforts seemed useless. In that splendid city we rang up the curtain on our opening night with exactly three people in the audience, and the next night we didn't even ring the curtain up.

Completely discouraged, we decided to forget the city idea and mailed some "coming" bills down the river intending to continue with our regular course.

The following day, our last in the city, we all voted to forget about the possibility of an evening's performance and go uptown and take advantage of the city lights for one day at least. But just at dusk a large, magnificent, disabled yacht, with a jolly party aboard, drifted helplessly in against our showboat and tied up for repairs. When its captain and owner found out what we were, he offered us twenty-five dollars to play *Ten Nights in a Bar Room* for his out-of-town guests who had never seen a showboat before.

Disgusted and discouraged as all of us were, for twenty-five dollars we would have played *Strange Interlude*.[1]

You may not believe it, but old *Ten Nights in a Bar Room* was an instant hit, a sensation! They applauded our cotton-stocking heroine and stood up in a body and cheered Joe Morgan's denunciation of the demon rum. They laughed at our stale river jokes and thought our villain, Harvey Green, with his handlebar mustache, was the funniest human being they had ever seen on any stage, and hissed and booed him to their hearts' content.

It was all new and confusing to us to see our earnest river classic go so completely haywire in such a

[1] *Strange Interlude* by Eugene O'Neill was produced by John Golden in 1928.

strange manner. We didn't know what it was all about, but we knew that our audience was having a good time. After the show they took our entire company aboard their gorgeous yacht and entertained us in royal fashion. There we learned that they had not been kidding us as inferior actors, but on the contrary, considered us finished comedians. They had taken the play as a satire or something like that, and thought we were smart showmen to present it in that way. And we didn't argue with them. They had been our guests, in a manner of speaking, so we remembered our manners as hosts and let it go at that.

Mr. Moses Strauss, managing editor of the *Times Star*, was a member of the party and insisted that we stay over for another night or two and see what happened.

"I have a hunch you're going to go over big," he confided to me. "Take a look at the paper tomorrow morning."

The next morning I was up before the paper boys had put on their pants, and when the papers finally arrived I stared straight at a four-column headline about Bryant's Showboat and a story which gave us the works. You would have thought, reading it, that we were the greatest and the funniest show in the entire world.

That night we repeated *Ten Nights in a Bar Room* and played to standing room only. Night after night the Queen City amusement lovers had the

time of their lives on our boat. Our down-river engagements were forgotten. Business came so fast
that we had to install a telephone on board the boat
and were selling seats to out-of-town people three
weeks in advance. Families came from near and far
to check out Cincinnati's new toy. Rolls Royces
rubbed noses with Fords trying to find parking
space on the waterfront. Requests for favorite old-
time melodramas began coming by mail, and we
changed from *Ten Nights* to *Nellie the Beautiful
Cloak Model*[2] and from *Nellie* to *Bertha the Sewing
Machine Girl*[3] so fast that we wore out half of our
scripts. Characters who had been buried for generations were dragged out of their graves to moan and
groan and curse and pray their ways through their
sob-wrenching stories.

Of course I reveled in it. It wasn't Broadway, but
still it was a first-class city. We were headed at last
in the direction I wanted to go. Often, as I looked at
the capacity audience out front, I would think of
New York. If Cincinnati liked our show as much as
this, Broadway would eat it up!

While we played in Cincinnati we gave several
charity performances in appreciation of the city's
splendid hospitality. The saddest of these was one
which we gave for the population of an institution

[2]*Nellie the Beautiful Cloak Model*, a melodrama, was written by Owen Davis when he was doing frivolous theater.

[3]*Bertha the Sewing Machine Girl*, a melodrama, was written by Theodore Kremer and produced in New York in
1906.

for the blind. When we stood on the stage and saw the patient men and women, to whom the priceless gift of light had been denied, laughing, and apparently having a good time as the attendants tried to explain the action of the play to them, it was sometimes quite difficult to go through with our lines correctly.

But even our blind audience packed into its composite person less drama and pathos than did three hundred crippled children who came to us on another day. All of them were seeing an old-fashioned showboat for the first time. Many of them had never before even feasted their eyes on the beautiful olive-green waters of the river.

The Cincinnati Rotary Club furnished special buses which brought them to the river. From the buses those who could hobble along on crutches came aboard under their own power. The rest were carried or brought up the stage plank in wheel chairs. Many of them were kept on carefully restricted diets, but for this day all prohibitions were removed and they were given peanuts, popcorn, and red lemonade—as much as they could hold! I watched them cramming peanuts down their throats and gulping their lemonade with faces as solemn as that of a preacher lining out hymns. Their poor hungry hearts had been silent so long, their twisted little bodies had known so much pain, they had learned to expect so little from life, that they didn't know how to be gay.

When the curtain went up on the first act I faced them with a greater longing for happiness than I had ever known—yet it was not my happiness I was thinking about, but theirs. I wanted terribly to see them relax, to see them show some of the gaiety which is the birthright of every child. I found myself uttering an incoherent prayer that I could find a way to bring them that gaiety, if only for an hour. I wanted terribly to be a better comedian than I had ever before conceived—the kind of comedian that could make crippled children forget, for awhile, that they were cripples. For the moment, my desire for a big time success on Broadway, for the kind of success George M. Cohan knew, faded before my desire to make those children happy.

But as the action began I saw that they were taking it just as they had the popcorn and peanuts and lemonade—with solemn faces and big, burning eyes. They were being so incredibly good! They seemed afraid that if one of them were to giggle they would all be put out.

Finally I could stand it no longer. I stopped right in the middle of my own lines and held up my hand to the other actors, stopping the show. Then I stepped to the front of the stage and addressed the children themselves.

"Listen, kids," I pleaded. "Can't you laugh? This is your day on the showboat, you know. The whole works is yours as long as you're here. Do anything you want to! Laugh if you think we're funny. That's what we're trying to be! Tell us we're punk if you think we are. But please have some fun! We like the sound of your voices. We'd love to hear you all laughing together. You don't have to be afraid of making too much noise. The fish in the river won't mind, and we'll like it. Isn't there just one little giggle in the lot of you?"

Just then a little girl with golden hair hanging to her shoulders, but so feeble that she had been carried onto the boat, let out a gay titter in a high-pitched, half-frightened voice, and I began to laugh with her—half because I wanted to encourage her and half because I had to do something to keep from crying.

"That's the ticket!" I shouted. "Any more giggles anywhere to give away?"

In a moment the whole crowd was laughing, not because I had said anything funny, but because they suddenly discovered that it was fun to laugh and no one was going to tell them that they shouldn't. After they had laughed awhile we went on with the show, and from then on it was a riot. Often we had to stop and wait for them to laugh themselves out so that they could hear the lines.

The little girl who had started it, apparently feeling like a pioneer, outlaughed and outshouted all the rest of them until, completely exhausted, she fell off her chair in a dead faint and we had to carry her to the front of the boat where the cool river breeze revived her.

As a result of our success with all types of audiences in Cincinnati, our original three-day engagement in the Queen City has been extended to seven years, and I hope will continue for at least seven more. During one of those joyous summers we played for thirty-eight continuous weeks tied up at the foot of Lawrence Street, until we were afraid that the rest of our river audience would never welcome us again after so long a desertion.

It was toward the end of the 1931 season that the unexpected happened, and brought the matter of the big time cities so close to us that something had to be done about it. Charles Collins,[4] the Chicago drama critic, hearing that we were playing Cincinnati wrote a piece for the *Chicago Tribune* about it, asking plaintively, "Why can't Chicago have a showboat season?"

After all, Chicago was a river town, too, even though the engineers had turned the river on its head, by thinking that they knew better than God which way it should flow, and made it into a canal.

George Wintz,[5] the producer, read the story and immediately phoned us at Cincinnati. I remember that when I answered the phone I had the impression that he thought he was talking to a taxi driver.

"Bring your showboat up the Chicago River," he said. "I'll meet you at the foot of Madison Street."

[4]Charles Collins (1880–1964) was a drama critic for the *Chicago Tribune.*
[5]George Wintz was a theater producer in the 1920s.

It was plain that Mr. Wintz had never navigated a showboat, and I instructed him as gently as possible over the long-distance phone (at his expense) in the ways of river craft, explaining patiently that it would be quite impossible unless he wanted to send a crew of house movers down to bring our showboat up by land.

"All right," he said cheerfully, "wait a minute while I talk to somebody—oh, never mind, I'll call you back."

A few hours later he was back on the phone and full of enthusiasm.

"All right," he said, "it's all fixed up. You're set to play in the Studebaker Theater."

I think I just let the phone receiver hang in the air that day; I was so scared. I talked it over with Mother and Dad and Florence and Jo and gradually we all got enthusiastic about it except Dad, who was hesitant.

"I've had enough of big cities," he said. "I'll bet there isn't a restaurant in the place where I could get a good slice of brown bread and butter."

By this time the season was over, so, with the Chicago venture still undecided, we took the boat to Point Pleasant, where we tied up for the winter and began to consider what we would do with ourselves until spring. Meanwhile, we kept getting letters, wires, and phone calls from Wintz urging us to come at once. Finally we all ganged up on Dad and told him we were going.

"All right," he said. "You go on. I'll stay and take care of the boat while you go and sleep your lives away in that place!"

Florence and Jo packed some baskets of sandwiches and made rolls of our bedding and we all got on a bus and headed north. (Later we learned that we had loaded ourselves down uselessly with blankets; hotels charged just as much whether you brought your own bedding or not.)

Inwardly I was a strange mixture of elation and nervousness. Cincinnati had been, as I had believed there, only the start. I was on my way at last to the big time, the metropolitan audiences and critics who would recognize the ability which would give me my place in the sun.

Mr. Wintz met us and took us at once to the Studebaker. As I walked in and saw its size, my knees began knocking together. The first half-dozen rows would seat as many people as our entire showboat, and that was only the beginning of it. The seats stretched back and back and up and up into seeming infinity.

"This isn't a theater," I said in awe, "it's a cathedral. Nobody will be able to hear us or see us in this huge building!"

Next to it, in the same building, was the little Playhouse, which had been used in turn for small theatrical productions and high-class motion pictures, and I pleaded with Wintz to let us play there instead. It seemed much more nearly the right size for a scared troupe of river actors, and more like a showboat. But he only laughed and said that the Studebaker wouldn't be half big enough once we began to jam them in.

There were financial arrangements to be made and I had to wire Dad to ask what to do about them, and he, who had been opposed to the trip from the first, left us to figure it out for ourselves.

"Whatever you think best, Billy," he wired. "The city is yours. I'll keep the river."

But behind his brusqueness was the affectionate assurance that he would back us in whatever we decided to do. And he was there for the opening, taking his old parts in the cast and his bows with the rest of us.

I'll never forget the excitement of that opening night. Amy Leslie[6] was there in the front row, the late Anton Cermak,[7] then mayor of Chicago, Edith Rockefeller McCormick,[8] Commander Eugene McDowell (who later entertained us all aboard his yacht, the *Mizpah*), Sport Herman, Ted Lewis,[9]

[6] Amy Leslie (1860–1939), whose stage name was Lily West, was the first woman to become a significant theater critic. She worked for the Chicago *Daily News*.

[7] Anton Cermak (1873–1933) was the Mayor of Chicago who was assassinated while he accompanied President Franklin Delano Roosevelt on a visit to Miami, Florida.

[8] Edith Rockefeller McCormick (1872–1932) was a Chicago philanthropist.

[9] Ted Lewis, whose given name was Theodore Leopold Friedman (1891–1971), was a vaudeville and night club entertainer.

Fanny Brice[10]—and they led in the loud and full-hearted welcome the Windy City gave us.

I didn't sleep much that night for happiness. For hours I lay awake, gazing into a future to which I had looked forward so long! I was in the big time at last, headed for the recognition I had wanted so long. And there seemed little point in sleeping just then when in a few hours I would be able to read what the Chicago critics had to say about us.

When the papers arrived in the morning I had long been waiting impatiently, with no thought of breakfast. I seized them with all the avidity of a young man reaching for a letter from his sweetheart, and turned the pages feverishly until I came to what I was seeking. And when I found it I sat for a long time, gazing into space, confused, hurt, let down. I couldn't understand what it meant. Only one of them said anything about my ability as an actor, and what he said was like a knife thrust into my heart. I was only a clown, a monologist, a Raymond Hitchcock,[11] a Will Rogers,[12] a Fred Allen,[13] an Al

[10] Fanny "Brice" Borach (1891–1951) was a famous comic and torch singer who worked for Flo Ziegfeld and later achieved success as a radio celebrity with the character "Baby Snooks."

[11] Raymond Hitchcock (1865–1929) was a successful comic actor in the first two decades of the twentieth century.

[12] Will Rogers (1879–1935) was a vaudevillian, actor, humorist, and syndicated columnist.

[13] Fred Allen (1894–1956) began as a vaudeville performer and later became a radio actor and writer who was known for his wit.

Jolson[14] (and I never sang a Mammy song in my life!) a philosopher, a connoisseur of garlic; but, in the minds of these mighty ones, apparently I was not an actor!

I could have comprehended this simple denial of my ability, and set it down to lack of discernment on the part of the critics, if it had not been mixed with praise of their own sort. But they had obviously liked me in all of these ways I did not understand. All of the things that I was not, that I had never tried to be, that I could not comprehend, they said I was, and praised me for it.

"Billy Bryant is great—truly a Will Rogers of the river," Ashton Stevens[15] reported in the *Herald Examiner*. "There's only one Captain Billy—a Raymond Hitchcock in the making," Claudius Cassidy[16] said in the *Journal of Commerce*. Already I was two persons, and neither of them had ever played the kinds of parts I had always played so successfully! Charley Collins became equivocal in the *Tribune*. "What a play! What a troupe!" he wrote. "A night

[14] Asa Yoelson or Al Jolson (1888-1950) was perhaps the most distinguished variety performer of his era. He performed in the first full-length sound film—*The Jazz Singer*.

[15] Ashton Stevens (1872-1951) was an ascerbic theater critic who spent most of his career in Chicago working for the Hearst newspapers.

[16] Claudia Cassidy (1905-1980?), not Claudius, was a tough-minded theater critic for the Chicago *Journal of Commerce* and later the *Chicago Tribune*. During her years as critic for the *Tribune* she was the most influential critic in the Middle West.

worth remembering." And it occurred to me that one would remember the Johnstown Flood, too, if he had been there. Lloyd Lewis[17] was more enthusiastic. "Nothing better in the Loop," he wrote in the *News.* Gail Borden,[18] to my continuing amazement, picked out what I thought was the least important part of the whole thing—the little piece I spoke in front of the curtain to our new audience. "Billy Bryant's curtain speech is the best I ever heard," he wrote. "He knows his garlic." And Fritzi Blocki followed in the *American* by calling me "a genuine backwoods philosopher."

But the crowning blow came from C. J. Bulliet[19] in the *Post.* "Billy Bryant is the worst actor that Chicago has seen since David Warfield[20] attempted to play Shylock, but as a monologist he is in a class with Will Rogers, Fred Allen, and Al Jolson."

Now I was four other fellows—but only as a monologist. I didn't know what their acts were like and probably they had never heard of me. I wasn't a

[17]Lloyd Lewis (1891–1949) was an author and popular historian who wrote primarily about Lincoln and the Middle West.

[18]Gail Borden (1905–40) was the theater critic of the Chicago *Daily Times.*

[19]Clarence J. Bulliet (1883–1952) was the art and theater critic of the Chicago *Daily News.*

[20]David "Warfield" Wollfeld (1866–1951) achieved success first as a comedian portraying long-bearded Jewish immigrants but went on to serious roles and played starring roles for David Belasco. His portrayal of Shylock was so bad that it was legendary.

philosopher, I protested angrily, but a great comedian who had played star comedy roles. I made audiences howl along the river from Pittsburgh to
New Orleans, and could do the same in Chicago if
they would give me a chance. Was I going to have to
sing "The Green Grass Grew All Around" for them
to prove that I was not what they were saying I was?

Bulliet's crack about my acting ability was, of
course, the hardest blow of all. I'd never read as
frankly uncomplimentary words about myself in a
newspaper. All the write-ups in the river newspapers praised me and the whole troupe to the skies,
since I wrote most of them myself. I didn't get the
real flattery in the notices simply because the thing
I was looking for, the thing I wanted—recognition
of my ability as an actor—was not there.

And so, as week followed week and we packed
the Studebaker every night with an enthusiastic
throng, I became more and more puzzled. There
was no question that we were a hit. Yet no one
would praise me as an actor! That fact smarted and
hurt, and I wondered how I could convince them.

After six weeks at the Studebaker, *Elizabeth the
Queen*, which had arranged previously for the use of
the theater, squeezed us out, and we moved to the
Cort. The first night at our new location I went
down to the theater a little late, with barely enough
time to dress before the curtain. When I got near
the front door I saw a small crowd standing outside,
looking up with rapt attention at the sign over the

entrance. As I came closer I saw that the group was made up entirely of members of our own cast, staring in a daze at their names in bright lights for the first time.

Someone had heard about our river version of *Hamlet*, and the critics had been clamoring for it. Remembering what an unseemly mess it had been on the river, we put it off as long as possible, but at last gave way. I went over it again and tried to get it straightened out a bit before putting it on before the sophisticated audience we expected at the Cort. But we didn't have anyone in the cast who seemed up to the role of the melancholy Dane himself, so I went hunting.

I found the man one day at the corner of Randolph and Dearborn streets, right there in Chicago. He was leaning against a mail box when I first saw him, and he looked so hungry and sad that I decided he would be perfect. There seemed to be that far-off look in his eye, and that remaining touch of elegance under the shabby exterior of his clothes, which marks, the world over, the old trouper who has been "at liberty" too long.

I spoke to him, and the way he accepted my invitation to lunch reminded me of all the tragedies I have seen on the stage. When I found that he was not only an actor, but had played Hamlet before, I was overjoyed and hired him on the spot for ten dollars a week, with board and room thrown in. We were both very happy that night.

All of us meant well when we started out on the *Hamlet* performance the next night. But we forgot our lines as thoroughly as we had on the river, and everyone but Hamlet himself began ad-libbing two minutes after the curtain went up. But the new member of the troupe, the man I had picked up on the street corner to play the title role, staring scornfully at the rest of us, played the part of Hamlet straight and with a definite ability. It was very confusing to all of us to have such a finished actor on the stage with us in our river Shakespeare. In ten minutes we had all given up, except him, and were saying anything which came into our heads whenever he stopped speaking. The play would have gone completely to pieces had he not kept strictly to his lines and held it together.

In my curtain speech that night I tried to make an especial apology for our acting. "To be a ham and not know it is pitiful," I said, "but you'll have to confess that to be a ham and admit it is something beautiful."

The next morning I picked up the papers with fear and trembling. What would they say about the way we played Shakespeare? But, to my surprise, the attention of the critics had been drawn, not to our terrible butchery of Shakespeare's masterpiece, but to the acting of the man I had picked up on a street corner. They called our Hamlet a star in no uncertain terms.

And that spoiled everything. On that day I was

greeted by a very superior and greatly wronged actor. He was the best Hamlet Chicago had seen for
years. The critics said so. Did I think he was going
to work for ten bucks a week and cakes? He wanted
seventy-five, and a contract, and no compromise
would do. He wanted the star's dressing room. He
wanted his name in lights out in front. There was
no reasoning with the man.

I mollified him as well as I could, but when I got
to the theater that evening I found him so drunk
that it was impossible for him to go on the stage. We
tried everything we could to sober him up, but it
was no use. At one point I asked one of the boys to
give me a hand so that we could throw him out of
the window, thinking a good ducking in the river
would straighten him out, but I remembered just in
time that we were not on the boat and that it
wouldn't do anybody any good to break his neck by
throwing him into an alley off Dearborn Street.

Finally, ten minutes after curtain time, I went out
in front of the curtain to make my apologies, and
there, way down in front, I saw Lloyd Lewis and
Charles Collins and Ashton Stevens, whose pane-
gyrics had made our Hamlet's hat too small for him.
At that point I could cheerfully have wrung their
necks. But I couldn't get to them without jumping
over the footlights, so I just pointed my finger at
them and accused them.

"You ruined a perfectly good actor," I shouted,
"by telling him how good he was. Now you've got

to watch *The Bird in the Gilded Cage* because your beloved Hamlet is lying in the alley drunk as a result of your flattery."

After we had played our regular river repertoire for a few nights we all unwittingly had a visitor who was to change our course once more. John Golden, the New York producer, having read of our Chicago performances, wired a friend of his to see our show and report on it. When the friend wired back that it would be a riot in New York, Golden got in touch with Wintz and Wintz flew to New York to make arrangements for that Times Square appearance, about which I had been dreaming for so many years.

In spite of our success in Chicago, in spite of the enthusiasm of the critics, I left gladly. We had been a hit, to be sure, but I was still confused about the way they had taken us. They had praised us to the skies, had been the utmost in hospitality and appreciation, but they took us as clowns. No one would take our acting seriously. Now we were going to the theatrical hub of the world, the island which has made and broken more actors than any other whole continent, Manhattan. We were going to Broadway, home of the biggest critics in America. We would show them, and through them the world, what we were like!

Needless to say, the night we opened at the Golden Theater in New York I was more nearly incapacitated for facing any audience than I had ever been before in my life. I don't know yet how we got through the first act. But just as the curtain was falling and I was getting ready to step out for the curtain speech I always gave after the act, I was handed a wire from Ashton Stevens, the Chicago critic. It read: "Just be yourself in your curtain speech tonight and New York is yours." I wanted to rush to the phone and call Chicago to thank him, I felt so grateful for that one encouraging word.

But the real thrill of friendship came as I finished my curtain speech. As usual, I ended it with an invitation to all and sundry to come up on the stage and meet the troupe. The first one who bounded over the footlights was O. O. McIntyre, the famous columnist, and one of the grandest fellows who ever trod the earth. He is probably the most widely read columnist in America. His rural back-home style of writing is read and loved by millions, and the reason is, it seems to me, that he is always for the underdog. His happiest moments seem to be when he can tell the world the name of some small-town boy who has made good in the big city. And, in his private life, he practices what he preaches in his column. If any proof were needed he furnished it that night in the Golden Theater.

Taking me by the hand, as though it were the proudest moment in his life, he led me through a group consisting of a host of his famous friends. It was one of the most distinguished groups of men and women I have ever seen collected in one spot at one time. Such a group was old stuff to him, but to

John Golden and The Golden Theater, New York City
Courtesy New York City Public Library

me it was as confusing as a September river fog. It seemed to make him very happy as he introduced me to Fannie Hurst,[21] Roy Howard,[22] Rube Goldberg,[23] James Montgomery Flagg,[24] David Warfield, Bruce Barton,[25] Gene Tunney,[26] Alfred E. Smith,[27] Charles Francis Coe,[28] Irvin S. Cobb,[29] Charles Dana Gibson,[30] and dozens more as I tried in vain

[21]Fannie Hurst (1889–1968) was an American novelist and short-story writer. Many of her works were made into films.

[22]Roy Howard (1883–1964) was a journalist who founded the Scripps-Howard newspaper chain.

[23]Reuben Lucius "Rube" Goldberg (1883–1970) was an author and Pulitzer Prize-winning cartoonist whose name became synonymous with complicated contraptions designed to perform simple tasks.

[24]James Montgomery Flagg (1877–1960) was an American author and illustrator.

[25]Bruce Barton (1886–1967) was an American advertising executive who wrote *The Man Nobody Knows*, which depicted Christ as the forerunner of the American businessman of the 1920s.

[26]Gene Tunney (1897–1978) was a heavyweight champion of the world who was famous for his long-count fight with Jack Dempsey. He also had something of a literary bent.

[27]Alfred E. Smith (1873–1944) was a Democratic politician, governor of New York, and presidential candidate in 1928.

[28]Charles Francis Coe (1890–1956) was an author and penologist whose books were often turned into films. He was also the general counsel for the Motion Picture Producers and Distributors.

[29]Irvin S. Cobb (1876–1944) was a humorist, journalist, and short story writer, who relied on Kentucky local color.

[30]Charles Dana Gibson (1867–1944) was the illustrator who created the "Gibson Girl," a type of young woman who was representative of America in the 1890s.

to take on the air of a Broadway sophisticate and carefully avoided bringing up such subjects as trout lines and fish.

He soon realized that the whole thing was about to be too much for me and that I was then on the verge of a very bad case of knee tremors, so he offered consolation in a voice full of friendliness.

"Brace up, Kid," he said. "Don't worry about this layout, because we're all just a bunch of brush-apes in dinner coats."

Our kind of tall-grass showboat acting had awakened memories of the past in him and he never stopped to consider what the rest might think of him as he sprang over the footlights. He only knew that he was one of us from the same river bottom-land, and he was answering the call of "All hands on deck" which my nervousness had transmitted to him. What a riverman's friend!

Back in the audience that night (as I learned the next day when he gave them to me) he handed his friends pages from a little loose-leaf notebook and on these pages each of them wrote a message for me. The little book which contains them is now one of my greatest prizes.

Here are some of the things that are in it:

"To a lot of earnest actors, with my admiration. Irvin S. Cobb."

"Swell! Rube Goldberg."

"Begin with the speech. It's grand. Charles Dana Gibson."

"The best of its kind in the country. Grover A. Whalen."[31]

"Great! James J. Bush."

"With you on the stage, why have a curtain? Bob Davis."

"Great stuff! Jesse L. Lasky."[32]

"Billy Bryant is a big hit in the city as well as on the river. Arthur William Brown."[33]

"Ten Nights in a Bar Room and one grand night in John Golden's Theater. Fannie Hurst."

"A long, long run on Broadway! Bruce Barton."

"Simply delightful. David Warfield."

"With thanks for the best curtain speech I ever heard. Rupert Hughes."[34]

"A great show! O. O. McIntyre."

"Terribly amusing. Gene Tunney."

"Perfect. F. P. Adams."

"Wish the Theater Guild were as good. Maurice Wertheim."[35]

"Unique, Julius Miller."

[31] Grover A. Whalen (1886–1962) was a New York merchant, philanthropist, and civic leader.

[32] Jesse Lasky (1881–1958) was a Hollywood film producer and executive.

[33] Arthur William Brown (1881–1960) was an illustrator and cartoonist for the *Saturday Evening Post* and other popular magazines.

[34] Rupert Hughes (1872–1956) was a novelist, biographer, and dramatist.

[35] Maurice Wertheim (1896–1950) was a banker, philanthropist, and co-founder of the National Theatre Guild in New York.

All are written in pencil and signed. And there are other pages, too, with great shaggy signatures scrawled on them: Alfred E. Smith, Judge Dike,[36] James Montgomery Flagg, and others, all enthusiastic guests of ours that first night in New York.

Again, as in Chicago, I waited for the papers the next morning, my lips dry with nervousness. This was to be the real test. What the New York critics said would really tell whether I was to be recognized as an actor or not.

The first one out was Percy Hammond's[37] in the *Herald Tribune*, and again I had the same confused feeling I had known in Chicago. "In Billy Bryant, New York has found a clean, refreshing clown," he wrote.

The afternoon papers were no better. John Mason Brown,[38] in the *Post*, sympathized with the audience before giving praise. "It must be hard to sit through Billy Bryant's *Ten Nights in a Bar Room*," he wrote, not having sat through it himself. "But his curtain speech is not to be missed."

"More fun than a barrel of Barrymores," Robert Garland[39] said in the *World Telegram*.

---

[36] Judge Norman S. Dike (1862-1953) was a member of the New York State Supreme Court.

[37] Percy Hammond (1873-1936) was a distinguished and very caustic theater critic in both Chicago and New York.

[38] John Mason Brown (1900-69) was the drama critic for *Theatre Arts Monthly*.

[39] Robert Garland (1895-1955) was the drama critic for the Baltimore *American*.

"Bryant is headed for the Palace or some exclusive night club," said Lee Mortimer[40] in the *Mirror*.

"A likable bad actor with a lucky personality" was the description of me by Arthur Pollock[41] in the Brooklyn *Eagle*.

"Bryant is an American Balieff,"[42] the *American* decided.

"It's worth dropping in at the Golden to hear Bryant's speech and the song, 'She's More to be Pitied than Censured,' "[43] Burns Mantle[44] conceded.

I was still too stupid to get the point, still too confused to appreciate the praise I was getting. We were being unusually well received, as a matter of fact, but all I could see was that not one of them had said that I was a great actor. I didn't want to be "an American Balieff," whoever he was. I didn't want to be headed for the Palace or a night club. I wanted to be recognized as a fine actor, like Ezra Kendall, Francis Wilson,[45] or George M. Cohan.

[40] Lee Mortimer (1903?–1963) was a journalist, radio commentator, and amusement editor of the New York *Mirror*.

[41] Arthur Pollock (1886–?) was the theater critic of the Brooklyn *Eagle*.

[42] Nakita Balieff (1877–1936) did a notorious monologue and was known as a "Russian Gossip."

[43] "She's More to be Pitied than Censured" was written by William B. Gray and epitomizes the maudlin sentimentality of the 1890s.

[44] Burns Mantle (1873–1948), a distinguished critic of the New York *Daily News*, was the editor of *Best Plays*, an annual anthology that was published from 1920 until his death.

[45] Francis Wilson (1854–1935), comedian, actor, author and later served as president of Actor's Equity.

They were all crazy, these critics, I told myself. I
had played Fagan in *Oliver Twist* better than Nat C.
Goodwin[46] ever had, and here they were praising
me as a clown!

Day-after-day I went on with this sting in my
heart, and night-after-night we kept packing the
theater with enthusiastic audiences. It was plain
that, whether they liked us for acting or clowning,
we could get, and hold, New York audiences. If we
wanted to play it their way, we could go on from
one success to another here. But was I willing to let
them get away with this "clowning" legend?

And so, when I received word that John Golden
wanted to see me in his office, I went with mixed
feelings. What would the great Golden say?

When I reached the door of his first private office
(and there were three of them) I was met by his private secretary, Miss Jean Dalryple who looked at me
(as only a Dalryple can) and then looked at me
again to be sure she had seen something. She always
gave me the impression that her job was the worst
on earth, and although a very attractive woman, she
looked more like a foreign missionary bound for
China than the smart theatrical woman she really
was. As she thumbed me aft to the next private office, I murmured to myself, "My God, what a type
for Desdemona in our *Hamlet!*"

[46] Nat C. Goodwin (1857–1919), a notorious comedian,
won fame for his grotesque and broad humor but changed
his style after 1900 to gain success as a sophisticated actor.

When I finally reached Mr. Golden's office he introduced me to Mr. Frank Craven[47] who was just leaving. As I lifted up his arm and shook his hand vigorously, I knew from the expression on his face, he never again would recall the incident. Standing in front of the great producer, John Golden, as he sat behind a mammoth mahogany desk chasing a pencil up and down his fingers, I was scared stiff.

"Billy," he finally said as he came around and placed his hand on my shoulder, "I'm leaving for Florida in the morning and I wanted to say goodbye to you. As far as your New York engagement is concerned, I feel sure that you will have a good season on the river next year."

He then took from his desk a book entitled *Stage Struck*[48] and autographed it for me.

"I want you to have this book of mine because I admire you," he said. "You are a good loser. That makes you a good showman. I sat through your performance the other night for the first and last time. So did Percy Hammond, Lee Mortimer, Stephen Rathburn, John Mason Brown, Burns Mantle, Arthur Pollack, Brooks Atkinson,[49] Robert Garland,

[47] Frank Craven (1875-1945) performed on the New York stage from 1908 until 1944.

[48] *Stage Struck*, John Golden's autobiography, was published in 1930. Portions of it had appeared in the *Saturday Evening Post*.

[49] Brooks Atkinson (1894-1984) was the Harvard-educated theater critic of the New York *Times* from 1924 to 1960 and was the city's most influential reviewer.

and all the rest of the twelve apostles, and we all agreed that you looked good from out front and have a marvelous personality. You have a splendid voice and speak lines nicely. Your wardrobe is lovely; you make up nicely, and can dress a stage beautifully. But—YOU CAN'T ACT!'"

Then he quickly added, "But you are in a class by yourself alone in front of a curtain, and some day George White[50] or Earl Carroll[51] will be after you, unless the sheriff gets there first."

That's John Golden. One minute he will stab you to the heart with his cruel, frank criticisms, and the next, sweep you off your feet with the most beautiful sort of flattery. Later, in my dressing room, with tears of defeat rolling down my cheeks, I silently fought it out alone, finally admitting the painful truth. The New York and Chicago critics had been right in their judgment of my acting ability, and from that moment on I knew that the funny, red-nosed, big-mouthed, baggy-panted Bill Bryant of the river would never be the George M. Cohan of the cities.

And while I was trying to swallow this bitter

---

[50]George "White" Weitz (1890–1968), dancer, director, and producer, staged thirteen editions of his so-called *Scandals* between 1919 and 1939. He was convicted of morals charges because of activities that took place at a raucous party he gave after a play.

[51]Earl Carroll (1895–1948), a lyricist and producer, achieved success and notoriety because of his musical plays that stressed off-color jokes and scantily clad women.

truth the show continued to pull and our engagement kept on successfully for ten weeks. It looked as though Lee Mortimer had been right. If I wanted success in clowning parts it was apparently there for me. But was that the kind of success I had sought in the cities? My mind went over it again and again, and meanwhile the show went on. I don't know how long a run we would have had if it hadn't been for some of the boys and my little daughter Betty.

One of the things we had looked forward to in Chicago and New York was the taste of metropolitan food. On the boat we ate the same products of family cooking over and over again. Now we were in the center of fancy restaurants and could order almost anything we wanted from their bills of fare. But I began to notice, as winter wore away, that one after another of our troupe would pore over the lunch menu, scowl for a while, then sigh and say "Bring me some beans—and prunes for dessert."

Things couldn't go on that way for long. I knew something was about to happen, and it did at a matinee. Curtain time came and Mack Franks wasn't anywhere around. We held the curtain for fifteen minutes for him and then put on the show without him. He came in just as the last act was over, with a far-away look in his eyes and seemingly no consciousness of the fact that he had missed the show. As I came offstage, ready to bawl the daylights out of him, he completely disarmed me by giving me an appealing hound-dog look.

"Gee Cap," he said longingly, "I was down at the Battery and they got some of the damndest fish in tanks down there you ever saw. You could catch 'em with your hands, only the guards won't let you."

I could have stood even that. But the next day was one of those days in early spring when it seems as though you'd jumped right into summer. The trees in Central Park were all covered with little green leaves that looked like a lacy veil, and the ground just asked you to lie on it and go to sleep in the sun. Betty and her mother went for a walk in it. When they came back I could see in Betty's face that the cause was lost. She held something tight in one of her fists and when I asked her what it was she didn't want to tell me. Finally she opened up.

"Aw, gee, Dad, it's just an old fish worm came crawling out of the grass in the park," she said, and looked a little sheepish. Then she looked up at me hopefully. "Bet they're bitin' at the mouth of Bull Creek above Waverly," she said, and grinned.

Then I gave in.

"I'll bet they are too, Honey," I said. "Let's go!"

Two weeks later we closed and headed south. I left New York behind with a sense of relief and peace. We had done it at last, met the big town, taken it in our stride, and found out what it was like. Now we were going home, to the river.

We wouldn't have to come again.

XVI

All Rivers Lead Home

ALL THE WAY back to Pittsburgh and down along the Ohio River I kept seeing and feeling the warm anticipation of spring, and I found myself saying over in my mind, just because they sounded so good to me, the names of a lot of little creeks, and sand bars, and landings that I knew; places like Little Yellow Creek, Whiskey Run, Sun Fish Bar, Petticoat Ripple, Cow Creek, Grand Hog Landing, Funk's Bar, Fish Gut Creek, Lonesome Hollow Creek, Pumpkin Patch Landing, Owl Hollow Run, Forty Winks Creek, Haunted Hollow Landing— their very names were music in my ears.

As we approached the river and our boats at Henderson, the first sound I heard which had any special significance was the scratching wheeze of a practically worn-out cylinder phonograph record playing "Red Wing." There was Duckfoot King on his shanty boat, sitting in a tipped-back chair, pipe in mouth, listening in complete contentment to his one record (it was several years after this that he traded it for "Pony Boy")—the record which he had played hundreds of times before, and it was sweeter music in my ears than any I had listened to from Broadway orchestras!

I stood on the head of our boat and breathed deeply, filling my lungs with the pure river air which they had missed so long. Frost was out of the ground and the sticky mud shores were drying rapidly under a warm south wind. The willow and sycamore trees which lined the bank were leafing out in a variety of colors which ranged from yellow to a deep blue-green. Shanty-boat row had come to life again. Gunny sacking, newspapers, and other stuffing had been removed from broken window panes to let the fresh cleansing wind in, and the boats' tenants were bailing out their john boats and flats in shirt sleeves and bare feet. Fishermen, setting their trout lines in a serious silence across the river, witnessed that fish were biting on worms again. Everything was alive with spring.

Sitting on the deck, I took off my shoes and stockings and began kicking my heels against the side of the boat and there were tears of happiness and wonder in my eyes. I had wanted so badly and for so long to make the big time on Broadway. I had wanted to be a big shot in the Gotham manner. Yet here I was, happy as a kid, that New York was behind me and I was back on the river again. I couldn't tell why. And suddenly I remembered a short sentence that was spoken many years ago: "Render unto Caesar the things that are Caesar's." New York was for New Yorkers; the river for its own. And I was a riverman. I had come to it originally by accident, perhaps, but I knew suddenly that I would stay with it now by choice so long as I lived.

Jumping to my feet, I went along eagerly to inspect the boats and see what they needed for the spring that was at hand.

We opened our season surrounded by the friendliness and loyalty of our old audiences. All of our old friends wanted to hear about our "trip" to Chicago and New York, and we told them as well as we could, omitting the disappointments and heartache that went with the glamor and excitement.

But it was not until late summer that I really shook off the last of my residual desires for the kind of success I had dreamed of in the big cities.

It was at Ste. Genevieve, Missouri, on the upper Mississippi, in August, and hot as it can only get hot in Ste. Genevieve. We were there for a one-night stand and had barely got the boat shipshape for the evening's performance when a large black sedan arrived in a cloud of dust carrying a stately old lady, her maid, and chauffeur. These she dismissed at the top of the levee and proceeded on foot alone down the stony wharf toward our boat.

She must have been nearing her eightieth birthday, and her silvery hair glistened in the bright sunshine of that late afternoon. She wore a black silk dress and an old-fashioned poke bonnet with ribbons that came down the sides and tied under her chin. She carried a cane and a small old-fashioned bag, and walked with a slight limp.

Without any hesitation she hobbled up the gangplank as if she had been expected and addressed Dad in a crisp, incisive voice which would win admiration and respect from anyone.

"Who's the owner of this tub?"

Amazed at such a blunt river expression in the mouth of this old lady who bore all the marks of wealth, Dad was speechless for a moment. Then he rallied and answered her with all of the chivalry which the Dr. Sam Bryant of old had learned.

"I am, Madam," he said drawing himself up. "And most happily, since you are interested. I am at your service."

Out of breath from her walk over the cobblestones and up the gangplank, she surveyed us all critically.

"Who's the captain?" she asked finally.

"My son, here," Dad answered pointing to me.

Again her piercing coal-black eyes made a critical appraisal with me alone as their focus this time, until I felt as though there was nothing about me that she didn't know.

"So you're the captain, eh?" she said at last, and I thought there was a twinge of sarcasm in her voice, but I could have hugged her for the way she carried herself at that age.

"Yes, Ma'am," I confessed. And then, to live up to my reputation for being a blundering fool, I asked her if she wished to purchase some tickets for the evening's performance.

The Modernized Bryant's Showboat

Courtesy Kent State University Library, Kent, Ohio

"No, I don't," she curtly replied. "I can imagine what that would be like. I just want to see your steamboat, that's all." And we were thunderstruck as she puckered up her sweet little brow and said, "You better tighten up that spring line there. If you get a good upstream wind, it'll trip your spars."

With that she started back toward the steamboat, walking rapidly, and I followed, wondering who she was, where she came from, and where she had got her river talk and knowledge.

As she reached the aft end of the showboat she whirled like a flash and faced me.

"Say," she said, "is this boat planked crossways or for'd and aft?"

Before I could answer her, she was off again at a lively clip. She crossed the deck of the *Valley Belle* and paused at the foot of the steps leading to the boiler deck. Here she reached up and gave the bell cord a quick jerk which was answered by a rather flat, dull sound from overhead.

"Cracked," she said accusingly, looking at me with disgust.

"It's a very old bell," I ventured apologetically. "It was cast in Pittsburgh in 1848 and has been on the *Valley Belle* for over fifty years." But she only grunted, as if to say, "You ought to be ashamed of yourself."

Once on the boiler deck and out on the for'd castle, she glanced down at the deck below and snorted again.

"Humph! No steam salvage. This can't be much of a boat."

She climbed another flight of narrow steps to the hurricane roof, where, with trembling hands, she opened the small door into the pilothouse and stepped inside. The scorching sun beating down upon the glass enclosure and tarpaper roof created a suffocating heat, but she seemed not to notice it. With feeble hands and evident emotion she carefully rang each of the handling bells, suiting the action to the word.

"That's the come ahead and the stoppin' bell," she said softly as she listened to its clear notes echoing up through the trumpet from the engine room below. "And this," she began hesitantly, "is the back . . ." She stopped short and looked at me with a frightened expression as if her memory were about to fail her. I nodded my head silently and encouragingly, as if we were being watched by hundreds of spectators.

"Yes, I was right," she resumed, ignoring my gesture of assistance, "it's the backing bell. And this," she said with a sigh of relief, "is the emergency gong." And again I nodded my head in approval, and said nothing.

Fatigued by this time from the heat and her exertions, she slowly rolled the huge pilot wheel over with great effort until the rudders were hard down. I tried to help her but she would have none of it and waved me aside impatiently.

At last, clearly exhausted, she leaned against the pilot wheel for support, laid her cheek affectionately against its circle, and softly murmured, "It's all just the same, just the same."

I choked up and a lump came into my throat. I looked on helplessly, longing for something to do or say.

When she faced me again, tears were streaming down her withered cheeks and she looked then as she must have felt, a very tired old lady. She swayed slightly as I quickly stepped to her side and helped her to a shaded spot on the pilothouse bench. Then I left her for a moment to call down to the galley for a glass of cold water.

Later, when she was comfortably seated in a wicker chair on Mother's front porch, she told us, between sips of tea and bites of toast and English black currant jam, the story that all of us had been longing to hear.

She had been born and raised (up until she was nineteen years of age) on the lower Mississippi, which was then the broad highway of the nation. She had had her full share of the careless happiness of childhood along the shores of that mighty stream and the fine free adventures that it always affords, and she remembered them all. There was the river, the islands, the forest beyond, and most of all the famous steamboats of that period. The walls of her luxurious home in Chicago were lined with pictures of such famous old river steamers as the *Grand*

Republic,[1] *J. M. White,*[2] *Sultana,*[3] *Kate Adams, The Buzzard,*[4] *Bostonian,*[5] *Fleetwood,*[6] *Buckeye State,*[7] *The Morning Star.*[8]

Her father had been a riverman all his life. Born out back of Vanceburg, Kentucky, on Kenny (Coconnique) Creek, he had, as a boy, helped his father float flats of tan bark and salt from Pomeroy Bend and Sandy Springs to southern ports with only the aid of pike poles and side sweeps. In the

[1] Originally the *Great Republic*, the *Grand Republic*, a side-wheel, wooden hull packet, was built at Shousetown, Pennsylvania in 1867. The *Grand Republic* was famous for carrying record loads of cotton. The vessel burned at dockside in St. Louis in 1877.

[2] *J. M. White*, a side-wheel, wooden hull packet, was built at Jeffersonville, Indiana, by Howard in 1878. It was the ultimate in design for a cotton boat. The vessel was destroyed in a spectacular fire at Point Coupee Parish, Louisiana, in 1886.

[3] *Sultana*, a side-wheel, wooden hull packet, built at Cincinnati, Ohio, by Moore and Richardson in 1863. The vessel upbound from Memphis in April, 1865, exploded with the loss of almost 1600 lives.

[4] *The Buzzard* is not listed in *Way's Packet Directory*.

[5] *Bostonian* is not listed in *Way's Packet Directory* but there are several vessels named *Bostona*, any of which could have been what Bryant had in mind.

[6] *Fleetwood*, a side-wheel, wooden hull packet, was built at Cincinnati, Ohio, in 1880. The vessel was retired in 1894 and used as a barge.

[7] Probably the first of three vessels of that name, it was a side-wheel, wooden hull packet launched in Shousetown, Pennsylvania in 1850. The *Buckeye State* was dismantled in 1857.

[8] This could have been any of seven vessels by that name that were licensed between 1856 and 1901.

same manner they had also floated thousands of logs from the Big Sandy River to the mills at Cincinnati. As a deckhand on the famous *J. M. White*, her father married her mother, who was then the chambermaid of that grand old packet, and in later years she herself was born, during an ice break-up, in the dingy forw'd cabin of a small steamboat at Cairo Point. In 1851, on the steamer *Falcon*,[9] Jenny Lind[10] had held her in her arms and sung to her many of the songs that made that great artist famous during her concert tour along the Mississippi River under the management of P. T. Barnum.[11]

At the age of eight she had helped her mother in the kitchen (washing dishes and waiting on table) on the steamer *Atlantic*[12] of the Lightning Line that operated out of New Orleans.

She told us about the greatest poker game ever played aboard a steamboat by Mississippi River

[9] *Falcon*, a side-wheel, wooden hull packet, was built at McKeesport, Pennsylvania, in 1851. Renamed the *Queen City*, the vessel was lost off the Scioto Chute, probably in 1859.

[10] Jenny Lind (1820–87), the so-called "Swedish nightingale," was a famous soprano who came to America under the sponsorship of the showman P. T. Barnum and became a sensational success.

[11] Phineas T. Barnum (1810–91) was a circus impressario and producer, who became famous for the expression that a "sucker" is born every minute.

[12] There were several vessels named *Atlantic*. This probably refers to the *Atlantic*, a side-wheel, wooden hull packet, that was built at Jeffersonville, Indiana, in 1859 and dismantled in 1867.

gamblers. It happened on the old *Atlantic* in 1859. A planter, M. Jules DeVereaux, with a Mr. Parker from New York, Mr. Alberti Gallanti of Havana, Cuba, and Mr. Carrico of Montreal played with $37,255 in gold before them—played poker continuously from the time the boat backed out at Red Church Landing, eighteen miles above New Orleans, until the porter called New Albany, Indiana, several days later. They had played all the way up the Mississippi and three days into the Ohio, had their meals and drinks served to them in their cabin, and had smoked fifty packs of cigarettes, five boxes of cigars, and run up a bar bill of $971.50.

She had watched her father help to scrape and oil the hull of the steamer *Natchez* prior to its great race with the *Robert E. Lee*[13] in 1870. In her late 'teens, from the top of a high cottonwood tree in the famous Natchez Bend, she had watched these two grand old steamers race for the supremacy of the South. No wonder she loved the rivers. Her father finally became a bona fide master and pilot, after which she and her mother made their home in New Orleans.

During a visit to an aunt in Chicago, she received word that her mother and father had been drowned while on the big side-wheeler *Mississippi*, which sank while making a landing thirty miles above Natchez.

[13]This legendary vessel was a side-wheel, wooden hull packet built at New Albany, Indiana, in 1856.

A short time later she married a Chicago business man who amassed considerable wealth. He was a kind, lovable, and considerate man, she said, but nevertheless she wished a thousand times, after her marriage to him, that he had been just a Mississippi River deckhand, like her father.

Until the day she visited us, she had never returned to the Mississippi shores that had been both cruel and kind to her during her childhood and early youth.

The sun was sinking over the tops of the sycamore trees and high willow banks that grace that wooded Missouri shore when she finally said goodbye. She kissed my mother, and I was hoping that she would kiss me, too. I helped her up the levee where her maid came running to her assistance, but she quickly stopped her, exclaiming, "Go back—Go back—I see enough of you at home!"

Twilight shadows lengthened as the natives gathered on the wharf in small groups waiting for the calliope and band concert. At the water's edge, laughing children were skipping rocks on the surface of the muddy stream, and the joy of youth was in the air. Moved by a sudden impulse, the old lady reached down for a small rock, and tried to throw it into the swift current of the river. But her arm was feeble, and the stone landed only a short distance in front of her. Then she laughed childishly and we went on.

As we continued up the wharf, Jo, at the calliope,

began playing the evening serenade, "When You and I Were Young Maggie."[14] The gallant old soul smiled as she leaned heavily upon my arm. Tears dimmed my eyes and my face was soon as wet as a morning fog at Brush Creek Island.

At the door of her car she bade me goodbye. As I clasped her frail hand in mine she said, "You've been awfully nice to a cranky, old lady today, and you forgive me, don't you?"

I bit my lips and nodded yes. She paused for a moment and then bluntly said, "Can I do anything for you, son? I've got money now."

I glanced down at our splendid steamboat and showboat brilliantly illuminated with hundreds of lights, at the many people swarming around the box office to purchase tickets, and shook my head.

"No. Twenty years ago you might have helped us, ma'am," I said. "But now it's too late to save us what we went through then. We don't need it now."

I stood watching her car until all that I could see was a cloud of dust on the road, and then walked back to the boat. That night I found my comedy part a bit difficult to play with conviction. All the slapstick antics had been taken out of me that afternoon. I could not brush away from before the eyes of my mind the spectacle of that staunch and sweet

[14]The lyrics to "When You and I Were Young Maggie" were taken from a poem by George W. Johnson and the music was composed by James Austin Butterfield of Chicago, who published the song there in 1866.

old lady, pining away in homesickness for the life she loved.

As we were leaving the stage after the final curtain that night, my little daughter Betty came up and put her hand in mine.

"What are you lookin' so sad for, Daddy?" she asked. "You have been as quiet as a graveyard all evening."

I caught her up in my arms and kissed her.

"Just happiness at being on the river in August I guess, honey," I told her. "You know sometimes happiness makes you look about as sad as sadness. It's just the same as in a play. Some of the plays that make people cry at the towns along the Big Sandy make 'em laugh in Cincinnati. Things are strange that way. Sometimes it's hard to know whether you're playing a tragedy or a comedy."

She took my word for that and we went out front to join the departing audience (as we always do on the river) and talk and laugh with them until long after the time when any theater audience in the city would have gone home or to night clubs. After the show we were just a happy group of friends, swapping river yarns with our audiences and hearing all that had happened since our last trip. I looked at them and thought of our audiences in New York and Chicago. Aside from a chosen few new friends who had taken the trouble to hunt us out in our dressing rooms (and whose friendship I shall cherish so long as I live) there would be no one there whom I would recognize if I were to go back the next year.

But here were people I had known for years, men and women and children who would come to our show year after year. Some, who had come to us first in the arms of their mothers, squalling like mad and sometimes stopping the show when a property gun would be fired on the stage, were now strapping young men and beautiful girls almost ready for marriage. Boys and girls whom we remembered as adolescents were now leading their own children by the hands. We had grown up in the show business with these people. We had shared good fortune and calamity, birth and death, with them. They were a part of us.

As the crowd thinned I noticed Betty with a group of children who were urging their parents to let them stay longer, and I thought back over the brief years of her life, and the part the river had played in it.

I saw her as she was on that first day of her life, her pretty baby blue eyes looking unseeing across the blackened Monongahela River at Elizabeth, Pennsylvania. I saw her strapped in a highchair in the pilothouse when she could sit up, laughing with the gurgling music of an infant as she watched me maneuver the boats in and out of the landings, around islands, sand bars, towheads, and dug chutes. I saw her later as she got her first lesson in numbers by counting the government beacon lights

Betty Bryant as a Young Performer
Courtesy The Public Library of Cincinnati and Hamilton County

along the shores, and the advancing red and black floating buoys that marked the outline of the river channel.

I thought with pride of her expert knowledge of river signals, which enabled her, before she was ten years old, to know what every whistle meant. I remembered how, only that morning, she had been up at the peep of dawn after a late crowd the night before, hustling around on the bank and helping to untie the ropes while bossing the deckhands, who good-naturedly humored her childish desire to lead. I remembered how (following a custom which she initiated herself) she had brought coffee up to me in the pilothouse as soon as we were under way, and then had gone down to relieve Shorty, the engineer, so that he could get his breakfast, answering the whistle signals and handling the throttle almost as well as he could himself. And then, because it was a late show the night before and we hadn't taken time to clean up, she had helped the boys sweep the peanut shucks and empty Crackerjack boxes out of the auditorium so that they would have time to eat their breakfast before we landed.

I thought of her gaiety in the water, swimming like a muskrat and laughing like an angel, of her hundreds of playmates scattered along every inland stream we have touched, and the receptions they staged for her whenever we made port, and how she would bring her friends onto the boat, where their enjoyment in the show would be heightened by the fact that she played the piano or saxophone or did her imitation of George M. Cohan as a featured portion of the show.

She was as thoroughly a child of the river as any bullfrog or muskrat and, through her life on our showboat, was filling a place in thousands of lives along the rivers' shores with a vital success which the city would probably never have accorded her. And the last shred of my endless longing for a big time career—for a lifetime like that of George M. Cohan's—vanished.

The next morning, before the sun was well over the eastern ridges, I lay in my bunk listening sleepily to the sounds of the men untying the shore lines and getting ready to move. Lazily, I was aware that I should be getting up and going about the business of the day, but it was good to lie there a little and remember the old lady of the day before and the pleasant peace of mind which had come to me in the evening.

I was shaken out of my sleepy thoughts by the sound of tapping at the window of my stateroom. Looking up, I saw it was Betty, peeping over the sash at me.

"Goin' to sleep your head off?" she called, in perfect imitation of my father. I grinned at her and she laughed back at me.

"She's all ready, Daddy," she called then. "Want me to back her out?"

I sprang out of bed.

"You and me together, Honey," I called back. "I'll be right there."

Under my breath I amended that a little.

"You and your Mother and I, Honey, together on the river so long as I can hold a pilot wheel! And Mother and Dad, too, to the end!"

EPILOGUE

WHEN Billy Bryant wrote *Children of Ol' Man River* he was shrewd enough to know that he was telling a good story and not writing the history of modern showboating. He was too busy talking about his own experiences and feelings to see how other people and events fit into a historical perspective. Therefore, although many of his comments about his time are interesting and informative, what happened to showboats, their owners, and entertainment after 1907, when the Bryants launched their first boat, the *Princess*, is a totally different narrative than one that concerns Billy Bryant's adventures on the river.

The decade that included the First World War was one that brought significant changes to America's economy and social character. It was also a time when intense competition forced major changes on the showboat fleet. From the point of view of the owners of the eight large showboats that plied the Ohio and Mississippi Rivers there was simply not enough audience to go around. For example, in 1910, even without the Bryant's *Princess*, which had a limited seating capacity of 140, these eight floating palaces contained more than 6,400 seats.[1] If the

[1] The *Goldenrod*, 1,300; *New Sensation*, 960; *Wonderland*, 900; *Greater New York*, 850; *Sunny South*, 800; *Cotton Blossom*, 700; *Water Queen* 624; and *New Era*, 300.

season was of regular length, each boat averaged 290 performances, and if they played to houses that were three-quarters full—the financial break-even point—they required an annual audience of roughly 1.5 million—too much to expect from the markets they could reach.[2]

As boats grew larger and navigational restrictions came to pass, many of the older markets were no longer open to them. The bayou country and the Alabama and Tombigbee Rivers were closed to the largest of boats. This was also true for the upper reaches of the Kanawha, Green, and Cumberland, all of which had at one time been rich showboat country.

The need to seek out new audiences led a few showboat owners to try to navigate rivers west of the Mississippi, such as the Missouri. Commercial freight steamboats had been on that river long before the Civil War, but river-packet operators were always wary of the mighty Missouri. The river, like here sisters to the south—the Red and the Arkansas—was treacherous. Because the Missouri was fed by many tributaries that rose in the Rocky Mountains and others that gathered water on the plains, it was subject to unpredictable flash flooding as well as fast and twisting currents if heavy rains fell anywhere in its watershed, even hundreds of miles away. Moreover, the Missouri tore constantly at its

[2]The data is drawn from Reed, *A History of Showboats on the Western Waters*, pp. 332–33.

banks, changed its course repeatedly, and usually carried large amounts of dangerous debris.

The owners of the exceedingly low-draft steamboats—some that could operate in one foot of water—with high-pressure engines to fight the current and with only a handful of crew members could afford to take risks on the Missouri. For a fragile showboat with a less powerful tow, the Missouri was a formidable challenge. Only acute competition would drive a showboat owner onto that river in a search of profitable untapped audiences. Actually the gains did prove commensurate with the potential losses. The *Wonderland* went up the Missouri in 1913–14 and made money because people in the river towns demanded two shows a day, but neither the Missouri, nor the Red, nor the Arkansas ever presented a potential audience as rewarding as the more placid rivers east of the Mississippi.

Although many small showboats had been sunk or damaged during the decades after Gus French launched his first *New Sensation*, very few of the newer, large, and lavish types had been lost. But tragedy was about to stalk the owners of the big boats. In 1916 the *Illinois* went down at Foster, Kentucky, because of a fire—the most dangerous threat to any wooden boat. In use as a motion picture theater, it was at a time when film was highly flammable and difficult to handle because the catch reel had not as yet been invented and loose film was caught in baskets before rewinding. The *Illinois* became a total loss as a result of an explosion in the projection room—an event to prove that risks faced by boat owners who showed movies—and many did to stay competitive—were greater than the dangers of the river itself.

In April, 1917, the *Greater New York*, its tow the *Robert Dodds*, and *French's New Sensation*—all owned by Captain Ed Price—were tied up at the Red Shaft colliery above Newburgh, Indiana, when a heavy wind storm swept the Ohio Valley. The water level rose swiftly, and two of the vessels broke loose. The *Greater New York* was thrust on her side, the *Robert Dodds* was forced under water so deep that only the very top of its upper cabin was visible. The *New Sensation* survived but was so badly damaged that fully a month elapsed before it was able to continue the season. When the river receded the *Robert Dodds* was pumped out and refloated but the *Greater New York*, which had set a standard for opulence and grandeur, had to be dismantled.

In January, 1918 the *Cotton Blossom* and her tow, the *Jewell*, were tied up at Mt. Vernon, Indiana. The boats, caught in a premature heavy freeze, had laid up for the winter. Although they seemed quite secure, having been safely at the wharf for almost three months, the ice in the Ohio River began to shift. Both boats were dragged from their moorings: the *Cotton Blossom*, with its bow on the bank, was broken in half, and water surged over the *Jewell*'s lower deck.

The destruction of the *Wonderland* in the summer of 1918 is more than the story of a river accident; it also explains a good deal about the nature of the showboat business. Only a year earlier the *Wonderland* had been damaged and refloated, but when it broke loose from its dock in 1918, as its owner later told a Cleveland newspaper reporter, "I told them to let her go and go she did." [3] Why had the owner of a premier showboat built less than a decade earlier been willing to "let her go?" John W. Cooley, who owned the *Wonderland*, was something of a romantic, but his reasons for abandoning the showboat were probably quite pragmatic; he could no longer afford the operation. He had employed the best entertainers and crew, and he had sought audiences from remote locations, but to no avail. The combination of competition and the wartime mood of the country had hurt business. [4]

Even Captain Ralph Waldo Emerson, feeling the wartime pinch in the summer of 1918, sold the *Goldenrod*—the most impressive of the great showboat fleet—to a group that planned to tie it up near an arms plant at Nitro, West Virginia, on the Kanawha River to provide entertainment for the workers. The enterprise failed, and Emerson had to eventually retrieve the boat.

[3] *Ibid.*, p. 383; Graham, *Showboats*, p. 105.
[4] Two other showboats were lost during the war years: the *Hippodrome* (formerly the *Sunny South*) sank in 1917; and the *Dixie* sank in 1916.

There were, however, new showboats being built during these years. In fact, several showboats were launched as late as the 1920s, but they were all much smaller than the huge water palaces floated before the war.[5] Most were comparable to Billy Bryant's second showboat, which seated less than 500. Many of these, like Bryant's, were family operated. And contrary to Captain Ralph Waldo Emerson's motto coined before 1910, "After the Minnows Comes the Whale," in real-life showboating, after the whales came the minnows.

It is ironic that the Bryants launched the *Princess* in 1907 just when competition among the finest showboats on the river was becoming knife keen and, further, they floated their second showboat— *Bryant's Showboat*—during the war when many of the larger showboat owners were hardest hit because of declining audiences. The boat owners were not alone. All traveling theater—circuses and serious drama along with showboats—was suffering because of changes in America's lifestyle. The smaller isolated towns that had made up the basic audience for traveling companies were gradually being linked by interurban trains and paved roads. Inexpensive automobiles allowed people to travel to larger cities where they experienced first-rate movie houses. It all added up to audiences becoming increasingly more sophisticated.

[5]The exception was the fifth showboat named *Cotton Blossom*, which seated 700 and was built in 1939.

The motion picture that was produced on location or with special effects—such as chase scenes or erupting volcanoes—and a new breed of successful dramatic actors wrought a revolution in American entertainment. The traveling companies with their third-rate casts and cheaply painted scenery looked shoddy by comparison. Many simply folded.

Interest in showboats was revived strangely enough through the publication of a series of magazine articles by Edna Ferber that were eventually published as a book in 1926 under the title of Show Boat. Ferber knew little of showboats but her romantic tale of love and passion on the river was turned into a Broadway hit and a highly successful movie filmed on the *Cotton Blossom*. The public enjoyed the book, relished the music by Jerome Kern and Oscar Hammerstein and flocked to see the film that starred Irene Dunne, Alan Jones, and Paul Robeson, and began going to showboats as much out of curiosity as in search of entertainment. The excitement generated by Ferber's novel, a brilliant stage play, and a blockbuster movie did not last because showboat productions did not live up to audience expectations.

There is no doubt that the best showboats were providing quality vaudeville, comedy, melodrama, and serious plays. Performances were honest, devoid of sexual inuendo, and straightforward. Most owners believed in the Victorian manners and morals that were built into their shows. But America's tastes were fast changing. The era of the Roaring '20's was at hand, and many people—even those in the smaller towns—began to view nineteenth-century, middle-class Victorian ways in a different light. The showboat variety acts—clowns, acrobats, magicians, jugglers, animal trainers, all the characters of the vaudeville community—could be taken at face value. They were part of the day-by-day entertainment world, where people laughed at themselves or were victims of their own naiveté. To a certain extent variety acts could compete with the movies, but they were quite expensive; and audiences tired of seeing the same performers and craved change and greater novelty.

When it came to drama, the situation was worse. Theater audiences had mixed responses to showboat performances. On the one hand they wallowed in nostalgia, wishing that they could recapture the life of the romantic theater of *East Lynne*, but on the other hand they enjoyed a certain urban postwar cynicism that made the plays presented on the showboat stage seem absurd.

Actors found it impossible to present a melodrama, which was a mainstay of the showboat theatrical repertoire, as a legitimate dramatic form. All during the nineteenth century, audiences accepted melodrama for what it was—a sentimental form of low tragedy that stressed a rigid sense of moral justice. The melodrama's simple categories of good and evil as well as its plot were taken seriously. Women in

the audience wept at the plight of the innocent heroine and, legend has it, men became so emotionally
involved in the play that they rose from their seats
to threaten the evil villain and had to be reminded
that it was, after all, only a play. Little wonder that
showboat drama seemed stale and dated.

The only way to make melodrama acceptable to
this changing audience was as a burlesque of a serious form. A true burlesque should be understood
for what it really is: a form of drama that employs
humor as criticism. This humorous criticism accepts
the virtues and values of the story line but scoffs at
lack of subtlety with which they are presented.[6]
The American audience of the 1920s had not completely rejected traditional moral values but scoffed
at their simplistic presentation as a serious form of
melodrama.

Billy Bryant capitalized on this national mood.
He denies that he purposefully initiated this trend,
asserting only that he discovered the success of the
burlesque melodrama only by accident because his
company's acting was so bad as to make virtually
any performance a burlesque of the original. But
whether the Bryants were so bad as to burlesque
any play they tried to do seriously or whether Billy
Bryant recognized the national temper, the Bryants

[6]Showboats did not produce satire, a form of criticism that
employed humor but that rejected the values expressed in
the plot. Richard S. Pollak, "An Analysis of the Selected
Plays by Billy Bryant as Performed During His Showboat
Career," (Ph. D. diss. Kent State University, 1975), pp. 2–5.

turned a vice into a virtue and were the first company that pandered to post-war cynicism.

Billy Bryant encouraged audience participation
in various ways that earlier actors would have
abhorred; hissing the villain, cheering the hero, and
shouting warnings, jeers, and advice to the characters on the stage. He also apologized to the audience
for the miserable nature of the show. As a result of
his successful adaptation of the burlesque melodrama, *he made money*. Even more significant, the finest
showboats turned to this kind of burlesque in order
to compete. Today, *melodrama means what Billy
Bryant made it*—a burlesque of a serious play. Bryant, in fact, wrote nine plays that were essentially
burlesques, and he had the temerity to parody
Shakespeare by turning the tragedy of the melancholy Dane into *Hamlet and Yeggs*.[7]

The use of the burlesque melodrama made the
showboat in the 1930s welcome to the sophisticated
audiences in large cities where showboats had not
been successful for a generation. But even burlesque
melodrama could not reverse a national trend in
taste and opportunity for unique entertainment.
It was the improved quality of radio reception and
programming, and more importantly, the motion
picture theater—many of whom out-grandeured the
floating palaces—which meant that only a declining
portion of the theatergoers would be attracted to

[7]G. Harry Wright, "Heyday and the Decline of Showboat
Theatres," *Dramatic Magazine* (April, 1949), p. 10.

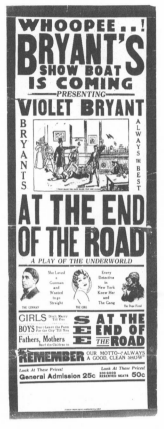

Posters Used by Bryant's Showboat

Courtesy The Public Library of Cincinnati and Hamilton County

the showboat. These beautiful barges had become akin to the traveling circus, attended annually by families with small children, young people reveling in nostalgia, and an older generation that enjoyed the innocence of burlesque. The showboat had become as much a piece of Americana as the melodrama it produced.

On the eve of the Second World War there were several large showboats remaining on the river, but only a few after it. In 1941 the *Hollywood*, which was owned by Ed Price and Ralph Waldo Emerson, was demolished by ice near Paducah, Kentucky; in 1942 the *Water Lily*, the one boat that had only showed movies and presented vaudeville had sunk; that same year the last big showboat, and the fifth named *Cotton Blossom*, burned; in 1943 the *Dixie Queen* was converted to an excursion boat; and *Bryant's Showboat* was converted into a wharf boat that same year. At the close of the war only the venerable *Goldenrod*, which was tied up at St. Louis and made permanent as a showboat by encasing it in a steel hull, and the *Majestic*, which became a student showboat operated at different times by Hiram College, Kent State University, and Indiana University, remained in service. Although "Opryland USA" launched a modern showboat at Nashville in 1985 that seated 670, the era of the "floaters" had truly come to an end shortly after the final curtain of the Second World War.

Billy Bryant was fifty-three when he sold his

showboat. A dedicated showman, he took his company on tour and tried to recapture the showboat spirit for inland audiences. He was not successful. In an article entitled "Captain Billy's Flop," a New York *Times* columnist reviewed Billy's show at Forester's Hall in Chicago. He put his finger on why Billy had difficulty attracting a wartime audience. Even a public eager for escapist material felt Billy's venture "not sufficiently strained to be funny and not authentic enough to be a museum piece. . . . " The reviewer concluded that "Everybody in Chicago loved Billy, but nobody saw him. . . . "[8]

At the close of the war Billy talked about building another showboat but he surely must have known that the era had passed. He pursued the vaudeville circuit in small towns and tried to keep high visibility as a performer in the eyes of New York's Broadway theater critics. Billy was well enough known as a character in 1944 for the New York *Times*' Lloyd Lewis to conjure up a mythical conversation between Billy Bryant and Billy Rose, New York's leading impresario of spectaculars, in which Rose agrees to build a huge showboat and go into a partnership with Billy if Bryant will give up burlesque melodrama—plays like *Her Dead Sister's Secret*—and produce *Macbeth*. Lewis, of course, with a proper sense of irony demonstrates Rose's lack of knowledge, bad taste, and misunderstanding of melodrama by having him insist that Mae West be

[8]New York *Times*, June 17, 1943.

Billy Bryant in Later Life
Courtesy Cincinnati Post

cast as Lady Macbeth. In the end he has Billy Bryant walking away totally confused.[9]

Always looking ahead, Bryant became a pioneer in the field of television entertainment. WNBT, a National Broadcasting Company affiliate, prepared a telecast based on his life in 1946. Billy made a guest appearance. The show was novel in the sense that it was a television version of a radio program taken from a series entitled the American Cavalcade. In 1948 Billy Bryant's *Children of Ol' Man River* became the basis for a television series entitled "Captain Billy's Mississippi Music Hall." It was produced by the Columbia Broadcasting Company for a season on Friday evenings from 8:30 to 9:00. As before, Billy made a guest appearance.

His time in the spotlight slowly faded in the years that followed. He joined the Colston Leigh Lecture Bureau and became a comic "platform spieler" for women's clubs and college students. He occasionally found a vaudeville spot where he could perform as a song and dance man as well as a comedian. His brand of humor remained essentially the same, devoid of anything that was not wholesome and fit for the whole family. Eventually he retired to Fort Lauderdale, Florida, where he died at age seventy-nine.[10]

[9] *Ibid.*, October 8, 1944.
[10] Billy's parents were also long lived: Sam Bryant died in Gallipolis, Ohio, in 1948, at the age of ninety-two, and Violet Bryant died in Gallipolis, Ohio, in 1949, at the age of eighty.

The obituary in the stage magazine *Variety* was unusually wise in writing about his life. The author of the obituary noted that when Billy's boat was in drydock after the showboat season he often played in the best vaudeville houses and that his burlesque of *Hamlet*, which included dancing girls, was highly successful.[11] The obituary also conceded that he was virtually unknown to big city audiences. But the author added with genuine insight, "Bryant had to be inventive [to succeed]. Many of the West Virginia audiences [where his showboat often played] comprised Bohemian and Polish miners who did not know about Hamlet's soliloquy. So he sawed a woman in half instead."[12] There was a critical truth here that Billy Bryant himself might not have grasped. He learned to burlesque Shakespeare for sophisticated audiences that recognized his performances as a spoof but he could also appeal to a culturally deprived public that craved escape from the desperately hard life of the coal-mining towns and the hard-scrabble farming communities of the Ohio Valley.

Billy Bryant was not a great actor, and he may not have been a great entertainer, but he brought happiness into the lives of many people. At the close of each of his showboat performances, Billy Bryant would often apologize to his audience by saying that he was sorry the acting had not been

[11] *Variety*, January 31, 1968.
[12] *Ibid.*

better. He had no reason to be ashamed of the way he acted during his lifetime. If all the world is indeed a stage and all the people players, then Billy Bryant acted his role with consummate skill and verve, bridging generations of the theater and river technology to earn a lasting place in showboat history and as the author of his delightful, informative, and pseudo-self-deprecating memoir. Like Bryant himself, *Children of Ol' Man River* will be appreciated for a long time because it will bring both a smile and a chuckle into the lives of many people.

Index

INDEX

List of The Lakeside Classics

The Lakeside Classics